CRIMES OF PASSION

CRIMES OF PASSION

TREASURE PRESS

First published in Great Britain by Verdict Press
Produced by Phoebus Publishing Company in co-operation with Verdict Press
This edition published in 1983 by Treasure Press, 59 Grosvenor Street, London W1
Reprinted 1984, 1985
© 1973/1974 BPC Publishing Ltd
© 1975 BPC Publishing Ltd

ISBN 0 907812 28 7
Printed in Shenzhen, China

Contents

Foreword

MEN and women have been moved to kill, cheat or steal for many reasons, mostly discreditable, but there is one reason that can evoke some sympathy in the mind of the observer. That is when the mind has become obsessed, even deranged, with passion based on love.

Some crimes of this kind have been caused by jealousy, as when Ruth Ellis coolly emptied her revolver into the body of the lover who was deserting her and then waited for the police to come and arrest her: or when a well-known member of New York society interrupted the performance of a play by shooting the distinguished architect whom he believed had seduced his wife. Many such murders occur when a husband tires of a wife or a wife of a husband; when a girl tires of her lover, or a lover of his mistress. Some occur when a wife and her lover are glad to get rid of her husband, like Ruth Snyder and Judd Gray, or Edith Thompson and Frederick Bywaters. In such cases, when one hand strikes the blow are both equally guilty? This is a question that has been debated in many legal arguments.

Passion may spring from desire to avenge a wrong, as when Lieutenant Massie took the law into his own hands to punish his wife's rapist; or it may spring from a sense of rejection, as when Marie de Morell framed her accusation of rape against an innocent young officer.

Crimes of passion are often committed without forethought, and their perpetrators surrender themselves or are quickly identified. But some have remained unsolved: did Adelaide Bartlett poison her husband for love of a Wesleyan minister? If she didn't, how did chloroform get into his stomach? Were the New Jersey clergyman and the soprano in his church choir killed by his wife and her outraged brothers, or did they die at the hands of the Ku Klux Klan?

The French, with their innate understanding of the intensity of human love when it is thwarted, make allowance in their legal code for the *crime passionel*. In this book we can see examples of what this can mean.

The Champagne Murder

Thaw and White

New York socialites had packed into Madison Square Garden for the opening of a new musical, *Mamzelle Champagne*. The show was not going well. In the informal atmosphere of the roof garden, where everyone sat at tables instead of in conventional theatre seats, people moved about, chatting with friends. Suddenly there was a gunshot, followed by two more. Every eye turned to Stanford White, at 52 America's most distinguished architect. Slowly his elbow slipped from the table at which he had been sitting alone. The table overturned with a tinkle of breaking glass, and White slumped to the floor with a bullet in his brain and two more in his left shoulder.

Over him, unmoved, a smoking pistol in his hand, stood Harry Kendall Thaw, 34-year-old playboy and wastrel son of a Pittsburgh railroad and coke magnate. There was silence for a moment. Then Thaw, the pistol held above his head, made his way out of the roof garden to join his wife, Evelyn, and two guests in the elevator lobby.

They had all got up to leave a few moments earlier at Evelyn's instigation

SENSATIONAL SHOOTING: The gunman was the son of a railroad magnate . . . the victim was the most famous architect in all America.

because the show was so boring. She had reached the lobby with the guests before realizing that her husband was not with them. Then came the shots. "Good God, Harry, what have you done?" she asked in bewilderment as he joined them with the pistol still clutched over his head.

Meantime, back in the roof garden, screaming women fought their way to the

HER BEAUTY was as vague and intangible as that of a lily, or any other frail or delicate thing. It lay over her face like a gossamer veil . . . and she haunted Harry Thaw even in his cell, according to a newspaper cartoonist on the New York "Evening Journal".

HE MISSED his love in jail, but he did not forgo all his pleasures. Prison breakfast (right) was lavish for Harry Thaw, a man of notorious and costly escapades.

Culver

exit. The manager tried to restore order by jumping on a table and shouting: "Go on playing. Bring on the chorus." The shock of having a murder committed before their eyes, however, seemed to have paralyzed both musicians and chorus girls. Then a doctor fought his way through the stampeding audience to White's side. He lay in a pool of blood, his face blackened and unrecognizable from powder burns. He was already dead.

Out in the elevator lobby, a fireman disarmed Thaw, who did not offer any resistance. A few moments later a policeman arrived and arrested him. Together they walked to the nearest police station in the Tenderloin—a district notorious for its prostitution, lawlessness, and graft. There Thaw identified himself as "John Smith", a student, of 18 Lafayette Square, Philadelphia. A visiting card found on him when he was searched, however, revealed his real name.

Great party-goer

Thaw made no comment. "Why did you do this?" the sergeant in charge asked him. "I can't say," Thaw answered laconically. Several reporters had tracked him down by this time, but Thaw—at least until he had consulted his lawyer—refused to make any further statement.

The shooting took place on the night of June 25, 1906. The next day it dominated the front pages of newspapers across

the United States. Even the New York *Times,* not given to sensationalism, ran the heading:

THAW MURDERS STANFORD
WHITE
Shoots Him on the Madison
Square Garden Roof
ABOUT EVELYN NESBIT
"You've Ruined My Life," He
Cries and Fires
AUDIENCE IN A PANIC
Chairs and Tables Are Overturned
in a Wild Scramble
For the Exits

Stanford White, a big man with a thatch of red hair and a moustache to match, was a national figure. He has been credited with being the greatest single influence in beautifying the rather drab, brownstone New York City of the nineteenth century. Madison Square Garden itself, with its amphitheatre for horse shows and prize fights, and its theatre, roof garden, restaurant, and arcade of fashionable shops, was his creation. So were the memorial arch at Washington Square and the Hall of Fame at New York university.

But there was another side to the dignified architect. He enjoyed mixing in theatrical and Bohemian circles, was a great party-goer, and, although married, had a quick eye for a pretty girl. In fact, it was only the stage manager's promise to introduce him to a chorus girl who

had taken his fancy, that kept him sitting through the dull *Mamzelle Champagne.*

For his part, Thaw's life had consisted of one notorious escapade after another. During a brief spell at Harvard, he had devoted himself almost exclusively to studying the finer points of poker. Later, he tried to ride a horse into one of several exclusive New York clubs which had barred him. He had also driven a car through a display window, lost $40,000 in a single poker game, and thrown a party in Paris at which his guests were the French capital's leading whores.

Unspecified services

The bill for the Paris party, including jewellery and trinkets handed out to his guests for unspecified services rendered, was said to be $50,000. It was hardly surprising, therefore, that on the death of his father, Thaw found himself cut off with an allowance of $200 a month until such time as he showed himself responsible enough to handle his $5 million share of the $40 million estate. However, his doting mother, Mrs. William Thaw, enabled him to resume the wastrel's life he enjoyed by upping his allowance again to $80,000 a year.

As might be expected, it was sex that led to the tragic crossing of the paths of White and Thaw. Thaw's wife was the former Evelyn Nesbit, a photographer's model who graduated to the chorus of

STRAW-HATTED and elegant, Harry Thaw pictured in happier times with one of his society girl companions.

the famous musical *Floradora*. She was one of the beauties asked nightly: "Tell me, pretty maiden, are there any more at home like you?"

She had an oval face, copper curls, hazel eyes, a voluptuous mouth, and a splendid figure. When Thaw eventually came to trial, and his wife was called to give evidence, columnist Dorothy Dix, wrote: "Her beauty consists in something as vague and intangible as that of a lily or any other frail or delicate thing. It is something that lies over her face like a gossamer veil, infinitely appealing . . ."

Despite, or possibly because of, her apparent frailty, White had seduced her when she was just 16. Thaw had married her on April 4, 1905 — 14 months before the shooting — when she was 20. In the interval, he had twice lived with her as man and wife on trips to Europe, and had caused a major New York scandal when the two of them were evicted from a hotel where they were again cohabiting.

In the events which followed the shooting, the principals fell into roles as clearly defined as those in an old-fashioned melodrama. White was the aging roué, seducer of young girls . . . Thaw the chivalrous avenger, who dwelt so long on his wife's dishonouring that he eventually had a "brainstorm" and killed the man who had wronged her . . . Evelyn, the young innocent, brought to a life of shame by a man she looked upon almost as a father, now standing loyally by the man she loved, the man who had made an honest woman of her.

Mrs. Thaw, Senr., who was in England visiting her daughter, the Countess of Yarmouth, also announced that she was returning to the United States to stand by her son. "I am prepared to pay a million dollars to save his life," she said.

Thaw's trial did not begin until January 21, 1907. In the intervening seven months, White underwent a character assassination in the newspapers that was unprecedented for an American of distinction moving in respectable society. There were so many tales about his amorous activities that, for even half to be true, he would have had to have slept with a large proportion of the women and teenage girls in New York.

A typical story concerned a 15-year-old model, Susie Johnson, who had been the highlight of a Bohemian party which White attended. She had risen out of a giant pie and exhibited her charms — "lilliputian, tender, rose-coloured breasts, and evasive hips, proclaiming precocious puberty" — clad only in a wisp of chiffon.

White was so taken with her, the story in the New York *Evening Journal* went on, that he plied her with champagne and, when she was in a stupefied condition, took her back to his apartment — "furnished with Oriental splendour" — and seduced her. Later, he turned her out penniless. "Girls, if you are poor, stay in the safe factory or kitchen," were the last words of the story which, it was said, Susie had told to a friend before dying at the age of 23 and being buried in a pauper's grave.

The campaign of slander and vilification against White was masterminded by Ben Atwell, a press agent hired by Thaw's mother. Mrs. Thaw Senr. also backed a play based loosely on the construction which the yellow press put on the known events.

Gave girls swings

It featured three characters named Harold Daw, Emeline Hudspeth Daw, and Stanford Black. On his first appearance, Black brutally assaulted a blind man who was asking for news of his beautiful young daughter. The Girl in the Pie incident was featured in another lurid scene. The play ended with Daw shooting Black during a performance in a roof garden theatre, then declaring from his cell at The Tombs (where Thaw was being held awaiting trial):

"No jury on earth will send me to the chair, no matter what I have done or what I have been, for killing the man who defamed my wife. That is the unwritten law made by men themselves, and upon its virtue I will stake my life."

There is evidence that the episode with Susie Johnson did take place at a party, given by an artist friend, which White attended. It seems probable, however, that the seduction part of the tale was inspired by what happened to Evelyn Nesbit before she became Mrs. Harry Thaw, and was seen as a useful overture to the story she would tell in court.

Evelyn first met White in the summer of 1901 when she was 16 and a girlfriend took her to lunch at the architect's apartment on West 24th Street. A second man was there but left after the meal. White then took the two girls upstairs to a room where there was a red velvet swing. He gave the girls swings in turn. "Right up to the ceiling," Evelyn recalled. "They had a big Japanese umbrella on the ceiling, so when we were swung up very high our feet passed through it."

White did not lose touch with his new discovery. He met her mother by arrangement and suggested that Evelyn should have some dental treatment. He sent her a hat, a feather boa, and a long red cape.

Throughout, he always behaved with the utmost correctness. "At supper," said Evelyn, "he wouldn't let me have but one glass of champagne, and he said

I mustn't stay up late. He took me home himself to the Arlington Hotel, where we were staying, and knocked at my mother's door."

Then came the day when Evelyn's mother decided to visit friends in Pittsburgh, but did not like to leave her daughter alone in New York. When he heard of this, White immediately offered his services. "You may leave her with me in perfect safety," he said. "I will take care of her." He also made Evelyn promise that she would not go out with anyone but him while her mother was away.

Mirrors round bed

White paid for her mother's trip and, the second night after her departure, sent a note to the theatre – Evelyn by this time was appearing in *Floradora* – asking her to a party at the West 24th Street apartment. When she got there, however, there were just the two of them. "The others have turned us down," White explained somewhat lamely.

He suggested they should have something to eat nevertheless, and afterwards offered to show her the rooms she hadn't seen on her previous visit. He took her up some tiny back stairs to a bedroom. "He poured me a glass of champagne," said Evelyn. "I don't know whether it was a minute after or two minutes after, but a pounding began in my ears, then the whole room seemed to go round."

When she came to, she said, she was in bed. All her clothes had been torn off. White, naked, lay beside her. There were mirrors all round the bed. "I started to scream," she said. "Mr. White tried to quieten me. I don't remember how I got my clothes on or how I went home, but he took me home. Then he went away and left me, and I sat up all night."

White called the next day and found her still sitting in a chair, staring out of the window. "Why don't you look at me, child?" he asked. "Because I can't," she replied. Then he told her not to worry because "Everyone does those things". She asked if the *Floradora* sextet, and various people she had met with White, made love. "They all do," he said, adding that the most important thing was not to be found out, and making her promise not to say a word to her mother about what had happened.

Amid all the subsequent mudslinging, Thaw, the "chivalrous avenger", did not escape. Before the trial one enterprising reporter unearthed details of a suit brought against him by a girl named Ethel Thomas in 1902. She told how, at the start of their relationship, Thaw had lavished affection upon her and bought her flowers and jewellery.

"But one day," she went on, "I met him by appointment, and, while we were walking towards his apartment at the Bedford, 304 Fifth Avenue, he stopped at a store and bought a dog whip. I asked him what that was for and he replied laughingly: 'That's for you, dear.' I thought he was joking, but no sooner were we in his apartment and the door locked than his entire demeanour changed. A wild expression came into his eyes, and he seized me and with his whip beat me until my clothes hung in tatters.'"

Evelyn, too, it was said, had undergone a similar experience during the first of her two European holidays with Thaw. She had suffered so much at his hands, in fact, that, on her return, she had gone to Abe Hummel, a celebrated shyster lawyer, and sworn an affidavit about the way Thaw had treated her.

The trouble had begun while they were staying at Schloss Katzenstein, a castle Thaw had rented in the Austrian Tyrol. One morning she had come down to breakfast wearing only a bathrobe. After the meal Thaw accompanied her to her bedroom where, "without any provocation", he grasped me by the throat and tore the bathrobe from my body, leaving me entirely nude except for my slippers.

". . . His eyes were glaring and he had in his right hand a cowhide whip. He seized hold of me and threw me on the bed. I was powerless and attempted to scream, but Thaw placed his fingers in my mouth and tried to choke me. He then, without any provocation, and without the slightest reason, began to inflict on me several severe and violent blows with the cowhide whip.

Besought him to desist

"So brutally did he assault me that my skin was cut and bruised. I besought him to desist, but he refused. I was so exhausted that I shouted and cried. He stopped every minute or so to rest, and then renewed his attack upon me, which he continued for about seven minutes. He acted like a demented man. I was absolutely in fear of my life . . . It was nearly three weeks before I was sufficiently recovered to be able to get out of my bed and walk.

"During all the time I travelled with Thaw, he would make the slightest pretext an excuse for a terrific assault on me . . . He also entered my bed and, without any consent, repeatedly wronged me. I reproved him for his conduct, but he compelled me to submit, threatening to beat and kill me if I did not do so . . " It was on this trip, she also claimed, that she had discovered Thaw was a cocaine addict.

Why, people wondered, had she married a man who treated her so badly? Evelyn's motives seem clear – the desire for wealth and position. Thaw, it appears, was "persuaded" to marry her by White at her family's instigation. The alternative to this was a charge – backed up by the affidavit – of corrupting a minor (Evelyn had been only 18 at the time of her first European holiday with Thaw).

The trial, which began on January 21, 1907, did not end until April 11. Then, after being out for more than 24 hours while an inquisitive crowd of 10,000 milled around under the courtroom windows, the jury announced that they had been unable to reach a verdict. On the final ballot, it was later learned, seven had voted Thaw guilty of first-degree murder, five had voted him not guilty by reason of insanity.

Thaw was kept in custody until his second trial started early in January 1908. This time his "ordeal" was shorter. On February 1 the jury – after again being out for more than 24 hours – found him not guilty by reason of insanity, and he was committed to the New York state asylum for the criminal insane.

Escape by limousine

Attempts by his lawyers to get him released were protracted and unsuccessful, and, on the morning of August 17, 1913, Thaw escaped from the asylum. With the aid of a limousine waiting outside the gates, he then sought refuge in Canada. The next month, under heavy pressure from the U.S. government, the Canadian Minister of Justice agreed to return him to the United States.

Put in jail in Concord, New Hampshire, Thaw fought a long legal battle against being returned to New York. It was not until December 1914 – over a year later – that the U.S. Supreme Court decided that this should happen. Back in New York, Thaw faced another long trial at which most of the evidence given at the two previous hearings was repeated. Finally, on July 16, 1915, he was declared sane and not guilty of all charges.

It was a victory of money over justice, and over commonsense for, only 18 months later, he was indicted for kidnapping and brutally whipping Frederick Gump Junr., a 19-year-old Kansas City youth. Once again Thaw was declared insane, but a week-long court hearing reversed the decision.

His bizarre behaviour periodically made the headlines until his death in February 1947, at the age of 76, after a heart attack. A photograph at the time showed him bespectacled and shrunken, looking more like a retired business executive than the sadistic paranoic that he was.

FINAL TRIANGLE: was the appealing Evelyn (opposite) really a young innocent? Was White (inset left) a father-figure turned seducer? Was young Thaw (inset right) a chivalrous avenger?

ALMA RATTENBURY had been a beautiful woman, but she felt frustrated in her marriage to an older husband. She threw herself into a passionate love affair with their young house-boy (opposite).

Murder at the Villa Madeira

Mrs. Rattenbury

Mrs. Rattenbury

Mrs. Alma Rattenbury was outwardly a conventional married woman who lived an apparently impeccable existence with her ageing husband. Within the refined walls of their Bournemouth house, however, the respectability was torn away to reveal a cesspool of lust, licence . . . and — finally — murder.

THE small advertisement lay buried in the dull, grey columns of the *Bournemouth Daily Echo*. A more innocent and innocuous offer it would be harder to imagine:

"Willing lad wanted, aged 14-18, for house-work. Scout training preferred."

The "willing lad" who replied was a dim-witted 17-year-old named George Percy Stoner, a semi-literate who lived with his grandmother and worked part-time at a garage. No Scout training ever devised, however, would have prepared him for what he soon discovered was to be his main duty — sharing the bed of his employer's wife.

Mrs. Alma Victoria Rattenbury was no ordinary woman. She was that most overpowering of female types, the Frustrated Artist. Impulsive, passionate and unbalanced, she saw herself as a creative personality caught in the dreary and soul-destroying labyrinth of married life. Her talents were minimal — she wrote the occasional sentimental song — but her temperament would have done justice to a creative genius.

Dull, stodgy husband

Alma Rattenbury's unconventional behaviour made the contrast between her and her husband even more pronounced. Francis Mawson Rattenbury was a retired architect, a dull and stodgy man whose main interest in life was rendering himself unconscious every night with a bottle of whisky. There was little sexual contact between the couple and their rooms were set apart on different floors.

As if all this wasn't enough to create an unbridgeable gulf between them, Mr. Rattenbury was 66, while Mrs. Rattenbury was an attractive and well-preserved 37. The word "incompatible" could have been coined for them.

In this sexually explosive atmosphere, the arrival of Stoner as chauffeur-handyman acted like a detonator, but even in her most melodramatic moments, Alma Rattenbury could never have foreseen the appalling repercussions of her passion for her loutish and immature employee. For within eight months of Stoner walking through the respectable door of the Villa Madeira, in Britain's archly-refined town of Bournemouth, both he and Alma Rattenbury were on trial for their lives.

And her teenage lover

In court, prosecuting counsel would point at Alma Rattenbury and accuse her of dominating and corrupting her lover. The judge would thunder, "You cannot have any feeling except disgust for her." And Alma Rattenbury, dazed and shocked at the ghastly train of events she had set in motion, would only explain, "I loved him, that's all, I loved him."

The Mr. Rattenbury-Mrs. Rattenbury-George Stoner triangle that had been constructed so satisfyingly in the Villa Madeira had shattered under a strain unusual even in this fragile sexual geometry. It was not the customary case of the "wronged husband" demanding the return of his marital rights. Far from it. Throughout the affair, Mr. Rattenbury, complaisant, incurious and uncomplaining, happily confined his embraces to the whisky bottle. Nor did Alma Rattenbury tire of her teenage lover — the flame of her passion burned to the bitter and brutal end. What nobody could have expected was that — inspired by his novel and elevated position — the loutish Stoner would develop airs and graces; that he would start behaving like a jumped-up ladies' man, that he would make demands and throw tantrums, and that he would become insanely jealous of the timorous and undemanding Francis Rattenbury.

In barely six months, the festering jealousy of George Stoner had led to a bloody climax which would have been more in keeping with the stage of the Grand Guignol than the prim backcloth of the Villa Madeira.

At the trial at the Old Bailey in May, 1935, Alma Rattenbury relived the grisly night when Stoner came into her room and, as usual, climbed between the sheets. "At first, I didn't notice anything unusual," she told the court. "But a little later I noticed he was looking a bit odd."

Counsel: What do you mean — odd?

Mrs. Rattenbury: Well, he seemed agitated and I said 'What's the matter, darling?' and he said he was in trouble and could not tell me. I said 'Oh, you must tell me' and we went back and forth like that for two or three minutes. He said no, I would not be able to bear it. I thought he was in some trouble outside. Then I said that I was strong enough to bear anything and then he told me . . . he told me he had hurt Mr. Rattenbury. It didn't penetrate my head what he had just said until I heard my husband groan; and then my brain became alive and I jumped out of bed and went downstairs as fast as I could.

I cannot remember

Counsel: Did you stop to put any clothes or slippers on?

Mrs. Rattenbury: Oh no.

Counsel: Did Stoner say anything about how he had done it?

Mrs. Rattenbury: He said he had hit him over the head with a mallet.

Counsel: Anything more about the mallet?

Mrs. Rattenbury: That he had hidden it outside.

Counsel: What did you find when you got downstairs?

Syndication International

Mrs. Rattenbury: Mr. Rattenbury sitting on the chair and he . . . and he . . .

Counsel: I don't think you need trouble to describe exactly what you saw, but he was sitting in the chair?

Mrs. Rattenbury: I tried to rub his hands, but they were cold. I tried to take his pulse and I shook him to try to make him speak. I tried to speak to him, and then I saw this blood, and I went round the table and trod on his false teeth and that made me hysterical and I screamed. I cannot remember, only vaguely. I drank some whisky to stop being sick.

Counsel: You say you screamed. Did you scream for anyone?

Mrs. Rattenbury: Yes, for Irene Riggs, my companion.

Counsel: Did she come down?

Mrs. Rattenbury: Yes.

Counsel: Was that the only drink of whisky you had?

Mrs. Rattenbury: No. I took one drink of whisky neat and I was sick and then I remembered pouring out another. I cannot remember drinking the next one. I tried to become insensible, to blot out the picture. I cannot now remember anything, from putting a white towel round Mr. Rattenbury's head and the vomiting and treading on those . . . aagh.

Counsel: You can remember nothing more about the events of that night?

Mrs. Rattenbury: No.

The mallet-blows had shattered Mr. Rattenbury's skull. But what had channelled Stoner's jealousy into such an outburst of ferocious violence? Just a small and insignificant incident . . . only its timing had been disastrous.

By March, 1935 — only 5½ months after answering the advertisement — Stoner's vanity had grown out of all proportion. Day by day, theatrical posturing alternated with sulks and scenes. Mr. Rattenbury kept out of the way, disinterested by day and tipsy by nightfall. Every night, Irene Riggs, Mrs. Rattenbury's companion, watched Stoner swagger into his mistress's bedroom, but although she was

HAPPY FAMILY? Mr. and Mrs. Rattenbury hardly seem to be enjoying their trip to the Bournemouth sands (above). Passion and death would soon destroy all semblance of their so-called unity.

scandalized she said nothing. Mrs. Rattenbury was clearly besotted with him.

On March 19 — after asking her husband for £250 — Mrs. Rattenbury took Stoner on a trip to London. They stayed in the Kensington Palace Hotel for four days as man and wife, although listed in the register as "brother and sister". This was to be Stoner's introduction to the life-style of a gentleman-about-town. Mrs. Rattenbury took him to the most expensive shops, where fawning assistants fitted the bumpkin with fashionable suits, shirts, underwear, shoes and gloves.

She bought him expensive silk ties and crêpe-de-Chine pyjamas, and in a humiliating act of self-abasement paid £16 for a diamond ring, which she then accepted as a present. As if "cohabiting above his class" had not already turned Stoner's head, the dazzling experience in London completed his mental picture of himself as an elegant stud, a kept man in crêpe-de-Chine pyjamas. It was with his absurdly inflated ego that Stoner returned to the Villa Madeira.

But instead of entering as master of the house, Stoner returned with a bump to reality. Probably through the effects of alcohol, Mr. Rattenbury was in a depressed mood, and to cheer him up Alma Rattenbury suggested staying overnight with friends at Bridport. "Stoner will drive us," she told him. Stoner, however, had other ideas. He had no intention of reverting to his menial role as chauffeur-

handyman to the Rattenburys.

When Mrs. Rattenbury broke the news, Stoner produced an air-pistol and waved it at her threateningly. "If you go to Bridport, get this straight, I will kill you!" he said. Mrs. Rattenbury tried to placate him, but his eyes narrowed in an expression of half-witted cunning.

Vanity and pride

For some reason, the idea had lodged in his head that Mr. and Mrs. Rattenbury might share the same bed in their friends' house. "Ratz went to your room today — I saw him," he said. "You were both inside there and the door was shut. Think I'm blind? Think I don't know what was

going on? It'll be the same at Bridport, won't it?"

For once, Alma Rattenbury ignored his tantrums and stood her ground. It was a fatal psychological mistake. Stoner's vanity and pride — boosted by his extravagant fling in London — had been wounded. Whatever happened, he was not going to sit meekly behind the wheel and drive the Rattenburys to Bridport like some miserable servant. If Alma Rattenbury refused to cancel the arrangement, then he would have to think of some other way of stopping it.

At around eight o'clock on the evening of Sunday, March 24, Stoner appeared at his grandparent's home at nearby Ensbury Park and asked if he could borrow a wooden mallet. "I've got to put up a tent and I need to drive in some pegs," he explained. By 10.30 that night, everyone in the Villa Madeira was asleep — well, almost everyone. Padding along the corridor from her bedroom to the toilet, Miss Riggs was surprised to find Stoner leaning over the banisters in his pyjamas and listening intently.

From below came the muffled snores of Mr. Rattenbury, who had fallen asleep in the drawing-room, cradling his bottle of whisky.

RELEASED but broken . . . Alma leaves London's Old Bailey after being found not guilty of her husband's murder. But without Stoner she had no wish to live.

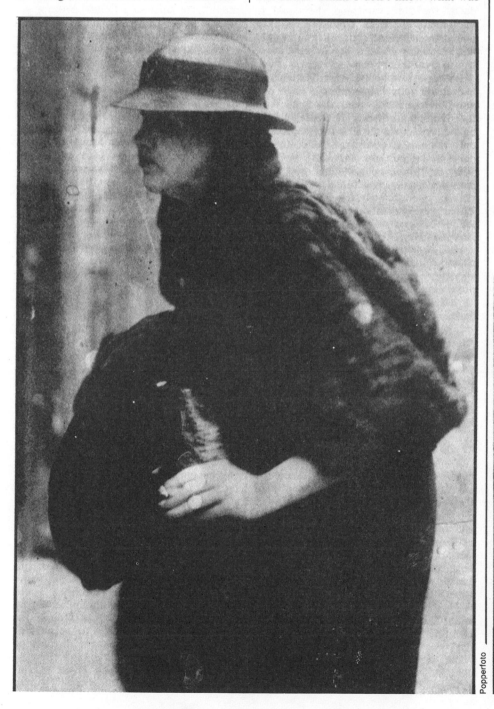

15

"What's the matter?" asked Miss Riggs. "Nothing," replied Stoner. "I was just checking to see if all the lights were out, that's all."

Miss Riggs returned to bed and was joined a few minutes later by Alma Rattenbury, who came in for her usual night-time gossip. She could talk of nothing else but the forthcoming visit to Bridport and how much she was looking forward to it. Whispering "Goodnight" excitedly, she left.

It was exactly 15 minutes later that Alma Rattenbury's piercing scream shattered the peace of the Villa Madeira. In the gruesome moment she was to describe so graphically at the Old Bailey, she had just stepped on her husband's false teeth, lying in the pool of blood flowing from his wrecked head.

"Oh look . . ."

Miss Riggs dashed downstairs to the drawing-room. The door had been flung open and Alma Rattenbury was standing in the shaft of light moaning, "Oh look . . . oh look . . . oh look." It was a sickening sight. Francis Rattenbury sat in his armchair, his head a scarlet mop. A rivulet of blood flowed down his clothes and spread across the floor. It was Miss Riggs who took control. She telephoned Dr. O'Donnell nearby and, to make sure he left immediately, sent Stoner to his home with the car.

Dr. O'Donnell took one look at Francis Rattenbury and phoned for a local surgeon, Mr. Rooke. Mr. Rattenbury was still alive . . . but only just. Despite the obvious and grisly evidence that Mr. Rattenbury had been attacked from behind by a blunt instrument, Alma Rattenbury started babbling about suicide. Her voice was hysterical. "Ratz was feeling depressed . . . we were going away . . . tomorrow, I mean, but that was this afternoon . . . he read me something out of a book . . . he said he admired a man who could do that . . . what it said, taking his own life . . . people do live too long, don't they, or at least that's what he thought."

Mrs. Rattenbury jumped to the piano, where a book was lying half-open. "Look, here it is, here it is," she stuttered. "Just where he put it . . . this is the book . . . where the man commits suicide . . . it's in it somewhere . . . he had lived too long."

While Mr. Rattenbury was rushed to hospital by ambulance, the distraught and incoherent Alma Rattenbury stayed at the villa. Emotionally unstable at the best of times and now demented by shock and alcohol, her condition had deteriorated frightfully by the time the police arrived at 2 a.m.

They were confronted with a grotesque scene. Still dressed in her nightclothes, Alma Rattenbury darted restlessly about the room babbling a stream of semi-gibberish. Her eyes were fixed and bulging and her movements were jerky and uncontrolled. She had put on her radio-gram and it was whooping away at full blast; as soon as one record finished, she put on another. Even more alarming, Alma Rattenbury had become drunkenly lecherous. She tried to kiss and paw the bewildered policemen, and had to be physically restrained from following one of them out of the house.

In her unhinged state, Alma Rattenbury presented the perfect picture of the drunken nymphomaniac and it was hardly surprising that suspicion first fell upon her rather than the saturnine Stoner. Indeed, she did everything she could to incriminate herself. Unknown to the policemen, the one rational thought that had somehow pierced her fuddled brain was to protect her lover.

Within a few hours, Alma Rattenbury had made four "statements", each one more incriminating than the last. With the radiogram blaring deafeningly, the police took down the first two statements only minutes after arriving. Mrs. Rattenbury described how she had "heard a yell" or "someone groaning" and, running downstairs, had found her husband sitting unconscious in his armchair. There was no mention of Stoner. Indeed, the police were still unaware of his very existence.

Half-an-hour later, while agitatedly pacing round the room, Mrs. Rattenbury suddenly exclaimed, "I did it!" The policemen scrambled for their notebooks. "I did it with a mallet," she continued dramatically. "Ratz has lived too long . . . it is hidden . . . no, my lover did it." At this point, Mrs. Rattenbury lost the thread of the sentence and drifted into what sounded like a feeble attempt at bribery. "I would like to give you £10 . . . no, I won't bribe you." But it was enough, however garbled. Alma Rattenbury had undeniably admitted her guilt.

"I did it"

The last statement under caution—even more halting and confused—came at around 3.40 a.m. "I did it," she repeated. "He gave me the book . . . he has lived too long . . . he said, 'Dear, dear' . . . I will tell you in the morning where the mallet is . . . have you told the coroner yet? . . . I shall make a better job of it next time . . . Irene does not know . . . I made a proper muddle of it . . . I thought I was strong enough."

The words were barely out of her mouth when Dr. O'Donnell returned from the hospital. He was furious. Mrs. Rattenbury was about to make another statement when the doctor intervened. "Have you cautioned this lady?" he asked the inspector in charge, with some asperity.

"No," said the inspector. "Well, look at her condition," snapped the doctor, who had just given her half a grain of morphia as a sedative. "She is full of whisky and I have given her a large dose of morphia. She is not fit to make a statement to you or anybody else."

Alma Rattenbury was carried upstairs to bed. But she was not allowed to rest. At 8.15—still half-drugged from the morphia administered only $4\frac{1}{2}$ hours earlier—she was charged with the attempted murder of her husband. Before she left the house, she made one final, disjointed statement. "I was playing cards with my husband when he dared me to kill him as he wanted to die. I picked up the mallet. He then said 'You have not got enough guts to do it.' I then hit him with the mallet and hid it outside the house. I would have shot him if I had a gun."

Talking too much

On the way out, Mrs. Rattenbury passed her little son John—only now aroused from bed, and white-faced and bewildered—the loyal Miss Riggs and the silent Stoner. "Don't make fools of yourselves," she told them. Only Stoner replied. "You have got yourself into this mess by talking too much," he muttered.

Stoner stayed silent for four days. On March 28, Francis Rattenbury died in hospital without ever regaining consciousness. By now, Stoner had been told about his mistress's incriminating statements. Plagued by conscience—and a genuine concern for Alma Rattenbury—he blurted out to Miss Riggs, "She is in jail and I have put her there. I am going to see her tomorrow and I shall give myself up. I want to be up at half-past six in the morning. Don't let me oversleep, now."

Miss Riggs didn't give Stoner a chance to change his mind. Forestalling the alarm-call, she telephoned the police and reported the conversation. That evening, Stoner was arrested and charged.

Nobody could ever claim that the passionate affair between Mrs. Rattenbury and George Stoner represented love at its most exalted and sublime, but faced with the hangman's noose, their devotion and loyalty to each other transcended the sordid details of their relationship. Each one was prepared to shoulder the blame for Mr. Rattenbury's murder, and vindicate the other.

Right up until the trial, Alma Rattenbury refused to withdraw her confession—until her legal advisers finally persuaded her that her own sacrifice would not make the slightest difference to the case against Stoner. Stoner himself instructed his lawyers not to suggest in any way that he had been incited or influenced by Mrs. Rattenbury, or that she had known anything about his intention to murder her husband. To help her own case, he refused to give evidence.

On the day of his arrest, Stoner had told the police: "Do you know that Mrs. Rattenbury had nothing to do with this affair? Yes, when I did the job I believed he was asleep. I hit him and then came upstairs and told Mrs. Rattenbury. She rushed down then. You see, I watched through the french windows and saw her kiss him good night, then leave the room.

"I waited and crept in through the french window, which was unlocked. I think he must have been asleep when I hit him, still it ain't much use saying anything. I don't suppose they will let her out yet. You know, there should be a doctor with her when they tell her I am arrested, because she will go out of her mind."

On May 27, 1935, George Stoner and Alma Rattenbury stood before one of Britain's sternest judges, Mr. Justice Humphreys, jointly charged with the murder of Francis Rattenbury. Local feeling against the couple had run so high that the hearing had been moved from Winchester Assizes to the Old Bailey in London. Both pleaded not guilty.

Stoner claimed that he was a regular cocaine addict and had been under the influence of the drug at the time. His defence was knocked right out of court by expert medical evidence which proved

that he had not shown the faintest signs of drug-withdrawal in the days immediately after his arrest.

But the strangest feature of the trial was Alma Rattenbury's almost total loss of memory. She could recall nothing of the events following the discovery of her husband's body. The combination of morphia, alcohol and shock—probably coupled with a psychosomatic "blackout" —had left her mind a complete blank. Earlier, she had described how she had tried to "blot out the picture" with whisky.

Apparently, she had been completely successful, for no efforts by counsel could make her see again that macabre night when the radiogram blared while she alternately flirted, babbled and wept in a bloodstained room.

"I cannot remember"

Her own counsel, Mr. Terence O'Connor, K.C., tried first.

Counsel: Do you remember the police officers coming?

Mrs. Rattenbury: No.

Counsel: Do you remember sending for Dr. O'Donnell?

Mrs. Rattenbury: I cannot remember anything.

Realizing that the line of questioning was getting them nowhere, Mr. O'Connor turned to a more constructive approach:

Counsel: Mrs. Rattenbury, did you yourself murder your husband?

Mrs. Rattenbury: Oh, no.

Counsel: Or take any part whatsoever in planning it?

Mrs. Rattenbury: Oh, no.

Counsel: Did you know a thing about it till Stoner spoke about it in your bed?

Mrs. Rattenbury: Naturally, I would have prevented it if I had known a half —a quarter of a minute before.

To the court—half-expecting some kind of hideous, drunken degenerate to mount the steps of the witness-box—Mrs. Rattenbury had already emerged as a sympathetic figure. She was attractive and smartly dressed. Her voice was clear and her answers frank. Above all, she had a natural dignity which seemed to be completely out of keeping with the distasteful details of the case. Could such a sensitive woman really have conspired to bludgeon her husband to death?

Prosecuting counsel, Mr. R. P. Croom-Johnson, K.C., was less impressed. Undaunted by Mrs. Rattenbury's plea of amnesia, he decided to break down her mental block with a brisk approach:

CROWDS turned up for the funeral of Mrs. Rattenbury after her desperate suicide. The salacious details of the trial had aroused the usual interest . . .

Counsel: Are you seriously telling members of the jury that, practically from the time you were sick and poured yourself a glass of whisky, your memory does not serve you *at all*?

Mrs. Rattenbury: I can remember a few things, like in an awful nightmare.

Encouraged, Mr. Croom-Johnson asked "Tell me a few things you recollect on that night?" But it was a false start.

Mrs. Rattebury: Oh, nothing . . .

Impatiently, Mr. Croom-Johnson returned to jogging her memory on the night of the murder.

Counsel: Do you recollect Dr. O'Donnell coming?

Mrs. Rattenbury: I cannot.

Counsel: *What?*

Mrs. Rattenbury: I have tried so hard to remember, even with piecing together what I have heard, and I cannot.

Counsel: Dr. O'Donnell was a friend of yours and your medical adviser?

Mrs. Rattenbury: Yes.

Counsel: As a rule, a person calculated to soothe rather than excite you?

Mrs. Rattenbury: Yes.

Counsel: And you recollect *nothing* of Dr. O'Donnell that night?

Mrs. Rattenbury: No.

Counsel: Or a succession of police officers coming in?

Mrs. Rattenbury: No.

Time and opportunity

No amount of hinting or nudging could elicit more than a shake of the head or a firm "No" from the witness. Counsel took a logical detour and suggested to Mrs. Rattenbury that she had been a regular drinker, used to taking large quantities of alcohol—a tactic aimed at making the jury wonder why a couple of whiskies could have produced total amnesia. Mrs. Rattenbury agreed unhesitatingly. After this cunning short cut, Mrs. Rattenbury's brisk admission only brought counsel face to face once again with the brick wall of her loss of memory.

Counsel: About incidents, your mind is completely blank?

Mrs. Rattenbury: It might be somebody else you are talking about.

Counsel: Blank about people too?

Mrs. Rattenbury: Oh, yes.

Counsel: About conversations?

Mrs. Rattenbury: Quite.

With the long-suffering air of someone who knew exactly what answer was coming, Mr. Croom-Johnson held up a policeman's yellow notebook:

Counsel: Is your mind a complete blank about making a statement to the detective-inspector, which he wrote down in this?

Mrs. Rattenbury: I cannot remember that. I've tried and tried. Yesterday, last night, I tried to remember again that—

Counsel: Just look at the book. Do you see the words 'Alma Rattenbury'?

Mrs. Rattenbury: Yes, I see them. It is all absolutely double-Dutch to me.

Determined to evoke *some* flicker of recollection, Mr. Croom-Johnson moved on to midday of March 25, after Mrs. Rattenbury had been in the police station some hours. This time she responded.

Counsel: At the police station that morning, somewhere around 12.30, do you recollect writing a cheque for Stoner for £5?

Mrs. Rattenbury: I remember writing two cheques, one for Irene and one for Stoner, but I do not remember who I gave them to.

Counsel: Do you remember how much were they for?

Mrs. Rattenbury: £5 each.

Counsel: And who they were for?

Mrs. Rattenbury: Yes, absolutely.

Counsel: Up to that moment, according to your evidence, your mind is a complete blank for many hours?

Mrs. Rattenbury: I cannot even remember how I got the cheque book.

Counsel: So that from the moment you poured that glass of whisky, do you wish the members of the jury to believe that your mind is a complete blank, with the exception of one or two trifling things which you have told us, until you recollect about the two cheques at the police station at 12.30 on the Monday morning?

"That," replied Mrs. Rattenbury with some finality, "is absolutely true."

Throughout the trial, nothing could shake Alma Rattenbury from her story. But consistency is one thing, truth another. Would the jury believe in her loss

THE SEDATE STYLE of the Villa Madeira (below) gave no inkling of the high passions at play behind the walls . . .

of memory, so selective in its timing? And would there be any sympathy to spare for Stoner, now left with the full burden of guilt?

The night before the verdict, Alma Rattenbury sat late in her cell in Holloway Prison and wrote a number of letters. In one, she said, "I have quite made up my mind here to finish things should Stoner hang; it would only be a matter of time and opportunity." In another, she said, "If I only thought it would help Stoner, I would stay on. But it has been pointed out to me all too vividly that I cannot help him. That is *my* death sentence."

On May 31, 1935, the Old Bailey jury returned to their benches with their verdicts. Alma Rattenbury was found Not Guilty, and acquitted. George Percy Stoner was found Guilty and sentenced to death by hanging.

Three days afterwards, on June 3, Alma Rattenbury took a train to New Milton in Hampshire and sat for a while on the river-bank smoking a cigarette. She put her fur coat and handbag on the grass beside her and stared at the sun reflected in the water. The words of her own letter must have drifted through her mind . . . "I have quite made up my mind to finish things should Stoner hang; it would only be a matter of time and opportunity." A man walking along the opposite bank saw something glint in the sun. Alma Rattenbury had stood up.

Before the man could move, she had plunged a knife six times into her breast, with such ferocity that three wounds entered her heart. She sank into the water, which carried her gently away from the bank.

A few weeks later, George Percy Stoner was reprieved and his sentence commuted to life imprisonment.

Shots in the Mews

Mrs. Barney

Her lips were as tender as they had always been, but her lover had already succumbed . . . to a fatal bullet. Whose finger had been on the trigger? The Bright Young People of England's upper classes, mocked by the famous author Evelyn Waugh in his book *Vile Bodies,* had created a new sensation.

BETWEEN the Wars young members of London Society were beginning to displace servants and chauffeurs as tenants of the flats above the garages in the London mews. It was from this setting that twenty-seven-year-old Mrs. Elvira Dolores Barney went on trial for the shooting to death of her lover Mr. Michael Scott Stephen in the London mews where she lived.

Both Elvira Barney and Michael Stephen, who was a year younger than his mistress, came from "good" families. Mrs. Barney's family was particularly wealthy, her old Etonian father, Sir John Mullens, having got his knighthood from Lloyd George for his generous contributions to political party funds. Sir John and Lady Mullens had a house in fashionable Belgrave Square and another in the country, but their daughter Elvira did not live with them.

Even after her husband had left her, which he had done about two years previously, she preferred to live independently in a mews flat off Knightsbridge. After they separated, Mr. Barney had gone to America, where, according to his wife, he became a singer.

Elvira Barney and the lover she took, after her husband's departure, belonged to the gay social set known popularly as the "Bright Young People", who gallivanted round London and were satirized by Evelyn Waugh in his early novels like *Vile Bodies*. They drank far more than was good for them, tore about the town in bright-coloured sports cars and even brighter-coloured clothes, played absurd and sometimes unkind practical jokes, indulged in riotous parties, as well as in promiscuous sex, and generally made nuisances of themselves.

Extravagant sponger

Early in his life Michael Stephen had developed wild and extravagant habits and had been turned out of the house by his father. At the time of the tragedy he occupied a bed-sittingroom in the Brompton Road, when he was not sleeping with Mrs. Barney or some other woman. He described himself as a dress designer, but in fact he lived largely by sponging on rich women; during the period of his acquaintance with Mrs. Barney, he had been quite content to be kept by her.

Nor did the course of their relations by any means run smoothly. At times they would make love with fierce abandonment; at other times their relations were marked by stormy scenes, when they would quarrel far into the night.

The "crime of passion" trial of Mrs. Barney for the murder of Michael Scott Stephen began before Mr. Justice Humphreys at the Central Criminal Court on July 5, 1932. Sir Percival Clarke led for the prosecution and Sir Patrick Hastings for the defence. Hastings, who was one of the leading advocates of the day in civil actions, rarely appeared in a criminal court. He only did so on this occasion, after he had first refused the brief, at the urgent entreaty of his wife, who felt sorry for Mrs. Barney's parents because of the unfavourable publicity which their daughter's behaviour had reflected upon them.

In his opening speech to the jury, the prosecutor described the scene at 21 Williams Mews, Knightsbridge, in the early hours of May 31, 1932, when Dr. Thomas Durrant, a well-known London physician, had arrived in answer to a telephone summons from Mrs. Barney. Stephen was lying dead on the floor of the upstairs spare bedroom. He was fully clothed, and near his left wrist was a loaded revolver. "He can't be dead," Mrs. Barney cried hysterically. "I love him so . . . He wanted to see you to tell you it was an accident . . . Let me die, let me die. I will kill myself." Dr. Durrant put his foot on the revolver to prevent her seizing it, and managed to control her with great difficulty.

Mrs. Barney went on to tell him in disjointed and incoherent sentences what had happened. They had had a quarrel. Michael had picked up the revolver from a chair where it was hidden under a cushion. They struggled and while they were doing so the gun went off. She did not know how. He had told her, as he lay dying, to call a doctor.

Shortly afterwards Detective-Inspector Winter arrived and examined the revolver, which he found to have five chambers with

Popperfoto

Radio Times Hulton

THE FATED FACES
of Elvira Barney . . . with her
husband (above), who left
her; and with her mother,
Lady Mullens, in a picture
front-paged at the time
of the trial. Her life of
gallivanting was brought to
an abrupt and dramatic halt
by the death of Michael
Stephen (left). Had she
wanted to kill herself?

weeks before," said the witness, adding
that on this occasion it was Mrs. Barney
who did it.

At this point the judge intervened.
"You mean you saw Mrs. Barney fire?"

"Yes, my Lord," Mrs. Hall replied.
"She fired out of the window. That was
in the early hours of the morning."

The witness went on to relate how she
had heard Mrs. Barney screaming out of
the window at Stephen on this previous
occasion, telling him to go away before
she sent for the police. "He was outside
at Mrs. Barney's door. He asked for
money and was told to go away and fish
for it. He went away in the taxi he'd come
in, but he soon came back—walking." The
next time Mrs. Hall looked out of the
window, Stephen was walking away. Mrs.
Barney then looked out of her window
opposite and cried, "Laugh, baby, laugh
for the last time!" Then she fired.

"How was she dressed?"

"Oh, I don't think she had anything on."

"How do you know she fired?"

"I saw her and heard the shot."

Get out! I'll shoot

According to the chauffeur's wife, the
shot was accompanied by a puff of smoke.
At that moment, said Mrs. Hall, Stephen
was standing just outside Mrs. Barney's
front door. Then he went away and got
into a greengrocer's van, which was
standing in the mews. The witness added
that she had heard them quarrelling before,
"many times, and in the early morning".

"Did you ever hear any other shot?"
was Clarke's final question.

"No," said the witness.

The prosecutor's examination of the
chauffeur's wife had revealed a slight but
very important discrepancy, which
defence council Hastings was quick to
note. In Mrs. Hall's original statement to
the police, which had been repeated at the
preliminary proceedings in the magistrate's court before Mrs. Barney was committed for trial, Mrs. Hall had stated that
just before the fatal shot was fired she
had heard Mrs. Barney say, "Get out,
I'll shoot you!"

Indeed this had been emphasized by the
prosecuting counsel in his opening speech.
But in her evidence at the trial the witness
had significantly changed the words to,
"Get out, I'll shoot!"

It was a vital difference; but when he
rose to cross-examine Mrs. Hall, Sir
Patrick Hastings did not touch upon it at
all, for fear that she might go back on
the version she had just given the prosecutor. He decided instead to concentrate
on the earlier shooting incident. In answer
to his opening questions, Mrs. Hall
stated that the same morning, three weeks
before, she had seen Mrs. Barney and
Stephen leave the flat together.

"Did they seem to you to be on the best

two discharged and three live cartridges.

He then looked into the bedroom and
noticed that the bed bore traces of having
recently been occupied by two persons.
The police officer also noticed the mark
of a bullet on the wall. When Inspector
Winter saw Mrs. Barney, she flared up
and ordered him out of the apartment. She
refused to accompany him to the police
station until her parents arrived.

"I'll teach you to put me in a cell, you
foul swine!" she shouted at the detective.
However, when her parents arrived she
went quietly to the station; there she
made a statement to the effect that the
shooting had been an accident, following
a quarrel about another woman. "As we
were struggling together—it went off." At
first she did not think he was seriously
injured, but she telephoned when he
said, "Fetch a doctor."

The first material witness was most
important from the point of view of the
prosecution. She was Mrs. Hall, the wife
of a chauffeur, who lived in the house
opposite Mrs. Barney's in the mews.
Answering Sir Percival Clarke, she said

she had often seen Stephen there; in fact,
he had been there earlier the same night
when Mrs. Barney had invited some
friends for cocktails and she had seen the
visitors arriving and going away, after
which Mrs. Barney and Stephen left together. She knew their voices well, and
about two o'clock in the morning she
heard them having a row. The witness
went on to say she looked out of her
window and heard Mrs. Barney say, "Get
out, I'll shoot!" She said it twice.

"Did you hear any answer?" asked
Clarke.

"No, I only heard a shot," answered
Mrs. Hall. "It appeared to come from
Mrs. Barney's front room. When I heard
the shot, I heard Mr. Stephen shouting,
'Good God, what have you done?' Mrs.
Barney then screamed, 'Chicken, chicken,
come back to me. I will do anything I can
for you.' Mrs. Barney was crying and very
hysterical. The doctor arrived shortly
afterwards."

"Was that the first time you had heard
the sound of firing from that place?"

"There was some shooting about three

Sunday Pictorial

JUNE 5, 1932

KNIGHT'S DAUGHTER COLLAPSES

Dramatic Scene When Charged with the Murder of J.P.'s Son

PRISONER CARRIED FROM COURT

Mother Renders Aid to Pale and Distraught Woman— Flat Tragedy Sequel

SOCIETY WOMEN IN RUSH FOR DOOR

Pale-faced, distraught, almost unable to walk, a knight's daughter was assisted to the dock at Westminster Police Court yesterday to answer a charge of murder;

ANXIETY FOR FLYER LAST

No News of Man Who Jersey on

DANGER OF HE

Considerable anxiety was flying circles for Mr. B Polish-American airman, w nett Field, New Jersey, on fly across the Atlantic to
It was stated at the Croydon airport late last had been heard of the fl
Mr. Hausner's 'plane— plane—is not equipped w
His petrol supply is as in the air until this even

possible terms?"

"Very friendly."

Having established this point, Mrs. Barney's counsel asked the witness whether Stephen had spoken to her, after Mrs. Barney had fired the revolver and while Mrs. Hall was at her window. "Yes," she said. "That was before he got into the greengrocer's van."

"What did he say to you?"

Sir Percival Clarke immediately jumped up and objected that the answer to this question was inadmissible as evidence. In reply, Hastings submitted—on somewhat shaky grounds—that it was always admissible to give evidence of a statement accompanying such an incident as this, and the judge ruled in his favour. Hastings subsequently expressed the view that Clarke was "probably right" and that Mr. Justice Humphreys, who was a most experienced criminal lawyer, had strained the law of evidence in favour of the accused on this occasion when he allowed the witness to answer the question.

"What conversation passed between you and the young man?" Hastings repeated the question.

"I told him to clear off, as he was a perfect nuisance in the mews," said Mrs. Hall.

"What did he reply?"

"He apologized and said he didn't want to leave Mrs. Barney *because he was afraid that she might kill herself.*"

This admission was one of cardinal importance for the defence, since it corroborated the story which, Hastings knew Mrs. Barney would tell in the witness box —namely that she had fired the revolver on the first occasion with the intention of frightening her lover and making him

think that she was going to commit suicide.

Mrs. Stevens, wife of another chauffeur living in the mews, corroborated Mrs. Hall's account of the night of the fatal shooting except that she swore she had heard five shots in all. Hastings cross-examined her on this point.

"You say that you heard five shots?"

"I heard five shots altogether," replied the witness, "and a great many other people must have heard them too, but they are not public-spirited enough to come forward."

Here the judge broke in with a question. "Do you think you are quite sure that what you heard were pistol shots and not something else?"

Mrs. Stevens said she was quite sure they were pistol shots. In doing so, she showed how a witness can easily form a mistaken impression on a vital topic, since the condition of the revolver after the tragedy showed that only two shots in all had been fired.

The next witness was Dr. Durrant, who confirmed what had happened after he

arrived at Mrs. Barney's flat and how she emphasized that Stephen had accidentally shot himself.

"Did she appear to be passionately devoted to this dead man?" Hastings asked the doctor in cross-examination.

"Oh, yes."

"Did she kiss him after he was dead?"

"Yes, several times."

"And did her actions appear to you, so far as you could judge, to be absolutely sincere and genuine?"

"Certainly."

"Did you believe that she was telling the truth?" Hastings went on, conscious that he was taking a certain risk with this question. But the risk was justified by the witness's reply.

"I haven't the slightest doubt that she was telling me what she thought was the truth," said Dr. Durrant.

Next morning the prosecution called Inspector Winter, who described Mrs. Barney's behaviour when he went to the flat after the shooting. He then read out a love letter which he found there and which Stephen had written to his mistress,

DRAMA IN COURT: Witness Mrs. Hall (far left) . . . "laugh, baby, laugh". **Prosecutor Sir Percival Clarke (above, left)** . . . "inadmissible evidence". **Judge Humphreys (above)** . . . "straining the law". **Jurors (left, walking to the courtroom)** . . . verdict was greeted with cheers.

asking forgiveness for "all the dreadful, horrible things" he had done.

"I love you, only you, in all the world, little one." To this effusion Mrs. Barney had responded in kind. "You hand me the biggest thrills I've ever had, my sweet," she had written, "and all I hope is that we can go on being thrilled endlessly . . . I feel like suicide when you are angry."

In his cross-examination of Inspector Winter, Hastings elicited two important pieces of information. The first related to the earlier shooting incident, when Mrs. Hall had testified that she saw Mrs. Barney fire out of the window. The witness admitted that no trace of any bullet had been found in the mews, despite a very thorough search.

The second piece of information Hastings got from Inspector Winter, Mrs. Barney's defender regarded as a stroke of luck. It concerned the handling of the revolver after the shooting and, as Hastings observed afterwards, it showed that on this occasion the police had not acted with their usual acumen. Questioned

about the fingerprints on the weapon, the witness agreed that if two people struggled over a revolver it would be likely that the fingerprints would be indecipherable.

"Was this revolver examined for fingerprints?"

"Yes."

"Was it found that the marks on it were so blurred that no fingerprints were decipherable except one?"

"That is so."

"Whose was that one?"

"Mine."

The remaining prosecution testimony came from "expert witnesses". Sir Bernard Spilsbury, the government pathologist, who had carried out the postmortem, disposed of the unlikely theory that Stephen might have deliberately shot himself by showing that if he had bent his wrist to do so it would have been impossible to get enough power to fire the weapon at all. However, in cross-examination he admitted that one of Stephen's ribs had been fractured by the bullet and that it was clear from this that the line taken by the bullet was horizontal.

Robert Churchill, the well known gunmaker, stated in examination that the weapon was one of the safest made, weighing 13 ounces and having a 14-pound pull. Questioned about the discharge, he said this would make a loud report, but that there would be very little

smoke from the cartridges which were filled with cordite.

Hastings began his cross-examination of this witness with a dramatic gesture. When he was handed the revolver by the court usher, he immediately pointed it at the roof of the court. He then pulled the trigger several times to show how easily it could be done. In fact he did so with such vigour that he gave himself a sore finger. The gunmaker agreed that it seemed easy. Nevertheless, he persisted, the weapon had a 14-pound pull.

"What is the meaning of a fourteen pound pull?" asked the judge.

"The dead weight required to pull the trigger," the witness explained.

Further questioned by Hastings as to how it came about that some of the cartridges had been fired and others not, Mr. Churchill said that the cylinder could be rotated by hand.

"If two people were struggling to get possession of the revolver and the pressure exerted was not enough to fire it at first, the cylinder might be turned round."

"It might spin round," Mr. Churchill replied carefully.

"If the struggling persons are close, and one has the revolver in her hand and the other seizes her hand, would it go off?"

"It might," the gunmaker agreed.

"When the finger, not of the person killed, is on the trigger?"

"Yes."

The last of the expert witnesses, Major Pollard, said that he had examined a similar weapon and fired it. He found that it discoloured a glove on the hand of the person firing it.

"You mean that if one puts one's hand over the barrel of the revolver when it is fired it gets black?"

"Yes," said the expert.

Extensive bruising

This testimony concluded the case for the prosecution. Hastings opened his defence by telling the jury that the doctor in Holloway prison, where Mrs. Barney had been held since her arrest, had made a report on her. Hastings had been allowed to see the report through the courtesy of the prosecution, and he was now allowed to call the doctor to prove its contents without his being regarded strictly speaking as a witness for the defence.

Had the doctor been a proper defence witness, Hastings, by the rules of court procedure, would have lost his right to the last word with the jury; defence counsel's right if he calls no material witness except the accused person.

The doctor, who was also the prison governor, stated that he had examined Mrs. Barney on her admission to Holloway. He had found fairly extensive bruising on her arms and on her right thigh which might have been caused by fingers.

There were also cuts and abrasions on one of her hands.

"If she had been struggling with the revolver in her hand," Hastings asked the doctor, "would the marks be consistent with that?"

"Yes."

Hastings called only one other witness, the prisoner herself. Everything now depended on Mrs. Barney, whether she would be able to confirm the breach in the prosecution's case which her counsel had already made, or whether her story would be riddled with improbability when she came to be cross-examined. No wonder Hastings afterwards confessed to having been very anxious when his client entered the witness box.

Physical maltreatment

Elvira Barney appeared a lonely and pitiful figure, as she took the oath in a low and trembling voice. Then she looked up and saw her mother, who was sitting in the well of the court; for a moment Hastings thought she was going to break down, but she quickly pulled herself together and began to answer his questions, at first showing considerable nervousness. From the outset her counsel set out to create an atmosphere of sympathy for her with the jury, and to some extent he succeeded as he asked her about her unhappy marriage to a man who used to ill-treat her physically and whom she had been unable to divorce on account of his American domicile. Hastings then came to her first meeting with Stephen in the previous autumn and the subsequent ripening of their acquaintance to intense devotion on her part.

"Were you anxious to marry him?"

"Very."

"And from the time you became devoted to him did you in fact become his mistress?"

"Yes."

"And did you support him almost entirely?"

"Almost entirely," Mrs. Barney echoed her counsel's words.

Asked whether Michael Stephen had always been kind to her, the prisoner said he had not always been so and sometimes she was frightened of him; on one occasion she had called the police to her flat. She went on to say that one of the causes of the unhappiness which sprang up between her and her lover was that he used to gamble, and there was another woman that he used to go out with for this purpose. Mrs. Barney gave him money to gamble with when he came and asked her.

Questioned by her counsel about the revolver, Mrs. Barney explained that it had been given to her by a friend in Devonshire who had used it for shooting rabbits. She also stated that she had

THE FINEST SPEECH the judge had ever heard. No appeals to emotion, just a careful analysis of the facts . . . for the defence, Sir Patrick Hastings.

never called her lover "Chicken" at any time in her life. In spite of their periodic rows, her devotion to him was unbroken.

"But I loved him," she said, her voice almost at breaking point. "I adored him."

Coming to the occasion some weeks before the tragedy when she had refused to give him money, Mrs. Barney said she thought she would make him think she was going to commit suicide, so she went for the revolver and fired it at random. "I thought that he would think that I had killed myself," she explained.

"We now know," said Hastings, "that on the left-hand wall of your bedroom are the marks of a revolver bullet having been fired into the wall. When were those marks made?"

"On that occasion," she answered.

"He made love to me"

After she and Stephen returned to the flat on the night of the fatal shooting, Stephen was kind to her at first, but then his manner changed. "He made love to me and he was very angry because I did not respond in the way he wanted me to." She now spoke in faltering and embarrassed tones. "He said that perhaps my feelings had changed, and I told him that it was only because I was unhappy and could not forget what he had said to me. Then he said that he was not pleased with the way in which things were going and he wanted to go away the next day and not see me at all. That made me very unhappy. He got up from the bed and dressed. I asked him not to leave me and said that if he did I should kill myself."

"Did he say or do anything then?"

"He got up and took the revolver, saying, 'Well, you don't do it with this!'"

"Where did he go?"

"He ran out of the bedroom towards the spare room."

"What did you do?"

"I ran after him. We struggled for the revolver. He had it and I wanted it, and I kept saying 'Give it to me.'" She did not remember whether he said 'No'. But the more she wanted it the more he tried to get it away from her. "We were moving about in various positions . . . I was crying . . . I remember fighting and suddenly I heard a shot."

Again Mrs. Barney seemed about to break down, but after a few moments she recovered herself and was able to answer her counsel's remaining questions. They were crucial to her case.

"Have you ever in your life desired to shoot Michael Stephen?"

"Never."

"Has there ever been anyone in your life of whom you have been fonder than Michael Stephen?"

"Never."

"Did you shoot him that night?"

"No."

"Had you any motive for shooting him?"

"None."

Mrs. Barney had told her story. The only question in her counsel's mind, as he sat down, was whether her answer to the last question would be believed. The prosecutor began his cross-examination by suggesting to the jury that there was a motive, and that it was abundantly clear—jealousy of the "other woman" in the case. Stephen, she admitted, "liked going about with her".

"When he said that he was going to leave you, did you think that he was going to leave you for this other woman?"

"No."

"Whom did you think was going to keep him?"

"I thought that he would probably try to keep himself by gambling. He thought he was very successful at it."

"You loved him very much?"

"Yes."

"Were you jealous if he looked at or spoke to another woman?"

"No."

"Was the cause of your quarrels always money?"

"Yes," Mrs. Barney agreed. "Money and the gambling habits in which this woman encouraged him."

Clarke went on to allude to her temper. On this point, Mrs. Barney insisted that she had full control of it, though on the night of the fatal shooting she admitted that she got hysterical during the quarrel with her lover, whom she believed was going to leave her.

"Did you genuinely intend to commit

LONDON HIGH SOCIETY had never known anything like it. Even the ever-so-glossy magazines condescended to cover the lurid Knightsbridge case.

in Williams Mews

MEASUREMENTS were taken by the police at the scene of the tragedy — Williams Mews, Lowndes Square

THE SHOT MAN: Mr. Thomas William Scott (Michael) Stephen, ex dress-designer in Paris, who was found shot after the party

THE ACCUSED: Mrs. Elvira Dolores Barney, daughter of Sir John and Lady Mullens who has been charged with murder

CHIEF INSPECTOR HAMBROOK, C.I.D., who was in charge of the police activities leaving the scene of the tragedy the day after

MR. AND MRS. BARNEY after their wedding in 1928. Mr. Barney was a member of a prominent cabaret turn—The Three New Yorkers

THE MOTHER AND FATHER OF THE ACCUSED: Lady Mullens, escorted by Mr. Coleman, solicitor for the defence, behind whom is Sir John Mullens

HOLLOWAY PRISON wherein Mrs. Barney awaits her trial on remand. Lady Mullens is seen moving from her motor-car to visit her daughter who, it is stated, has now recovered from her breakdown at the charge

THE SYMPATHY OF THE CROWD went out in typically English fashion to Lady Mullens when visiting Mrs. Barney in Holloway. The mother has paid several visits to her daughter since her removal on remand from police court to prison

LEA

suicide?" the prosecutor continued.

"The last time I genuinely intended to do it," Mrs. Barney replied.

"Did you say to him, 'Get out, I will shoot you. I will shoot'?"

"I said, 'Don't leave me. If you do, I shall shoot myself.' I did not want him to go."

The prosecutor's final question might conceivably have elicited a most damaging admission from the prisoner. But she parried it successfully.

"In the course of the struggle this pistol went off," said Clarke, as he picked up the weapon. "Whose finger was on the trigger?"

"I have no idea," answered Mrs. Barney.

On the whole, Mrs. Barney made a good witness, and she emerged little shaken by Sir Percival Clarke's cross-examination. Before she left the witness box to return to the dock, her counsel asked her a question or two in re-examination to rebut the suggestion of jealousy.

"Shortly before the tragedy did you go to see your solicitor?"

"Yes."

"Did you instruct him to make a will in which you left everything you have to Michael Stephen?"

"I did."

Actuated by jealousy

In his closing speech to the jury, which occupied the afternoon of the second day of the trial, the prosecutor emphasized the fact that Mrs. Barney had a hot temper, that she was actuated by jealousy —the strongest of all motives for a passionate woman—and that there was overwhelming evidence that she had shot and killed her lover during a quarrel.

Above all else, Clarke urged the jury not to overlook the fact that the dead man's clothes and hands were found to be perfectly clean. Even if Stephen had been holding the pistol by the butt, with his finger on the trigger, it was unlikely that the muzzle would be so far from his clothes as to fail to scorch them when the revolver went off.

The court adjourned for the day when the prosecutor had finished, and this meant that Sir Patrick Hastings for the defence had a night to reflect upon the lines his closing speech to the jury should take. He had no hesitation in rejecting any appeal to emotion or sentiment and in sticking firmly to a careful analysis of the evidence in his client's favour, while at the same time reviewing and disposing of the prosecution's strong points.

Hastings began by pointing out that the words "I will shoot you", which Mrs. Barney was alleged to have used and to which the prosecutor had repeatedly referred in his opening speech, were re-

Popperfoto

A YOUNG WOMAN with her life before her . . . or would she spend the rest of her years regretting their wastefulness? In the end, Elvira Barney couldn't escape her own potential for self-destruction . . .

duced to "I will shoot" by Mrs. Hall, the chauffeur's wife, who was supposed to have heard them. Might they not have meant "I will shoot myself"?

The same witness had also admitted that Stephen had told her he was afraid that Mrs. Barney might take her own life. If she had really tried to kill Stephen on the occasion of the earlier shooting incident, why was there no trace of any bullet mark in the mews? Then, from the very first moment of the arrival of the doctor and the police on the scene of the tragedy, her story had always been the same—"It was an accident."

This was supported by the doctor's view that in her hysterical condition she could not have invented this story. So why should she not be believed?

Lethal propensities

If the police had taken greater care, and if the revolver had been examined for the dead man's fingerprints before it was handled, there might have been discovered almost conclusive evidence that her account of the struggle was true.

"I am not going to beg for mercy and a lenient view of what has happened," said Hastings in conclusion. "I stand here and I claim that on the evidence Mrs. Barney is entitled, as of right, to a verdict in her favour. She is a young woman with the whole of her life before her. I beg you to remember that I ask you, as a matter of justice and of right, that you should say 'Not Guilty'."

In his summing up, Mr. Justice Humphreys described Sir Patrick's speech as one of the finest he had ever heard at the Bar, the more so because it consisted, as to nine-tenths of it, of a careful analysis of the evidence and was free from anything like a sentimental appeal. After his own review of the evidence, the judge ended by telling the jury that they could find the prisoner guilty of either murder or manslaughter or of nothing at all.

He felt bound to add one point which had not been covered by the prosecution. If the jury believed that Mrs. Barney was trying to commit suicide and if her lover's death resulted from his struggling to keep the revolver from her, it was open to the jury to convict her of manslaughter. This was because attempted suicide was an illegal act and a killing which took place in the course of furthering an illegal act amounted in law to manslaughter.

It took the jury less than two hours to reach their verdict—not guilty of either murder or manslaughter. The judge then ordered Mrs. Barney to be discharged and she left the dock to join her parents and friends in court. She was cheered by an enthusiastic crowd which had gathered outside the Old Bailey.

Poor Mrs. Barney. She seemed in a hurry to resume her former habits and even her lethal propensities. A few weeks after the trial, Sir Patrick Hastings took his car to the Continent for his usual summer holiday with his family. He was driving the vehicle up the steep hill from Boulogne on the Paris road, when a long, low car, driven by a woman, dashed round the corner behind him on the wrong side of the road, narrowly missing him and his chauffeur who was sitting beside him.

"Did you see who was driving that car, sir?" said the chauffeur indignantly. "It was Mrs. Barney!" She was on her way to Paris, where she eventually settled. She died there a few years later, filled with regrets for her wasted life.

The Peer in the Gravel Pit

Sir Delves Broughton

"TO Diana and Joss. I wish them every happiness and may their union be blessed with an heir." For a moment the court sat in stunned silence and then erupted into a babble of excited whispers. Even the judge, the eminent Sir Joseph Sheridan, looked startled. But he quickly brought the proceedings under control. "I would remind those present," he said, "that they are in a court of law." It was enough. There was silence once again. Mrs. Carberry, the witness, looked round the courtroom nervously. She was an intimate friend of the accused man, and knew that the words she had just pronounced could weigh heavily against him. Yet she had reported accurately what he had said, as he himself was later to admit.

Intimate party

In the dock sat 57-year-old Sir Henry "Jock" Delves Broughton, elegantly dressed as always, but looking watery-eyed and effete. He was on trial for the murder of Captain the Right Honourable Josslyn Victor Hay, 22nd Earl of Erroll, Baron Kilmarnock, Hereditary High Constable of Scotland and—though it did not appear as one of his titles—one of the most skilful and successful seducers of his time. A man who had specialized in bedding the wives and sweethearts of his upper-class friends, and who was described by one English divorce judge as "a very bad blackguard".

What was curious about the toast to "Diana and Joss" was that the lady in question was the beautiful, sexy young wife of the accused. And when Sir Delves Broughton spoke those words on the evening of January 23, 1941, at the Muthaiga Country Club, Nairobi, Kenya —during an intimate dinner party at which only Mrs. Carberry, Diana, Lord Erroll and himself were present—he was, in effect, giving his wife away.

Five hours later Lord Erroll, the "Passionate Peer", lay slumped on the floor of his car, which had nose-dived into a gravel pit just off the Ngong road, eight miles from Nairobi. He was dead, shot through the head at point-blank range with a .32 calibre revolver—murdered, the prosecution claimed, by Sir Henry Delves Broughton in rage and jealousy and as the result of a carefully planned plot. The toast was, in retrospect, simply part of Broughton's facade of sweet reasonableness which he used to disguise his lethal intentions.

From May 26 to July 1, 1941, a jury of 12 Kenya farmers and businessmen listened to the unfolding of the accusation

PASSIONATE PEER . . . Lord Erroll was well known as a successful seducer of women. Here, however, he appears at ease with his wife. She died in 1939.

Central Press Photos

THE RACES . . . Sir "Jock" Delves Broughton's life appeared to revolve around the racecourse. Like many fellow peers, he was devoted to extravagance.

and to Broughton's reply. It was a strange example of the workings of justice. In Europe and the East, World War II was rapidly building up to its full ferocity. Hundreds of thousands of armed men were at each others' throats with the full legal sanction of their respective countries. Yet here, in this tranquil British colony, one man found himself on trial for the murder of one other.

This grotesque contrast was not lost upon those taking part in the trial, and was responsible for some curiously futile and bitter arguments between counsels. Both sides reminded each other angrily on numerous occasions that there was "a war on"—as if justice had somehow lost its way in the struggle to maintain coherence, to distinguish between the criminal killing of one man and the legalized killing of thousands.

For the 26 days of the court action an audience of local socialites—several of them titled—and British soldiers on leave listened to the evidence and speeches. Every seat was occupied and many eager spectators stood throughout each day round the walls of the tiny courtroom. It was a *succès de scandale*. Murder in the highest echelons of the British aristocracy. For Western newspapers it was a heaven-sent source of juicy stories about vice in high places—a welcome relief from the gloom of war reporting.

The prosecution was led by the Attorney General of Kenya himself, Mr. W. Harrigan, K.C., assisted by the dour, punctilious H. E. Stacey. Harrigan was a

highly experienced court performer, passionately concerned with the cause of justice. He would be tough but fair. For Broughton and his solicitor, L. Kaplan, the choice of a defence lawyer had been difficult. Where, in Africa, were they to find an adequate lawyer not engaged in the war? Kaplan produced the answer. He wrote to Johannesburg, to the office of one of the most brilliant advocates South Africa had ever had, H. H. Morris, K.C.—who immediately cabled his acceptance of the case.

Morris had a well-known liking for difficult murder cases, and a reputation for winning them. He was dramatically secretive about his methods. When Kaplan met him on his arrival at Nairobi airport and began discussing the complexities of the case, Morris stopped him. "The answer," he said, "is simple. So simple that I almost mistrust it." But he gave no hint of his thoughts. When he entered the courtroom on the morning of May 26, 1941, the first day of the trial, he exuded an air of such confidence that some onlookers were already saying that the case was won for the defence. Once Mr. Harrigan began to unfold the evidence against Broughton, however, they were not so sure.

It was a simple and deadly story. The ageing Sir Delves had arrived in Kenya with his 27-year-old bride of one week on November 12, 1940. Marrying Diana Caldwell had been an attractive proposition for him. He was a man of enormous wealth and had been accustomed all his life to luxury, high living, and the possession of everything he desired. What could be a better accompaniment to his old age than a beautiful, passionate young wife?

On her side there was the lure of marriage to a rich aristocrat and the glamorous life that went with it. It also meant a substantial income of her own, for Broughton had made a marriage settlement providing her with £5000 a year. "Not something," Harrigan remarked, "that he would relish having to pay while waiting the obligatory three years for a divorce." Especially if he knew that the income would be shared with his successor, Lord Erroll.

Smells bad

The trouble began, the jury were told, almost as soon as the couple arrived in Nairobi. On their first day in town, they bumped into Lord Erroll, an old friend of Broughton's, and the three became inseparable. They dined together nearly every day at the Muthaiga Country Club, and when Sir Delves took a large country house at Karen, some 8 miles from Nairobi, Erroll was the most frequent visitor. It was not long before the dashing 39-year-old peer had captured the heart of Lady Broughton. The unsuspecting Broughton was slow to discover his wife's attachment. When he finally did so, the affair had gone too far.

"On January 20, 1941," Harrigan told the jury, "Broughton wrote a letter to his friend and neighbour Commander Soames: 'I have taken your advice, my dear Soames and spoken to Erroll and Diana. They say they are in love with each other and mean to get married. It is a hopeless position and I am going to cut my losses. I think I'll go to Ceylon. There's nothing for me to live in Kenya for.' On the same day," continued Harrigan, "Broughton reported to the police the burglary of his two Colt revolvers."

It transpired that on January 23, Erroll, Sir Delves and his wife had lunch together at the Muthaiga Club, where they discussed the "triangle" in which they were involved. Erroll, late that afternoon, described this meeting to his friend Lieutenant Lezard: "Jock could not have been nicer," he reported. "He has agreed to everything. As a matter of fact he has been so nice it smells bad!"

At dinner that night, where Mrs. Carberry was also present, relations were even more cordial. If Broughton was planning a murder, there was certainly no sign of it in his behaviour. "Never-

theless," went on Harrigan, "the fact remains that just a few hours after this, Erroll lay dead with a .32 calibre bullet in his head." The burglary, claimed the Attorney General, was pure invention. It was simply the first step in the plot to murder Erroll. Broughton had remained in possession of the Colt revolvers until after the murder—whereupon he had, no doubt, hidden them in a place which would probably never be discovered.

However, the jury learned, there was one weakness in Broughton's story. When he had first arrived in Kenya he and his wife had stayed with their old friend Commander Soames at his farm just outside Nairobi. On at least one occasion the three had engaged in some revolver practice. Broughton, as Soames later testified, used a .32 calibre weapon, and police, searching the practice ground, had found four .32 calibre bullets which matched those discovered at the scene of the crime. "All six bullets," announced the Attorney General dramatically, "came from the same gun."

Here Harrigan paused to allow his words to take effect. He was a scrupulously honest lawyer, but it was obvious that he was convinced of Broughton's guilt, and the jury was impressed by what he said. He proceeded to outline the events which took place on the night of the murder.

After dinner at the Muthaiga Club, Sir Delves, who had drunk "a considerable quantity" of whisky, went home in the company of Mrs. Carberry—leaving Lord Erroll and Lady Diana alone together. Broughton, however, in spite of his inebriated condition, remembered to give Erroll strict instructions to bring Diana home by 3 a.m. "A somewhat strange request in view of his abdication of her," Harrigan remarked, "but it gave him a perfect opportunity to commit the murder."

Miserable attempt

On arrival at Karen at around 2 a.m., Mrs. Carberry and Sir Delves retired to their rooms. He was "very tired", and she was suffering from a mild attack of malaria. About ten minutes later Broughton knocked at Mrs. Carberry's door to see "if she needed anything". At 2.30 Erroll and Diana arrived, talked for about ten minutes and then parted. Diana went upstairs to bed, and Erroll drove off down the long drive away from the house. At 3.30 a.m. Broughton again mysteriously knocked at Mrs. Carberry's door to see if she was well. "This," remarked the Attorney General, "was a most peculiar thing to do."

It was a miserable attempt, he claimed, to convince his guest that he had never left the house. But he *had* left the house. He had descended the stairs to await the arrival of the lovers, crept into the back of Erroll's car while the couple were

DIANA (left), though uninvolved in the death of Erroll, was the beautiful centrepiece of the tragedy. Background picture shows the house at Karen, Nairobi.

saying goodnight in the hall, and shot the peer as soon as the car was out of earshot of the house.

Harrigan admitted that his reconstruction of the crime left several questions unanswered. Could Broughton have got out of the house unseen and unheard? Was it possible for him to have returned to the house in time to knock at Mrs. Carberry's door at 3.30 a.m.? How did the car with the body inside it fall into the gravel pit? What had the accused man done with the murder weapon? How could he have disposed of it so efficiently, in so little time? These were interesting questions, the Attorney General suggested, but they were not vital to the prosecution's case. What *was* vital was proof that Erroll was shot by Broughton's gun —the gun which he claimed had been stolen three days before the murder.

Remote odds

"Proof" of this was supplied by two of the key prosecution witnesses, Maurice Henry Fox, the Senior Government Chemist, and Assistant Superintendent Alfred Harwich—both of whom had made a deep study of ballistics in relation to the identification of bullets and firearms. Fox explained that all bullets have on them, after being fired, the markings of the weapon from which they came. These markings were caused principally by the spiral grooves that are cut into the inside of the barrel, and which are designed to make the bullet spin round, thus giving it greater penetration and accuracy.

Not all revolvers, Fox added, have the same number of grooves, and they may twist either to the right or the left. These are some of the factors which allow an expert to distinguish the kind of gun which has been used. In this case Fox testified that the bullets found on Soames's farm were fired from a gun with five right-hand grooves.

"The two murder bullets," he stated, "were also fired from that weapon." But that was not all. Added certainty was given to this evidence by further information supplied by the government expert. He revealed that all six bullets had been fired with a "black powder propellant which is unobtainable in Kenya and has been out of general use for more than 25 years". The odds against two people having "black powder" bullets—and one of these was certainly Broughton—"were extremely remote".

"Are these your opinions, Mr. Fox?" queried Harrigan.

"No," replied Fox, "they are my conclusions."

THE CAR and the pit . . . The photograph (above) of Erroll's car in the gravel pit was taken on the spot by a Kenya police photographer. The Ngong road is just visible in the background, 200 yards away.

If the case had looked serious for Broughton before, it now appeared to be hopeless. On the face of it, there was watertight evidence against him. Everything seemed tied up; there were no obvious loopholes or loose ends. In addition to all this, Broughton was the most likely suspect by far—the only person who had a clear-cut motive for committing the crime. It was evident that Morris was faced with what seemed an almost impossible task. And so far in his cross-examinations, he had made little headway.

By the time Harwich and Fox were called to give their evidence, onlookers were beginning to murmur that Morris's reputation was a fraud. True, he had made efforts to chip away at the prosecution's case. But for the most part his efforts had been ineffectual. Only Kaplan knew about his mysterious remark at the airport—his "simple answer".

When he came to cross-examine Harwich, Morris delved deeply into the complexities of matching bullets to a

particular gun. He got Harwich to agree that without the murder weapon at hand the task of proving—beyond any doubt—that two different bullets were fired from it was difficult in the extreme. Nonetheless, Harwich, like Fox before him, stuck to his evidence. "All six bullets," he said, "came from the same weapon." He said it was a .32 calibre revolver with five grooves and a right-hand twist. It was then that Morris pounced.

"Tell the jury, Mr. Harwich, how many grooves there are in a Colt revolver."

"Usually there are six."

"Have you ever seen a Colt revolver which does not have six grooves?"

"No," replied Harwich, "I would say that they all have six."

"And is the direction of twist to the right or to the left?"

"It is left."

"The murder bullets could not then have been fired from a Colt, could they?"

Harwich agreed that this was so. To underline his point, Morris then asked Harwich what make of gun had been in the possession of Sir Delves Broughton three days before the murder.

"Sir Delves's two revolvers," answered Harwich, "were both registered as Colts."

It was, as Morris had first predicted, magnificently simple. But he was not finished with the ballistics experts. He returned to the question of identifying bullets as having come from a particular gun.

"In order positively to achieve this identification," he asked, "is a barrel required, or not?"

"It is," came the reply.

Calculated risk

For the first time Morris paused. The court was hushed and breathless as the famous lawyer turned to face the jury. "But, gentlemen," he said quietly, "there is no barrel. The claim that all six bullets were fired from the same weapon cannot be proved. Is that not so, Mr. Harwich?"

"It is."

It was a brilliant piece of advocacy. Morris had induced one of the prosecution's most important witnesses to refute his own evidence. So, even if Sir Delves *had* practised with a different gun about which no one knew, it was still impossible to prove that it was the murder weapon —unless that weapon could be found.

Having achieved inroads into the prosecution's case, Morris took a calculated risk. He advised his client to give evidence himself. It was a tense moment when—watched by the concourse of

LONELY ROAD to Ngong . . . The car, with Lord Erroll slumped in the front seat, was found in the gravel pit near the telegraph pole at centre of picture.

eager spectators who thronged the court, and by his glamorous wife, Diana—Sir Delves Broughton, tall and dignified, shuffled slowly across the court and took his place in the witness box.

The cross-examination of Broughton, which was conducted entirely by the Attorney General, lasted for three days. By any standards it was an exhausting ordeal. On two occasions Broughton became so fatigued by the insistent questioning that the court had to be adjourned to allow him time to recover. It soon became obvious, however, that he was no fool. Not only did he impress the jury with his apparent candour, but he used to great effect an impression which both he and Morris had subtly created for him—that he had a bad memory. To every dangerous question put to him by Harrigan, Broughton would reply in his weak-sounding high-pitched voice: "I do not remember."

Strange ending

It was an impressive performance, and Morris was clearly pleased with his client. Above all, Broughton had managed to evoke sympathy for himself as an honest man who was the victim of an unjust and unprovable accusation. When Broughton stepped down from the witness box Morris knew that the case was won. He returned to South Africa without even bothering to hear the verdict. At 9.15 p.m. on July 1, 1941, Sir Henry Delves Broughton was duly found not guilty and set free.

Apart from Broughton's own performance, the case had turned entirely on the ballistics evidence—and Broughton had good cause to be thankful for the homework that Morris had done on the technicalities of bullet identification.

The story has a strange ending. Sir Delves, reunited with his errant wife, departed for Ceylon as he had planned. There he suffered a serious fall which partially paralyzed him, and on his return to England, in December 1942, he committed suicide in a Liverpool hotel by taking an overdose of medinal. He left behind a confused and rambling note full of references to the trial, but added nothing to what was already known.

Did he kill Lord Erroll? He certainly had the opportunity and the motive. He would probably have been convicted but for Morris's flair and brilliance. For, while positive proof was lacking, there was plenty of suggestive evidence pointing in Sir Delves's direction.

What satisfaction it must have given him, if he was the killer, to have disposed of the seducer who had robbed so many husbands of their wives. And to have shown the unscrupulous Erroll that this time he had chosen to steal from the wrong man.

An Ice-Cool Murder

Ruth Ellis

Slight, determined, platinum-blond Ruth Ellis had a highly versatile career as a prostitute. Her boyfriend, David Blakely, unsuccessful as a racing driver, had even less fortune as a lover. Their relationship drove each to a consuming personal possession of the other . . . when death came it was an ice-cool murder.

IT WAS just after nine in the evening of Easter Sunday, 1955, and business was brisk in the saloon bar of the Magdala public house, at the foot of South Hill Park, a hillside road in the leafy North London suburb of Hampstead. As was usual for a Sunday, the pub's "regulars" were crowded around the bar, a fair cross-section of sports-jacketed young men, who talked mostly of cars and women,

and of girls who laughed just a little too readily and noisily. Mr. Colson, the landlord, occasionally joined in the banter, as any good publican must, but mostly he busied himself setting up his customers' continuous orders.

He did pause once in his routine, however, to attend to a Mr. David Blakely, a 25-year-old, good-looking racing driver whom he knew well. Blakely had come

into the Magdala with his friend, Clive Gunnell, a 30-year-old Mayfair car sales-man, and he was anxious to cash a cheque for £5. Mr. Colson obliged and, after spending some time drinking with his friend at the bar, Blakely bought three

MANAGERESS of a club, but not of her passions, Ruth Ellis (left) gave her boyfriend Blakely (inset) no chance.

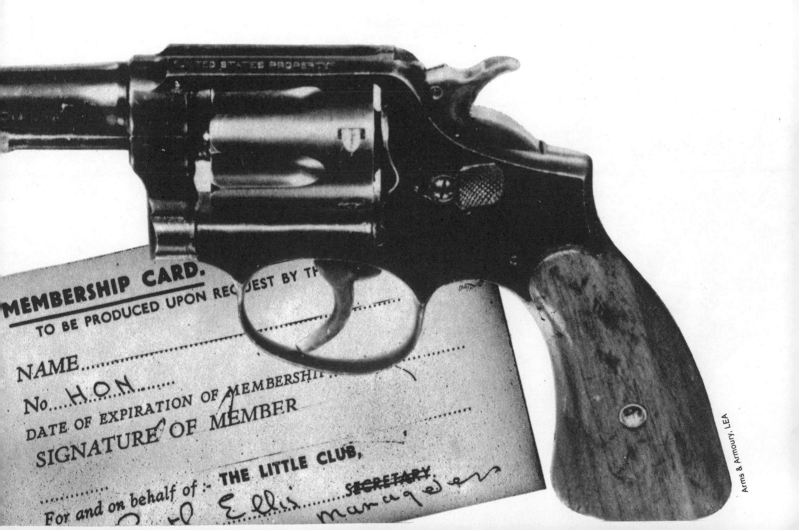

Syndication International

flagons of beer to replenish the stocks of a party to which he and Gunnell were now returning.

Waving goodnight to other regular customers, the two men left the bar and went out to Blakely's grey-green Vanguard van, parked at the kerbside immediately by the pub door. Gunnell waited by the passenger door while Blakely went around to the driver's side and — juggling with the flagon of beer he was carrying — searched in his pockets for his car keys.

Sinister tableau

Neither at that moment had noticed a slight, determined, platinum blonde walking down the hill, past a newsagent's shop, towards the pub. But she was observing Blakely carefully as she walked, and she called his name — "David!" Blakely, still having difficulty in finding his keys, took no notice and showed no sign of being aware that the girl was approaching him.

Finally, she stood beside him and as Blakely looked up he saw her swiftly open her handbag and take out a heavy Smith and Wesson ·38 revolver. She raised the gun and pointed it straight at Blakely, saying nothing, making no other movement. For a moment the scene was frozen as in some sinister tableau, the blonde appearing to be making an effort to hold the bulky revolver, the man staring mutely at her with the beer flagon still cradled in his arm.

Then, as if at the movement of a switch, the tableau sprang to life. Blakely turned and began to run towards the back of the van but, before he reached it, the woman fired two shots in quick succession. Blakely, who had assumed the stooped posture of a man fleeing for his life, reared up, slammed into the side of the van and stumbled forward again, appearing to reach out towards his friend Gunnell and screaming "Clive!"

Gunnell stood absolutely still, hypnotized by disbelief. But still the woman came on, walking in steady pursuit of Blakely, whose blood was already smeared along the Vanguard's side. "Get out of the way, Clive," she shouted and relentlessly followed Blakely, who had now stumbled around the other side of the van and was trying to stagger away.

Feminine cry

Again the woman fired and Blakely reacted with a sharp half-spin of his body, lurched sideways, and fell full-length on his face with his head parallel to the billboards outside the newsagent's shop. The blonde walked towards the inert form and fired more shots directly into it, until the emptied six-chamber gun clicked uselessly. She seemed totally oblivious of a sharp, feminine cry of pain uttered by a bank official's wife who had walked unawares into the incident on her way to the Magdala, and whose thumb had been struck by a misdirected bullet.

Blakely was dead, the final coursings of his blood covering the pavement and mingling with the frothing beer from the smashed beer flagon which he had carried with him to the last. Magdala customers, who had first dismissed the sound of shots as a car back firing, now poured out into the street and surrounded the body in a gabbling, shocked group.

Someone looked towards the blonde woman and screamed: "What have you done?" But she remained absolutely motionless, standing with her back against the wall of the pub, not a mark or bloodstain on her grey two-piece suit and green sweater. Her right hand still gripped the Smith and Wesson.

Completely unmoved

A tall, purposeful man strode from the Magdala and the woman spoke to him, quite calmly and distinctly. "'Phone the police," she said. The man studied her for a moment. "I *am* a police officer," he replied and, reaching out his hand, he took the revolver from her. She made no attempt to stop him and together she and the officer—Police Constable Alan Thompson, of "L" Division, Metropolitan Police—stood silently waiting while an ambulance arrived and took Blakely's body away.

UNSUCCESSFUL as a racing driver, Blakely had even less fortune as a lover. Clive Gunnell (far left) witnessed his death. Ellis (left) showed no emotion.

Following quickly behind the ambulance came a police car and, with the plain-clothes P.C. Thompson still at her side, the woman was driven to Hampstead police station, where she was given a cup of tea. She still seemed completely unmoved, drained of all emotion. She sipped the tea, turned her head so that the reflected station lights danced in her platinum hair like heliograph signals, and pronounced suddenly and solemnly: "My name is Mrs. Ruth Ellis. I am a model. I am 28 and I live at 44, Egerton Gardens —that's in Kensington."

Fragments of passion

While Ruth Ellis, born Ruth Neilson in the Welsh seaside town of Rhyl on October 9, 1926, reverted to silence and sat upright and trance-like on her uncomfortable police station chair, three C.I.D. officers had already opened their murder investigation.

At just after two in the morning the three came into the room where she waited, and one, Detective Superintendent Leonard Crawford, said to her: "I have just seen the dead body of David Blakely at Hampstead mortuary. I understand you know something about it. You are not obliged to say anything at all about this unless you wish to do so, but whatever you say will be taken down in writing and may be given in evidence."

HIDEOUT for Blakely was the home (left) of the Findlaters, pictured with the ill-fated couple (below) in happier times. Ellis had known where to find him.

Ruth Ellis looked directly at the be-spectacled detective as though the words of the official "caution" held no fears for her whatsoever. Then, softly but without hesitation, she replied: "I understand what has been said. I am guilty. I am rather confused." She then dictated a lengthy, coherent account of her past relationship with the murdered man, and of the kaleidoscopic fragments of passion, jealousy, and frustration that had cul-minated in the ultimate image of murder.

Her statement began with a reference to the Little Club, a sleazy upstairs drink-ing room in Knightsbridge catering daily from three in the afternoon until eleven at night to a regular crowd of boozy business-men and young, well-born drifters. It was here that the voyage towards murder was launched, over a gin-and-tonic served by Ruth Ellis, the manageress, to the attrac-tive new member, David Blakely.

To many men in the Belgravia-Knights-bridge, second-rank social world, Ruth was the Little Club's main attraction. In the argot of the times she was "that smashing blonde", and this was precisely why the club owner had installed her as manageress on a £15 a week basic salary, plus a £10 a week entertainment allow-ance. In addition to the money, he gave her a rent-free, two-roomed apartment with kitchen over the club.

Marriage mockery

It was the peak of her achievement for Ruth, the former waitress and machine-minder in a South London factory, who had longed to escape from her humble family background and move among a "better class" people. And she had done much to fulfil her ambition, from the tedium of service as a clip-joint hostess, to a highly versatile career as a prostitute.

In September 1944 she had given birth to an illegitimate son (by a French Cana-dian Serviceman who had a wife and two children back in Canada), and subse-quently she became the wife of George Ellis, a divorced dental surgeon from Surrey.

They were married in November 1950, when Ellis was 41 and she was 24, and she bore a daughter in October 1951. But Ruth's maverick life, and her hus-band's alcoholism, had made a mockery of the marriage from its very beginning, and the couple parted a month after their daughter's birth.

So it was that, even with two children to care for, Ruth Ellis had embarked upon yet another romance, at the Little Club, that afternoon in 1953 when she took young Mr. Blakely's order for a gin-and-

PUBLIC opinion swayed for and against the execution of the murderess. Her physical attractiveness created sympathy — and the interest of the press.

tonic. It was not an auspicious encounter. She had met him at another West End club a few weeks previously, had objected to some of his derogatory remarks about the hostesses, and called him a "pom-pous ass". He had displayed an equal antipathy towards her.

David Moffet Drummond Blakely, born the son of a Sheffield doctor on June 17, 1929, compensated with charm for what he lacked in natural ability and the will to find regular and useful employ-ment. Even though he was no Adonis — he was only five feet nine inches tall — there was a certain little-boy-lost look about his deep, brown eyes, with their long, almost feminine eyelashes.

Outward charm

When he was sober he could exhibit a great deal of well-bred charm and easy, confident manners. But when he had drunk too much, which he did fairly regularly, he could be truculent and stupidly offensive.

But Blakely's obsessive interest, which outweighed his taste for drink and casual encounters with women, was in racing cars. He raced, without not-able success, at a number of well-known tracks, including Le Mans in France. But he was neither able nor pre-pared to make the effort to acquire the kind of capital necessary for a serious

motor-racing career. He received a £7,000 legacy from the estate of his father, who died from a coronary throm-bosis in 1952, but most of that he quickly frittered away.

However, no problem seemed to diminish his outward charm and, despite her first reaction to him, Ruth Ellis began to show an increasing interest in the young man whose "better class" background she couldn't help but admire. Very soon she was sleeping with him in her apartment above the club. Occasionally, during the afternoons before the club opened, Ruth reverted to her call-girl role and enter-tained a number of regular "clients". But her sex life with Blakely was governed by affection, not money.

Simmering affair

At the time, Blakely was engaged to the daughter of a wealthy North of England businessman. Ruth afterwards stated:

"In December 1953 I had an abortion by him and he was very concerned about my welfare. Although he was engaged to another girl, he offered to marry me and he said it seemed unnecessary for me to get rid of the child, but I did not want to take advantage of him. I was not really in love with him at the time and it was quite unnecessary to marry me. I thought I could get out of the mess quite easily. In fact, I did so with the abortion."

Since she was "not really in love" with Blakely, Ruth saw no reason to allow him exclusive "privileges". She started to

encourage the attentions of one of his Little Club friends, a 33-year-old bachelor and company director. For the man, what began as rather pleasant love-making to an attractive woman rapidly flowered into passionate and sincere love.

Ruth's interest was no more than superficial. She continued to see Blakely and to keep their affair simmering, even if at a slightly lower temperature than before.

Whether or not it was the result which, deep down, Ruth Ellis had hoped for, this new affair heightened Blakely's desire. At her trial she recalled: "David was getting rather jealous. He asked me what I had been doing, and things like that, and, of course, I did not tell him . . .

"Our association began again at his insistence. It was very difficult. I was running a business and he was there all the time. He was entitled to walk in; he was a customer and he was hanging around the bar all the time. He was spending money in my bar. I could not tell him to go."

Emotionally upset

It was unlikely that she really wanted him to avoid her. Even though there was evidence that, despite all her bedroom experience, Ruth got very little satisfaction from sex, she could not be without the flattering attentions of men. Blakely's own capability for sexual fulfilment was of an equally low level – but despite this the unstable couple were now set on a course which drove each to a consuming need for personal possession of the other.

The ultimate tragedy was that the periods of possessiveness did not always coincide. Sometimes one would be in a feverheat while the other was cool – and then the roles would be reversed. This, inevitably, established an atmosphere of continuing jealousy.

At her trial at London's Old Bailey, Ruth recounted an occasion, after her divorce from George Ellis, when his ardour was at a peak and her's at a low ebb: "He 'phoned from the box just in the entrance to the club to my place upstairs and asked if he could please come up, and I said 'No'. After half an hour he came upstairs and I was fooling around in the flat, doing one thing and another. He was very emotionally upset and he went down on his knees, crying and saying: 'I'm sorry, darling. I do love you. I'll prove it.' He asked me to marry him."

She declined, but in February 1955 she found a one-room apartment at 44 Egerton Gardens, Kensington, and she and Blakely moved in together as "Mr. and Mrs. Ellis". But this was to be no cosy nook of regulated domesticity. Ruth continued to see her second-string lover, the bachelor company director, and he was lending Ruth money to pay the rent. Blakely had put such money as he had into the building of a new racing car – which, despite its

name, The Emperor, abdicated on its first race-track outing by falling apart.

At the Egerton Gardens apartment there were continuous rows, during some of which Blakely – who was drinking more than ever – beat Ruth and severely bruised her. These fights were followed by alcoholic reconciliations. Ruth again became pregnant and underwent yet another abortion. She insisted that the father was Blakely – but, in view of the presence in her life of the other lover, there could be no certainty about that.

By this time Ruth had brought her 10-year-old son to the apartment and he slept each night on a camp-bed while, in the same room, Ruth demanded Blakely's sexual attentions, more as a symbol of her possession of him than for physical need.

Lack of money, the strain of life with the constant noise of a boisterous and growing child, and hard, daily drinking began to tell on Blakely's nerves. He was not the first man to discover that a highly extrovert, attractive woman may be ideal as the life-and-soul of a party, but is not necessarily easy to live with.

In the Magdala public house one evening some friends, a young married couple named Carole and Anthony Findlater, found Blakely moody and despondent. "I'm supposed to be calling for Ruth at eight tonight, but I can't stand it any longer," he told them. "I want to get away from her."

He seemed, by then, to have grown afraid of Ruth, and he told the Findlaters he was worried about what she might do if he left her. Mr. and Mrs. Findlater did their best to calm his fears, and invited him to spend the week-end with them at their flat in Tanza Road, just a few minutes away.

Meanwhile, back at Egerton Gardens, Ruth waited for Blakely until 9.30 p.m. – then she rang the Findlaters. Ruth knew them and she knew that Blakely was a close friend of theirs. Anthony Findlater answered the telephone and Ruth asked: "Anthony, is David with you?" Findlater, enacting the protective role that had been agreed with Blakely, replied: "No." "Oh," said Ruth, "I'm very worried because he should have been back to meet me. Do you think he's all right?" With assurance, Findlater answered: "Oh, he's all right." Ruth thought she detected a slightly mocking tone in Findlater's voice and was convinced that Blakely was there.

Domestic tiff

From then onwards that evening she telephoned the Findlaters several times, but as soon as her voice was recognized the receiver was replaced. Later, angry and worried, she went to Tanza Road and saw Blakely's Vanguard van parked outside the Findlaters' flat. She rang the bell but no one answered. "I was absolutely

furious with David," she testified at her trial. "I just wanted to see him and ask for the keys back . . . I just wanted him to jump in the lake, or go and lose himself, something silly."

In her fury she turned her attention to the Vanguard. It had been partly converted by having its metal side panels replaced with glass windows, held in place by rubber strips, and she went to the van and thumped each window until it fell in. The noise this caused brought Anthony Findlater to his doorstep in pyjamas and robe, and Ruth demanded: "Where is David? I want to speak to him." Findlater replied that he didn't know where Blakely was, but Ruth persisted. "I know where he is," she shouted. "Ask him to come down!"

At that moment, a police inspector, whom the Findlaters had summoned by 'phone, appeared from the shadows and gently urged Ruth to go home. She declared: "I shall stay here all night until he has the guts to show his face!" After a further attempt at persuasion the inspector, unwilling to interfere in a domestic tiff, drove away.

Woman's giggle

But Ruth did not go home. She spent the whole night, walking around the Vanguard, huddling in nearby doorways – all the time watching the darkened windows of the Findlaters' flat. She was convinced that the Findlaters were deliberately trying to break up her affair with Blakely, and she was equally certain that Blakely must have found another woman. Overwrought and emotional, she decided that her "rival" must be the nanny employed to look after the Findlaters' baby.

At around eight in the morning Findlater and Blakely emerged cautiously from the flat. Seeing no sign of Ruth, who was concealed in a doorway, they inspected the damaged Vanguard and drove it away. Ruth went home to Egerton Gardens, gave her son some money and sent him off, alone, to spend the day at the London Zoo.

She then persuaded her ever patient second lover to drive her to the Magdala pub in search of Blakely. But he was not there and that Saturday night she was back watching the Findlaters' flat – more enraged and embittered than ever by the sound of what seemed to be a high-spirited party. An occasional high-pitched woman's giggle stoked her jealousy. She was certain it came from the nanny, and that Blakely was its inspiration.

The next evening, the evening of Easter Sunday, Clive Gunnell, another of Blakely's friends, brought his record-player to the Findlaters' flat and everyone there settled down to a few noisy hours of music. At about nine o'clock Blakely and Gunnell decided to go around to the Magdala and buy some beer and cigarettes.

Ruth, by now unhinged with jealousy and rage, arrived outside the flat just after the two men had driven away. When she saw that the Vanguard had gone she was sure that Blakely would be at the Magdala, and she set off towards the pub, on foot. In her handbag she carried the Smith and Wesson, given to her, she later claimed, "about three years ago by a man in a club whose name I don't remember".

As she walked she felt herself to be, she said, "scmehow outside of myself, in a sort of daze". She saw the Vanguard outside the pub, saw Blakely emerge, and fired at him. Four bullets entered his body, and the subsequent post-mortem showed that one—almost certainly the first—had been fired from less than three inches away.

Brief moments

Murder having been committed, the once talkative, ebullient Ruth Ellis entered into the cocoon of calm detachment in which the Hampstead police found her, and from which she never fully emerged. When she entered the prisoner's dock of the Old Bailey's number one court on Monday, June 20, 1955, her platinum blonde hair was as immaculate as ever, her voice as quiet and controlled as on the night of the murder.

The decisive question in the case took only a few brief moments to ask and be answered. Mr. Christmas Humphreys, Q.C., put it, on behalf of the Crown: "Mrs. Ellis, when you fired that revolver at close range into the body of David Blakely, what did you intend to do?"

Without hesitation, almost tonelessly, she replied: "It was obvious that when I shot him I intended to kill him."

Mr. Justice Havers warned the jury that, bearing that evidence in mind, it was not possible for them to return a verdict of manslaughter. It was as no more than a formality that the jury, of 10 men and two women, retired to their room for 14 minutes before returning a verdict of guilty. The black cap was adjusted on the judge's head, and Ruth Ellis stood, unmoving, as the sentence was pronounced.

When it was finished, Ruth turned and smiled faintly towards friends in the spectators' gallery. The last public sight and sound of her was a flash of her silvered hair and the clicking of her high heels on the steps leading down to the cells below the court.

She was taken to Holloway, the London women's prison, and—although her solicitor announced that there would be no appeal—there were strong pleas for a reprieve from leading supporters of the campaign for the abolition of capital punishment. The organizers of one petition collected 50,000 signatures. But others took a different view. The bank official's wife, whose right hand had been partly crippled by the stray shot from Ruth's gun, wrote in a London newspaper: "If Ruth Ellis is reprieved we may have other vindictive and jealous young women shooting their boy friends in public . . ."

OUTSIDE the Magdala public house (below), Ruth Ellis finally caught up with Blakely and riddled him with bullets.

Ruth Ellis said nothing more about the shooting and made no move to solve the mystery of how she had acquired the gun or whether anyone else had helped her with the murder plan. She showed no signs of remorse, although she asked for a photograph of David Blakely's grave, and kept it on her table in the death cell. She wrote to Blakely's mother to say she was sorry to have caused her "unpleasantness" but added: "I shall die loving your son, and you should feel content that his death has been repaid."

After she learnt that there was to be no reprieve, she sent a brief and cheerful note to a friend assuring her that she expected her execution to be no more alarming "than having a tooth out". She shed no tears and the woman who had been a call-girl, a lush, and a neglectful mother attained a death cell dignity that evoked admiration in the women prison officers assigned to watch over her.

Steady hand

On the morning of July 13 the solemn procession of officials came for her. She was given a tot of brandy and drained the glass with a steady hand. Then, after thanking the Holloway staff for their kindness, she walked—almost as if willingly—the few feet from the condemned cell into the execution shed. Ruth Ellis was the last woman to be hanged in Britain. Ten years later, in November 1965, capital punishment was abolished.

In December 1973 details of a statement about the murder gun—alleged to have been made to lawyers by Ruth Ellis just before her execution—were published in Britain. According to the statement, she said that a jealous second lover had given her the loaded ·38 Smith and Wesson and driven her on her final and fatal journey to Hampstead. She had not disclosed the details at her trial, she said, in order not to involve the man.

Had there been evidence during the trial that a second person was knowingly implicated in the murder it is possible—although by no means as certain as some commentators suggested—that Ruth Ellis would not have been hanged.

None of the police officers in the case believed her story that she had been given the gun "about three years ago by a man in a club whose name I don't remember". There can be little doubt that she must have practised with the gun. It was not the sort of weapon that anyone could use without some elementary instruction.

But in the kind of shady club world in which Ruth Ellis moved there were many men who had easy access to weapons. The fact that she either asked for, or accepted the offer of, a gun could well have been taken by the jury as added confirmation of her story that she had intended to kill Blakely.

Lana's Lover

Cheryl Crane

It began as a casual pick-up, this unlikely affair between the ageing movie queen and the smooth young gigolo and sometime hoodlums' flunkey. But then it grew, with the remorseless inevitability of a melodramatic tragedy, into obsessive love . . . and bloodshed. The death of Lana Turner's lover Stompanato at the hands of her precocious daughter Cheryl was just the beginning of her ordeal in an inferno of scandal.

GOOD FRIDAY, 1958, was drawing to its close when two senior detectives of the Beverly Hills police arrived at No. 730 North Bedford Drive, Hollywood. Officers already on the scene led them to a pink-furnished bedroom where lay the body of a well-nourished Caucasian male, dressed in casual clothes: shirt, slacks and woolly cardigan.

The dead man, Johnny Stompanato, had received a knife-stab in the stomach —a violent and painful end that, nevertheless, had left no imprint upon the corpse's darkly handsome, Latin features.

Stompanato was known to the police as a vaguely undesirable character who lived in the half-world of gangsterdom and whose name had been linked, in the scandal mags, with many of the top women stars of Hollywood. The latest of these names was Lana Turner: in fact, No. 730 North Bedford Drive was Miss Turner's home.

The blonde star was there. Face ravaged and make-up ruined with tears, she appealed to the senior of the two detectives, Chief of Police Anderson: "Can't I take the blame for this horrible thing?"

Anderson replied stolidly: "Not unless you have committed the crime. We'll find out all the facts."

Sun-kissed and athletic

The star's 14-year-old daughter by her second husband was in her own room. This was Cheryl. Tall and grown-up for her age; a typical Californian teenager; long-stemmed, sun-kissed and athletic.

Cheryl faced the detectives. "I stabbed him," she said. "I didn't mean to kill him. I just meant to frighten him."

There was a bloodstained knife in the bathroom sink. It had a nine-inch blade that tapered to a finely honed point. A man of Anderson's wide experience may well have speculated how little effort, and how little penetration, would be needed to kill a man with such a weapon. The kid was quite likely telling the truth.

The routine investigation of a homicide —refined by long and frequent practice— was under way; and the body of Johnny Stompanato, gigolo and possible small-time gangster, was borne off to its protracted obsequies that would begin on the post-mortem slab at the Los Angeles mortuary.

Already, through the night, the wires were singing the news of a top-flight scandal that would break the following morning.

Lana Turner, the super-star, was born Julia Jean Frances Mildred Turner in 1921, daughter of a San Francisco stevedore who was murdered in an alley for the sake of his winnings in a crap game.

At the age of 15, the girl was living

CHERYL'S father Stephen Crane (above) was sued by Stompanato's surviving brother. Ironically, Lana, pictured with lover and daughter on facing page, rose to fresh heights of stardom after the scandal.

with her mother in Los Angeles, where Mrs. Turner was working in a local beauty salon.

The day that gave Lana Turner to the world has gone down in the folk history of Hollywood. It was the day on which, dressed in skin-tight sweater, skimpy skirt and high heels, she was spotted in a soda fountain on Sunset Avenue by a journalist named Billy Wilkerson.

He should have had his face slapped for handing this truant high-school girl the oldest pick-up line in the Hollywood book: "How'd you like to be in pictures?" Except that Wilkerson was on the level: he had spotted something extra-special in the 15-year-old sweater girl.

Wilkerson fixed her up with an agent, who got her a small part in a murder drama called *They Won't Forget*, which

Mervyn LeRoy directed for Warners. She only played three short scenes; but *They Won't Forget* is only remembered for the breezy kid in the tight sweater. A star was born.

At 19, Lana Turner (the studio gave her the name) made her first venture into what was to be, for her, the familiar state of matrimony. This was to band-leader Artie Shaw. The marriage lasted two months, and drove Lana to a nervous breakdown. (Shaw fancied himself as an intellectual, and was disappointed when his bride's mind did not, in his opinion, match up with her physical endowments.)

Husband number two was a young executive of a hot dog concern named Stephen Crane. He asked her to dance at a night club, for a bet. Nine days later they were married; an impulsive act that could have led to a charge of bigamy, since Crane's divorce was not yet through.

The non-marriage was annulled, and before they could be properly joined in matrimony, Lana fell pregnant. The child was born five months after the second wedding. It was a girl, and because of the Rhesus Negative factor, its blood had to be changed every four hours by transfusion. They called the baby Cheryl. The girl who was later to admit to the killing of Stompanato.

It was some time after the break-up of her fourth marriage (to Lex Barker, the screen Tarzan; her third was to millionaire Bob Topping) that Lana became acquainted with Stompanato. In a manner that recalls Stephen Crane's pick-up, Stompanato rang her up for a dare and asked her to come out on a blind date.

It is a good indication of Lana's impulsiveness and naïvety that she responded to what she possibly regarded as a romantic and adventurous invitation. They met, and Stompanato played her along by telling her he was five years older than she; in fact he was five years younger.

At this time, Cheryl was 10, and spent her time between her maternal grandmother and various expensive private schools. Being the daughter of a superstar who was forever presenting her with new stepfathers could hardly have benefited the child's psyche, and her relationship with her mother left a lot to be desired.

"It's a meal ticket!"

At one of the schools she attended, Cheryl was told she must either write to her mother once a week or go to bed without any supper. She began her first letter: "Dear Mother, this is not a letter, it's a meal ticket."

In April, 1957, Cheryl was found wandering in a Los Angeles slum, having run away from convent school. She accosted a total stranger and begged him to help her find a hotel room, because, she said, she was being followed by three men.

This man had the decency to take the girl to the police station, where she told them she was upset because of a misunderstanding with her mother. Lana and her ex-husband Stephen Crane took her away from the station together. By now, Lana was deeply involved with Johnny Stompanato.

It was an affair that held all the elements of eventual tragedy. It began as a pick-up, and developed into a mutual obsession. There was the disparity of ages, tilted in his favour—though she did not know it till it was too late.

Believing her handsome Johnny to be older than herself, Lana cast him in the

SHE NEVER SAW THE KNIFE in her daughter's hand . . . and only when she lifted up her lover's shirt did Lana see his wound. Stompanato made a half turn and fell on his back, already in his agonized death throes, on the floor.

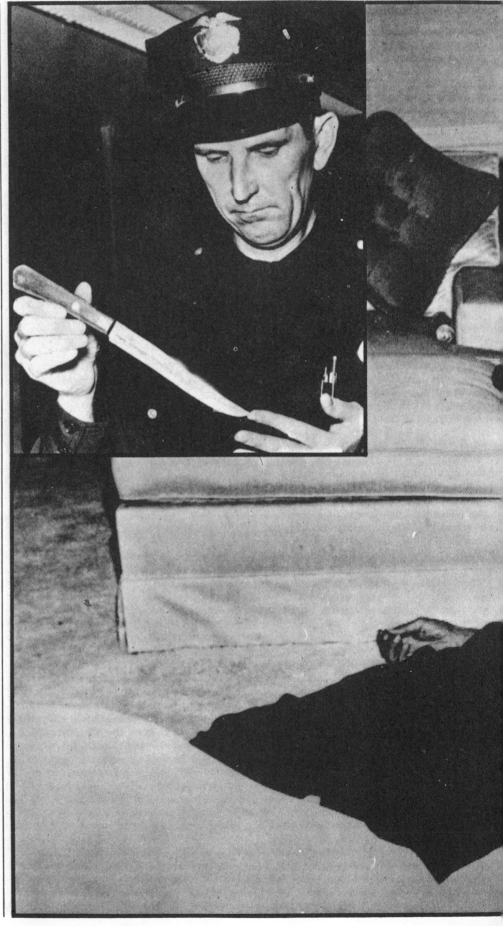

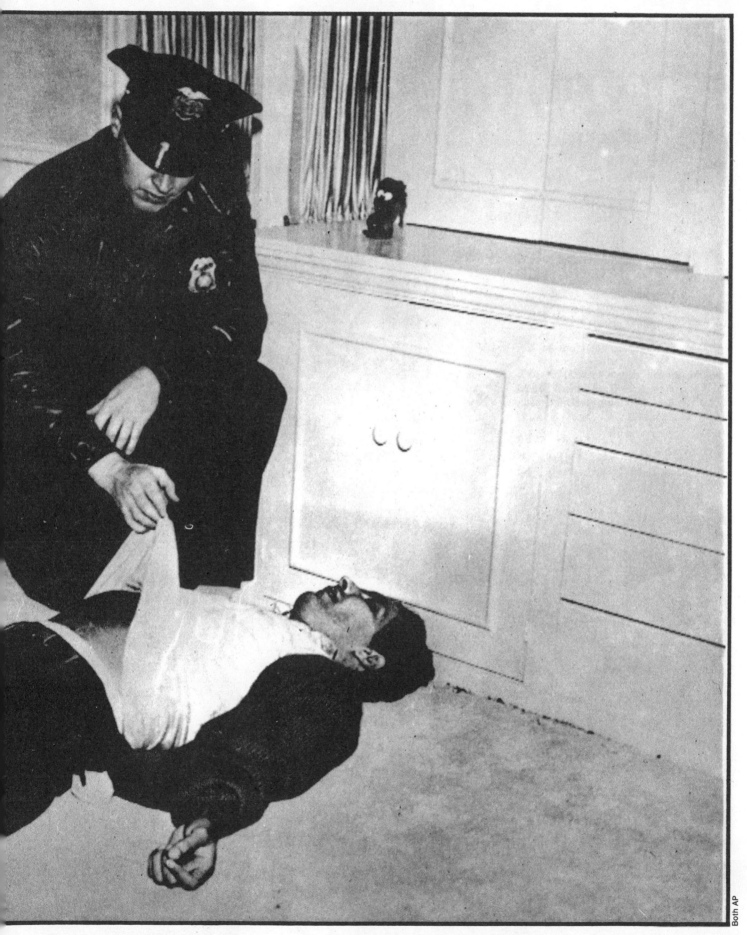

role of a father-figure: in her letters, she was always "Little Lana", and he was "Daddy" or "Papite". Her love letters, which were dragged out and splashed all over the newspapers after his killing, were innocent of eroticism or even passion. They were simply affectionate.

Stompanato's feelings for her were more complex. Whatever his intentions at the start, it is certain that, in the end, he loved Lana to obsession. No less than three women who had been in love with him have stated that "Lana was the real thing, and he loved her more than anyone in the whole world".

The trouble was, he was stuck with the lie about their respective ages. . . .

He was jealous. When she came to England to film, he was jealous of her leading man, Sean Connery—later to become famous as the screen James Bond. His violent rantings and his quarrels with Lana—he attempted to strangle her, and threatened to slash her face with a razor—led to Scotland Yard

ordering him to leave England at once.

Notwithstanding all that, the lovers were soon holidaying together in Acapulco. The obsession was to pursue its preordained course – to tragedy. Cheryl's letters indicate that, far from disapproving, she was very happy about the relationship between her mother and the superficially personable Stompanato. She wrote to him from school, and her choice of phrases reveals a casual affection for her mother's lover: "Give my love to Mother. Write soon and be good. Love ya and miss ya loads, Cherie."

Not sentiments of which murder is usually made. But, then, the killing of a fellow human being can often be a very casual matter: 90 per cent of people who kill before midnight meet their own re-

flection in the morning mirror with no thought of the dreadful thing they are fated to do that day.

Lana and her Johnny returned to Los Angeles from Acapulco in March, and Cheryl was at the airport to meet them.

Sophisticated chignon

At 5 ft. 8 in. tall, she almost topped Stompanato. Relaxed and smiling, her hair done in a sophisticated chignon, lipsticked and wearing dark glasses, she made a mockery of her mere 14 years. She was home for the Easter holidays, from boarding school.

Still on holiday, Cheryl accompanied her mother to the Academy Award presentations at Hollywood's Platages Theatre. Lana had been nominated for her performance in *Peyton Place*.

Tragedy was only a bare week away. Good Friday, April 4, 1958, Cheryl paid a visit to her father, Stephen Crane. She returned home to North Bedford Drive around half past five, and went to her

room. She was watching TV when her mother walked in, followed by Stompanato. He was in a furious temper and abusing Lana, who turned and rebuked him for saying "such things" in front of her daughter. Some time after this exchange, Cheryl went down to the kitchen and took a carving knife. As she was to testify later, she did this "in case he tried to hurt Mother".

Terrible threats

Soon after, the row was resumed, this time in Lana's bedroom. Cheryl may, or may not, have heard the threats that her mother attributed to Stompanato. She said afterwards:

"No matter what I did, how I tried to get away, he would never leave . . . and I would have to do everything he told me or he'd cut my face or cripple me . . . he would kill me, and my daughter and my mother."

It was at this point that Cheryl opened the door and went into her mother's room. Lana pleaded with her not to listen, but to go back to her own room. After a moment's hesitation, the girl obeyed.

But soon after, the row blazed up again, and Cheryl opened the door again, to see Johnny Stompanato swinging at her mother with a jacket on a coat hanger.

Cheryl closed with the man; struck him in the stomach. Lana afterwards remembered that they came together, and then parted. She never saw the knife in her daughter's hand.

Stompanato was already dying. He made a half turn and fell on his back. Not till Lana lifted up his shirt did she see his

STOMPANATO'S BODY is carried from Lana Turner's elegant Hollywood home. Opposite are the mother, the daughter and the handsome Latin lover.

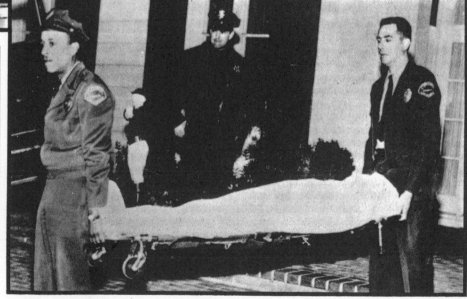

wound; and while her lover was in his death throes, the distraught star telephoned her mother.

It was Mrs. Turner who summoned the doctor, and in every way she showed an admirable presence of mind: while the doctor was giving Stompanato an adrenalin shot, she was trying mouth-to-mouth resuscitation.

It was no use. Johnny Stompanato's heartbeat faltered and faded away to nothing before the detectives arrived — and the doctor was smart enough to advise Lana to call lawyer Jerry Giesler.

Love letters

Stompanato had once been employed as bodyguard to the Hollywood gambler Micky Cohen; and Cohen was summoned to make a formal identification of the dead man. This he refused to do "on the grounds that I may be accused of this murder" — a cryptic statement that served to add an extra angle of sensation to what was already the biggest news story of the year.

Mindful that Stompanato and Cohen had always been close friends ("This was a great guy," was Cohen's epitaph on the dead gigolo), a newspaper editor asked the gambler if he knew of the existence of any love letters. Cohen came up with a pile of Lana's letters to her Johnny, from London, and also Cheryl's letters to her mother's lover.

How Cohen came by them is anyone's guess; it was suggested that his henchmen stole them from the dead man's flat. The letters were plastered all over the press of America, so that everyone was thor-

EPITAPH FOR A GIGOLO: "This was a great guy," said gambler Micky Cohen of his former bodyguard. By refusing to identify the body he added to the drama.

oughly acquainted with the relationships between the three parties before the coroner's inquest.

The inquest was held on April 11, and it was televised live on a nationwide hook-up. The biggest show of the season.

There was a sensational moment when an unnamed man got up and yelled: "This whole thing's a pack of lies! Johnny Stompanato was my friend. The daughter was in love with him, and he was killed because of jealousy between mother and daughter."

Jealous tantrums

It was Lana Turner's testimony that settled the issue. Gently guided by the skilful Giesler, she told the story of that fateful Good Friday evening. Not as Turner the super-star playing the role of her life, but as a distraught mother fighting for her child: confused, frightened, sobbing, completely broken.

Her story satisfied, for the same reason, both the requirements of the court and the criteria of good television. It was completely convincing. She gave the reason for the quarrel that evening. She had, at last, discovered his true age. The myth of the father-figure broken, she no longer needed to have around the man whose jealous tantrums caused her so much pain and embarrassment.

Stompanato, who loved his middle-aged super-star — after his fashion — could not

face up to the thought of losing her. So there was violent talk, and the beginnings of violent action. Lana told how her daughter had leapt to her aid — and all America wept.

The coroner's jury did not take long to arrive at a verdict of justifiable homicide, and Cheryl walked from the court a free person.

They buried Johnny Stompanato at his home town in Illinois. The dead gigolo's brother filed a suit for $800,000 damages against Lana Turner and Cheryl's father, alleging parental negligence; and lawyer Giesler arranged a settlement of some $20,000.

The wry coda to the Stompanato case was that Lana Turner, whose meteoric career had decidedly flattened by 1958, rose to fresh heights of stardom on the wave-crest of the scandal. And mostly in mother-and-daughter dramas with a strong autobiographical slant.

An Imaginary Rape

Marie de Morell

Lieutenant Emile de La Roncière (right) was well versed in the art of gaining a woman's heart—and her bed. But his troubles began when he failed to respond to the sexual fantasies of his commanding officer's daughter (above). Racked with frustrated desire, she plotted the ruin of the man she wanted.

THE courtroom clock showed midnight, a time when courts are usually deserted, the drama ebbed away, the contestants silenced, the crowds departed. This time, it was different. Stifling their yawns and sleepily rubbing their eyes, the spectators, counsel, judges and jurymen slowly filtered in until the court was full.

All eyes were on a large and heavily upholstered mahogany chair in the centre of the floor. It was unoccupied, but its very emptiness dominated the entire scene. Earlier, a doctor for the crucial prosecution witness, 16-year-old Marie de Morell, had informed a hushed court:

"The witness is afflicted with a convulsive nervous disorder, which recurs at certain hours. The first attack begins at four in the morning and continues until six. For the next four hours the patient is in full possession of her faculties but becomes disturbed again as the morning proceeds. This may last until midnight. The longest interval thus occurs between midnight and four o'clock in the morning, and it is during this period that Mlle de Morell could be brought into court with the least danger."

What terrible event had left a beautiful, 16-year-old girl a nervous wreck, subject to convulsions, afraid of the daylight and —like some anguished Cinderella-in-reverse—only able to appear after midnight? The prosecution had a simple word for it: Rape.

Like all similar labels, it was an oversimplification. The public preferred to think of Marie de Morell's ordeal as a seduction that had gone wrong. Other people had other words—words of anger, bitterness, and revenge, words of reason and calm, of protest and denial; but during the whole course of the trial nobody would utter the words that would accurately describe what had happened to Marie de Morell on that night of September 23, when a dashing cavalry officer entered her bedroom. Because nobody would have believed them if they had.

Her position demanded respect

One of the assisting judges was almost totally blind, an infirmity which seemed to spread to the entire Bench, for there are none so blind as those who refuse to see. And although the truth stared them in the face throughout the trial, they resolutely failed to see it. What obscured their vision? More than anything else, the fact that Marie de Morell came from a titled and influential family with the highest social connections. To cast doubt on her evidence would be to brand her as either wicked or half-witted.

In truth, she was neither. Present-day medical science has a word for girls like Marie de Morell, but it was unknown to judges, jury and counsel in the Paris of June, 1835, separated by almost a century

FAMOUS ARTIST Honoré Daumier was among the distinguished company who watched the Morell trial. Later he drew a portrait of Marie de Morell (opposite page).

from the modern concepts of psychoanalysis. Despite all the inconsistencies and insinuations in the evidence that was to come, Marie de Morell *had* to be believed. Her position demanded it.

There was no hint of the disturbing, telltale clues to come as the Presiding Judge, M. Ferey, took his seat and warned the court: "We must ask those present not to move about. We hope that curiosity will yield to the respect due to this witness's position."

The public gallery was packed with distinguished spectators, the authors Honoré de Balzac and Victor Hugo, George Sand —the mistress of Chopin, whose masculine attire shocked society—and the artist Honoré Daumier. It was not often that a Baron's daughter was seduced and assaulted by a General's son, and in the streets of Paris the public waited avidly for every syllable of scandal.

An almost unnatural silence greeted Marie de Morell's appearance. She was unbearably beautiful, dignified and grave in manner, her face half-hidden by a white veil brushed from the brim of an elegant straw hat. Gently, the Presiding Judge led her up to the events of September 23, 1834. At first, her voice was halting, gaining strength as she went on . . .

Marie: He put a handkerchief over my face and a rope about my body. He then trampled on me. He bit me. He said he meant to be avenged on me, my mother and father and Monsieur Octave d'Estouilly. I began to cry out but my voice was chilled with fear. I lost consciousness.

Judge: Did you hear a pane of glass break?

Marie: I didn't hear the glass break, but I heard an individual jump down into my room.

Judge: Why did you not cry out?

Marie: I was afraid.

Judge: How was this individual dressed?

Marie: He wore his greatcoat and a red forage cap.

Judge: Was he fully dressed?

Marie: Yes, sir.

Judge: Did he remove your dressing-jacket?

Marie: Yes, after he'd tied a rope around my body.

Judge: The rope didn't confine your arms, then?

Marie: No.

Judge: What kind of person was he?

Marie: It was Lieutenant Emile de La Roncière.

Judge: You were lying on the floor?

Marie: Yes, sir.

Judge: And did he lie on top of you?

Marie: He tried to, but he couldn't.

Judge: Did he undress in front of you?

Marie: No, sir. He bit me and struck me.

Judge: Did he strike you with a sharp instrument?

Marie: Yes.

Judge: Were the cuts made through your nightgown or underneath?

Marie: Underneath.

Judge: You fainted away?

Marie: Not completely.

Judge: Did you see the individual leave?

Marie: I saw him climb on to the window ledge and disappear.

Judge: Look at the accused and tell us whether you recognize him.

Marie: Yes.

Dashing cavalry officer

The eyes of all the spectators followed the accusing glance of Marie de Morell at the man in the dock, Lieutenant Emile-François-Guillaume-Clement de La Roncière, a 31-year-old officer at the exclusive cavalry college at Saumur—dark, handsome, immaculately dressed, the image of the dashing cavalry officer.

"What have you to say to that, La Roncière?" demanded the Public Prosecutor, M. Partarrieu-Lafosse.

"I affirm my innocence," replied the officer. "I insist that Mademoiselle de Morell's accusations are all lies. This I declare before God and before men."

The Lieutenant smiled and glanced down reassuringly at his father, the one-armed General de La Roncière, seated below the dock. Despite the light-hearted gesture, Lieutenant de La Roncière had nothing to smile about. The charges against him—forcible entry into the Morell home, attempted rape and malicious wounding—were grave. So far, the evidence against him had been unyielding. A conviction could ruin his military career for ever.

Only two other people knew the truth about what actually happened in Marie de Morell's bedroom. One of them, Marie herself had already given evidence

without lifting a finger to help him; the third person was yet to testify. But a new element had already shifted the emphasis of the trial—the mysterious affair of the anonymous letters.

On trial with La Roncière were Samuel Gillieron and Julie Genier, both former servants of Baron and Baroness de Morell, Marie's parents. They were charged with aiding and abetting La Roncière in entering the house and, by implication, placing his letters where they could be found; for although they had been anonymous in intent, they had clearly been written by the Lieutenant. And no letters could have been more damning.

They first fluttered into the case during La Roncière's interrogation by the Presiding Judge . . .

Judge: You are a Lieutenant with the 1st Lancers, attached to the Saumur cavalry school under the command of General Baron de Morell?

La Roncière: Yes, sir.

Judge: On a date in August, 1834, shortly after the arrival in Saumur of the Baroness with her children and governess, you were invited to their house. At dinner on that occasion you sat next to Marie de Morell?

La Roncière: Yes.

Judge: Afterwards, you said to her that her mother was charming and that it was a pity that she herself did not resemble her mother?

La Roncière: That is untrue. I would never speak to a young woman like that. Mademoiselle de Morell misunderstood me.

The anonymous letters . . .

Judge: About this time, a number of anonymous letters were found about the Morell house, and various circumstances pointed to you as their author. Several of them were signed with the initials E.R.

La Roncière: I have never written such letters, nor had anything to do with them.

Judge: They were addressed to Madame de Morell, to her husband, to Marie de Morell, to her governess, Miss Allen, and to a young officer who was a friend of the family, M. Octave d'Estouilly. At first the letters were amatory in tone, but presently became threatening. A letter to M. d'Estouilly, for example, says, "In a short time Marie de Morell will be nothing but a poor degraded creature. If you want her like that, they will throw her into your arms. In this way I shall revenge myself on her love for you." These letters were found everywhere about the house, even inside the piano. One of them ends with an extremely low expression.

La Roncière: I do not use such expressions, and I cannot have placed letters about the house.

Judge: Were you not acquainted with the manservant, Gillieron, who is accused

LIEUTENANT Emile de La Roncière, the dashing son of a General, trained at the Saumur cavalry school. The seduction trial brought his career to an end . . .

of complicity in this case?

La Roncière: I met him for the first time in Paris.

Judge: On Sunday, September 21 there was a reception at the Morell house. You were there. General Morell took you aside and asked you to leave. Is that correct?

La Roncière: Yes.

Judge: You asked for no explanation, but left at once?

La Roncière: Next morning, I saw Captain Jacquemin, who had been present. He told me that the matter was to do with anonymous letters, of which I knew nothing.

Hardly surprisingly, the court was puzzled at this unlikely sequence of events. Cavalry officers, eager to ingratiate themselves with their Command-ing Officer and his family, do not usually make derogatory remarks to the daughter of the house. Least of all do they write—for no apparent reason—abusive anonymous letters and then sign them with easily identifiable initials.

Somewhere in the cross-examination, the spectators felt, an important point had been ignored, left out or concealed. How right they were. The clue was in the fleeting reference to Marie de Morell's "governess." The one crucial point that La Roncière had not revealed was that, on the day after the dinner party, Madame de Morell—misunderstanding his reference to her daughter's looks—had sent the governess to the Lieutenant's lodgings for an explanation. The governess was no ferocious, grey-haired spinster but a lovely British girl of 20, Miss Allen. La Roncière lived up to his dashing and flirtatious reputation; within a few days, Miss Allen had become his mistress. For Lieutenant Emile de La Roncière it was to

Both Roger Viollet

become a catastrophic liaison.

If the evidence so far had mystified the court, the next sequence seemed even more incredible . . .

Judge: We come now to September 23, two days after you were asked to leave the Morells' house. That night, an individual dressed in a military greatcoat and forage cap introduced himself into Mademoiselle de Morell's bedroom. The man flung himself on the girl, removed her dressing jacket and committed an indecent act against her. Was this individual not you?

La Roncière: No.

Judge: Nevertheless, Mademoiselle de Morell has identified you. It was moonlight in the room and she knew you. The intruder also stated that he meant to avenge himself on her family, and two days previously you had been shown out of the house. Moreover, the intruder declared that he would mark the face of M. d'Estouilly, and the following day you

fought a duel with him. Was the intruder not you?

La Roncière: No.

Judge: This person threatened Mlle de Morell and struck her. Her feeble cries were eventually heard by Miss Allen, who entered, whereupon the individual left by the window. Miss Allen found Mlle de Morell with a handkerchief over her mouth and a rope about her hips. Further marks of violence were discovered later. Was this individual not you?

La Roncière: No.

Judge: A letter was found in the room addressed to Madame de Morell. It said, "Madame La Baronne, everybody shall know of your daughter's shame. She will soon have the results of my love, that is certain. I am going away. I shall not be able to enjoy the spectacle of your grief." It was signed "Emile de La Ron", breaking off at the first syllable of your name. The events I have described took place at half-past two in the morning. A few

hours later, M. d'Estouilly received a letter in which the writer said, "You are a coward and a wretch. I shall mark the seal of infamy on your face." M. d'Estouilly sent you a challenge and the duel took place that day. M. d'Estouilly was twice wounded, once in the arm and once in the leg. You denied that you were the author of any of the letters, but M. d'Estouilly continued to insist that you should confess.

La Roncière: He said, "Admit that you are the author of the letters and everything will be forgotten." Next day, I sent my second, M. Berail, to him. He still demanded a confession in writing.

Judge: Do you acknowledge authorship of a letter to M. d'Estouilly in which this admission is made?

La Roncière: Yes.

Judge: There were in fact two such letters?

La Roncière: The first letter admitted authorship only of the letters to M. d'Estouilly. But he further demanded that I should confess to having written the anonymous letters to the Morell family.

Judge: You did so?

La Roncière: Yes.

Judge: Why, if it was not true?

La Roncière: I trusted d'Estouilly. And I did not know then what those letters contained.

. . . Who kept writing them?

To even the most credulous members of the court the whole sequence of events seemed preposterous. The entire evidence was a daisy-chain of question marks. What officer in his right mind would try to rape his Commanding Officer's daughter . . . and then leave a letter virtually giving his name? Why hadn't Marie de Morell aroused the whole house with her screams? The Lieutenant was a strong and agile man, so why hadn't he overpowered the girl and forced himself upon her? Having made a successful getaway, why on earth implicate himself further by sending a challenge to d'Estouilly, a fellow-officer and a close friend of the Morell family? And if the Lieutenant had never written the anonymous letters, why confess to them?

Once again—unknown to the court—the truth was hidden between the lines of the evidence. The astonishing fact was that La Roncière *had* been the intruder in the military greatcoat and forage cap. But he had never intended to rape the General's daughter, nor had he attempted intercourse. As for the letters, La Roncière knew nothing about them. They had all been forgeries. After the duel with d'Estouilly, the Lieutenant had only agreed to his confession in the hope that the Morell family would then forget about the assault on their daughter.

It had been a serious miscalculation,

for on the day of the duel d'Estouilly had not even been informed of the assault. Worse than that . . . the anonymous letters continued to arrive.

After the duel, Lieutenant de La Roncière left for Paris. The letters still continued to turn up in the Morell house; one read, "Dear Mademoiselle de Morell, Soon there will be a bond between us, and in a few months you will be obliged to come to me on your knees to beg for a name for yourself and another." The manservant Gillieron was dismissed. The letters failed to stop. Another one addressed to Marie de Morell said, "Those you love most in the world—your father, your mother, M. d'Estouilly—will no longer exist in some months from now." The Morells gave notice to the other servant, Julie Genier. Still the letters kept appearing.

Adolescent hysteria

It was the repeated discovery of the letters—as much as the assault—that had forced M. le Baron de Morell to take legal action to protect his family's name. But if Lieutenant Emile de La Roncière had not written the letters, who had? And for what possible reason? Of the three people who knew the whole truth, two had already given evidence. The third now stepped into the witness box . . . Miss Allen, the pretty English governess and the Lieutenant's secret mistress. Only she could save La Roncière from ruin.

Judge: Tell us, Miss, what you heard on the night of September 23.

Miss Allen: I heard the muffled cries of Mademoiselle de Morell and the dull sound of someone speaking.

Judge: You were listening at the door?

Miss Allen: No, I was trying to break in. Presently, the noise stopped.

Judge: Was the door bolted?

Miss Allen: The bolt was half on. When I shook the door hard, it opened.

Judge: When entering Mademoiselle de Morell's room, did you see anybody, or a rope at the window?

Miss Allen: Neither a rope nor a person, only Mademoiselle, who lay on the floor with a rope round her body. There were bruises on her arms and a handkerchief over her face.

Judge: Was there blood on her face?

Miss Allen: Her nose was bleeding.

Judge: Was she wearing her dressing jacket?

Miss Allen: No, only her nightgown. There were teeth marks on one wrist, but the skin wasn't broken.

Judge: Did she say she had recognized anyone?

Miss Allen: Lieutenant de La Roncière, who had told her, "I have come for my revenge."

Judge: Has the dressing jacket been found?

IMPASSIONED PLEAS by Odilon Barrot, (inset) the Morell family lawyer, and the distinguished career of General Morell, Marie's father, helped sway the court . . .

Miss Allen: No, sir.

Judge: So we must suppose that the assailant took it away. Did Mlle de Morell mention whether the man was wearing breeches?

Miss Allen: No, she didn't mention anything like that.

Judge: Was the opening in the window large?

Miss Allen: Oh, yes, sir.

Judge: Where were the fragments of broken glass?

Miss Allen: Some inside and some outside.

Judge: What did you do with the fragments that were inside?

Miss Allen: I swept them into the fireplace.

The worst had happened. Miss Allen had told sufficient half-truths to satisfy the court, but had kept the real truth to herself. For Lieutenant de La Roncière, there was not a crumb of comfort in her evidence; he was now alone with a story no one would believe, even if he dared tell it.

It was a story of adolescent hysteria and sexual frustration inflamed by jealousy; a story of romantic intrigue confused by misunderstanding; a story of conspiracy compounded by deceit.

It began when Miss Allen became Lieutenant de La Roncière's mistress. At night she let him into the Morells' house and up to her room, which was connected to Marie de Morell's bedroom, by a communicating door. Through the door, the young Marie de Morell could hear their lovemaking. Frustrated sexual passion is a powerful thing; in an adolescent girl it can easily develop into a form of hysteria where fear and guilt transform the love-object into something to be persecuted and destroyed.

This is apparently what happened to Marie de Morell; her desire for the unattainable Lieutenant—so audibly enjoying himself in the adjoining room—was twisted into a compulsion to ruin him. And so the first anonymous letters started, forged by Marie de Morell to cast suspicion on the man she secretly coveted. In the beginning, they were addressed to her own parents, with the idea of forcing them to bar him from the house. It worked, and the Lieutenant was asked to leave before the dinner party on September 21.

But hysteria feeds on itself. Like anyone else gripped by a manic obsession, Marie de Morell found she couldn't stop. The letters became more frequent, more threatening, more indiscriminate in their targets. The one to d'Estouilly—a touchy social climber anxious to ingratiate himself with the Morell family—duped both men into a duel.

Even up to this point the whole affair could possibly have been smoothed over. Until La Roncière made his lunatic and apparently inexplicable attack on Marie de Morell.

On the night of September 23 he entered Marie's bedroom through his mistress's door. While Miss Allen fluttered helplessly in the background, he pulled Marie out of bed, lifted up her nightgown and snipped off some of her pubic hairs. It was madness, but it wasn't rape.

Confidantes together

La Roncière left the way he had come, taking Marie's bed-jacket as a souvenir. He also left the two girls in a frightening dilemma. Obviously, his assault on Marie de Morell—whatever the intention—could not be shrugged off, but nor could Marie reveal that the Lieutenant had entered her bedroom through the communicating door without compromising her friend and *confidante*, Miss Allen. A convincing story had to be concocted to explain the Lieutenant's dramatic entry into her room. Luckily, Marie's anonymous letters had already put the Lieutenant in an unfavourable light; the rest was easy.

Together, the girls broke one of the bedroom windows to give the impression that La Roncière had forced his way in from outside. A length of clothes-line was procured from the kitchen to support the story that Marie had been bound, and two more anonymous letters were forged— one to the Baroness and the other to d'Estouilly—which made it clear that the Lieutenant had been the assailant. Then a distraught Miss Allen rushed off to arouse the Baroness and tell her the story of Marie's ordeal.

The excited preparations took around three hours: just enough to wreck Emile de La Roncière's career for life. In court,

the two girls kept their secret. They revealed nothing of the conspiracy, and La Roncière's own misguided sense of gallantry prevented him from disclosing Miss Allen's part in the affair.

But no excuse—not the sealed lips of Marie de Morell and Miss Allen or the sense of honour of Lieutenant Emile de La Roncière—can explain why the three judges persistently closed their eyes to the truth. For as witness succeeded witness, one disquieting new fact after another should have led them to the single, inescapable conclusion that the two girls had lied to the court.

Monsieur Jorry, a glazier called to repair the damaged window, introduced the first element of genuine doubt. In a patient, matter-of-fact way—typical of a small French artisan—he described what he found.

Jorry: The pane was at the corner, at the bottom of the left-hand casement.

Judge: How was it broken?

Jorry: It was broken at the bottom, about five inches by four across.

Judge: If you had passed your hand through, would it have been possible to reach the hasp?

Jorry: No, sir, not without breaking the whole pane.

Judge: Did you find any fragments of broken glass?

Jorry: Yes, outside on the parapet.

Judge: Thank you. You say you visited the house on September 28. What makes you so sure of the date?

Jorry: Oh, I put the dates down in my book, sir. Everything goes down. Has to, you know.

Obvious evidence ignored

Jorry's flat and prosaic insistence that nobody could have opened the window from outside slipped right past the judges; so did his telling observation that the only broken glass he had found had been *outside* the window—a point confirmed by one of the Morells' servants, who found no glass inside Marie's room when she swept up immediately after the attack. The conclusions were obvious, La Roncière could not have entered from the parapet; yet somebody had broken the window from inside to make it appear that he had.

It was Monsieur Giraut, an architect from Saumur, who provided what should have been conclusive evidence that La Roncière could not have scaled Marie's wall and entered her bedroom window.

In a business-like manner, he unrolled plans of the side and front elevations of the house. Marie's bedroom window—on the second floor—overlooked a sheer drop of 28 feet to the River Loire. It *might* have been possible to clamber up, agreed M. Giraut, but it would have needed an army of men and a 28-ft. ladder. More-

THE TRUTH made no impression on the Court President (above), despite the efforts of Chaix d'Est-Ange, counsel for Lieutenant de La Roncière (below left).

over, the ladder would have left marks on the parapet, walls and guttering. In his examination of the walls he had found no marks whatsoever.

Like the monkey who covers his eyes to see no evil, the judges blundered on. More witnesses testified that La Roncière could not have entered the house from outside. Then came the bombshell.

One by one, four independent handwriting experts unanimously agreed that the incriminating anonymous letters had not been written by La Roncière, but by Marie de Morell. Hard on their heels, a paper expert confirmed that the notepaper on which they had been written belonged to the General's daughter.

It seemed inconceivable that the judges could ignore the implications of this evidence. But by now they had virtually committed themselves to believing Marie de Morell's testimony implicitly. There was to be no variation from the plotted course, even if it meant sailing right past the truth.

The boat had been rocked. But an

emotional appeal to the jury by Odilon Barrot, counsel for the Morell family, quickly restored the equilibrium as the trial neared its end:

"The whole of France, gentlemen, awaits your verdict anxiously. For we are concerned not merely with the private griefs of a single family; society itself as a whole must be helped to recover from the shock it has received. The case appears to me to be an embodiment of our age. There are people today who find a certain poetry in crime, they desire strong emotions at any price. And so every day we hear of new crimes, which go unpunished because their very novelty makes them seem improbable. Well, this is a case of that kind. Your justice, a reflection of divine justice, must make amends to the Morell family, the solemn reparation which this great family demands. The Morell family must not leave these precincts, to which honour alone has called it, dishonoured.

"No, before the law of this land of ours, great iniquities must be firmly put down. You understand me, members of the jury. You will not fail in your duty."

A man condemned in advance

A slightly different definition of duty was put forward by M. Chaix d'Est-Ange, counsel for Lieutenant de La Roncière, in his final speech:

"I am here to perform another duty. I am here to defend a man pursued against all justice by a powerful family, condemned in advance by blind prejudice. The prosecution have taken it as their maxim that the more serious a crime is, the less proof is needed to convict."

M. Chaix d'Est-Ange made a brave attempt at putting up the feeble points in the prosecution evidence and then shooting them down, but his pleas failed to penetrate minds that had been closed for days. Much more to the liking of the judges was the rhetorical fustian of the Public Prosecutor, M. Partarrieu-Lafosse, who reduced the case to a simple conflict between Beauty and the Beast . . .

"Members of the jury, you have to choose between a pure and stainless girl and a cavalry officer. If you seek an explanation for the hatred vowed by the accused to the Morell family, you have it in his expulsion from their house on September 21. On that day, his thirst for revenge was born, and vengeance is the key word in this case. The accused said to himself, 'I can't call General de Morell out, but I'll strike him in whatever a father holds most dear—the honour of his daughter. If this is talked about afterwards, he may think a marriage desirable. I will mark her with my claws all over her body, and if he asks for his daughter back, I shall reply with insults. Perhaps he'll be only too happy to buy my silence by giv-

PUBLIC PROSECUTOR Partarrieu-Lafosse reduced the case to a simple conflict between Beauty and the Beast. His efforts ended La Roncière's career . . .

ing his daughter's hand to the man who assaulted her murderously.'

"If, on the morning after the attack, M. le Général Baron de Morell had met La Roncière in the public street and run him through the heart with his sword, you wouldn't have found twelve jurymen in France to condemn that legitimate act on the part of an outraged father in his anger."

If the judges expected everything to be plain sailing from now on, they were to be bitterly disappointed. If was left to a juryman to introduce a new and disturbing note, with a request for clarification on a point of evidence briefly referred to by an earlier witness. It concerned a statement by a Monsieur Brugnière—a friend of the Morell family—which had not been read out in court.

Impatiently, the Presiding Judge shuffled through his papers and produced the statement. According to M. Brugnière, he had been at the Morell house one day in August when Marie, who had been standing by the window, suddenly cried out that a "cloaked man" had thrown himself into the Loire. They all rushed to the window, but there was nothing to be seen. They sent out a boatman, who also failed to find any trace of the man. The following day, Marie claimed to have received an anonymous letter from the drowned man saying he had killed himself for his unrequited love for her.

It was a text-book example of Marie's retreat into a fantasy world of repressed sexuality. Coupled with the clearly imaginary reference to the letter from the "cloaked man", the evidence could have been vital if only it had been produced at the right time. The fact was not lost on the juryman. "We ought to have heard of this incident before," he commented grumpily. "We could have questioned Mademoiselle about the fact . . . or vision."

The jury was out for six hours, long enough for Honoré Daumier to finish his sketches of the leading counsel for the magazine *Le Charivari*. The verdict was a crushing one for La Roncière. He was found guilty of attempted rape and malicious wounding and sentenced to 10 years in jail. His military career was over. The servants Gillieron and Genier were both acquitted. The trial, lopsided and off-balance, had limped to its predictable end; family honour had been satisfied.

In the cafés of Paris that night it was the sole topic of conversation. But even those who sympathized with the Lieutenant, who suspected that Marie had forged the anonymous letters, who were convinced that La Roncière could never have entered her bedroom through the window, and who guessed there had been some kind of conspiracy, all were faced with one unanswerable question: what insane impulse had led Emile de La Roncière to attack the General's daughter?

Ten years for an escapade

A few days later, in the private chambers of M. Ferey, the Presiding Judge, the question was answered. In a desperate attempt to alter the verdict against him, La Roncière told the judge the truth about the seduction of Miss Allen, the assignations in her room and the night he unbolted the communicating door and entered Marie de Morell's bedroom with a pair of nail-scissors taken from his mistress's workbox.

Why?

Little more than pique. His pride had been ruffled when he had been unaccountably shown the door by the Morells on September 21. In a drunken session with some fellow officers, he had vowed to get his own back. One boast led to another, and in the end he bet them 1000 francs that he could enter Marie's bedroom that night and seduce her. The bet was taken up, and he promised to produce some clippings of her pubic hairs as proof. It had been a crude and idiotic escapade, but he had meant no harm.

M. Ferey shook his head sadly. At least, the evidence now added up. But the trial had taken its legal course. There was nothing more he could do. There was no question of an appeal or a retrial.

Under military escort, ex-Lieutenant Emile de La Roncière returned to a decade in jail and utter ignominy. The victim of the most unlikely series of circumstances that ever ended a seducer's career . . . the malicious fantasies of a sex-starved teenager, the bruised honour of a noble family, drunken bravado, the determination of three judges not to recognize the obvious, misplaced gallantry, and the fact that Sigmund Freud, with his illuminating theories on repressed sexuality, was born 50 years too late.

The Duchess and the Governess

Duke de Choiseul-Praslin

She was goddaughter of the Emperor Napoleon; he was heir to one of the wealthiest dukedoms in France. Their marriage seemed to be the perfect match and the fact that they were so in love seemed a guarantee of future happiness. Slowly, however, the golden image began to crack; slowly their love gave way to hate. Until, one summer night in 1847, the crisis broke. It was a night which ended in violence, tragedy and a brutal, bloody death . . .

Archives Nationales

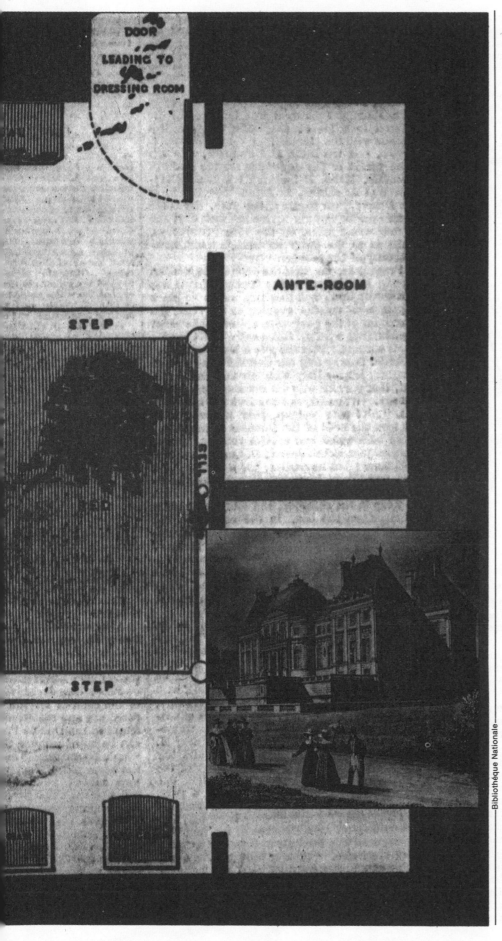

DOOR LEADING TO DRESSING ROOM

ANTE-ROOM

STEP

STEP

THE Duchess of Choiseul-Praslin's bedroom was in complete darkness within its closed shutters when, soon after dawn, her husband the Duke entered it soundlessly and alone. In the Duke's intention so early that day there was neither need for marital affection nor desire for physical comfort. In fact, he carried a knife and a pistol and there was hate in his heart.

The Duke put his hand over his wife's mouth and drew the knife clumsily over her throat, severing an artery. The Duchess awoke and screamed the first of many screams that were heard in the street on the other side of the park bordering the Praslins' Paris home. In a frenzy she gripped the blood-stained knife and badly gashed her hand.

Bloody handprints

Somehow, in the ensuing struggle the Duchess, a fat woman, but still young enough at 40 to command some agility, broke free from her maniacal assassin and ran across the room. She knew instinctively, despite the suddenness of the attack, the depth of her sleep, and the total darkness, the whereabouts of the three doors in the bedroom. Frantically, with blood pouring from her wounded neck and hand, she groped at each door in turn, leaving bloody handprints from wall to wall, from one door to another.

When she discovered that each door had been locked the Duchess, still screaming terribly, groped for and found the two bell ropes that summoned the servants. One she pulled so hard that it broke. Remorselessly the Duke chased her about the room, striking viciously with his knife, inflicting 30 wounds all over her.

The Duchess, maddened with pain and terror, struck back furiously at her tormentor. She bit and scratched him and in the darkness found her supper knife, left on her food tray from the previous evening, and struck the Duke with it. Like a wild beast caught in a trap, the desperate woman ran about the room, flinging herself from one corner to the next, trying to escape from the knife of her murderer. He hit her then with the butt of the pistol he was carrying, and next with a heavy candlestick which fractured her skull. From this blow she lost consciousness.

Servants, summoned by the frantic bell-ringing and the terrified screams, were already pounding at the bedroom doors. Uncertain at first what to do, they allowed precious minutes to pass before calling the police and a doctor. When they

BEDCHAMBER of the Duchess (left) was sealed off by her husband to prevent her escape. The Duke's château (inset) was the scene of the Praslin scandals.

at last entered the chamber they saw a scene of indescribable mayhem. The room was covered with pools of blood, in the largest of which was the broken body of the Duchess de Choiseul-Praslin. She was still just breathing. Minutes later, cradled in the arms of an anguished old retainer, she finally bled to death.

Of the Duke there was nothing for the moment to be seen. Those hurrying in and out of the Duchess's room were not so entirely distraught, however, as not to notice the columns of thick black smoke emanating from his bedroom chimney. It was the first of the obvious clues that the Duke was to leave that morning that within moments would eliminate all the suspects from the crime except himself.

The murder of Fanny, Duchess of Choiseul-Praslin, after 23 years of marriage, was a crime which stunned France in the summer of 1847 and which ever since has been the subject of intense conjecture over the characters of the tragic participants.

Early doubts

The Emperor Napoleon was a godparent when Alatrice-Rosalba-Fanny Sébastini, generally called Fanny, was christened shortly after her birth in the spring of 1807. Horace Sébastini, her father, was a Napoleonic general, and when his wife died from the effects of giving birth to Fanny, General Sébastini — with foreign conquests and military glory on his mind — placed his child in the care of a governess. Her name was Mademoiselle Mendelsohn and some historians believe she may have been a key figure, if a remote one, in the Praslin drama. The reason for that is that there is some evidence that Mademoiselle Mendelsohn was a lesbian.

Fanny was 16 when, while relatives were busy trying to arrange a match for her, she fortuitously met the man who was to become her husband. Her olive skin and dark looks, inherited from her father — who, like his mentor Napoleon, was a Corsican — fascinated Charles-Louis-Théobald de Choiseul-Praslin. And with such a suitor — a rich marquis, 19 years of age, heir to a dukedom and the great Praslin château of Vaux-le-Vicomte — there was no need for the Sébastini family to continue their search for a husband for Fanny.

Temperamental and psychological suitability in a socially correct marriage were not qualities that worried nineteenth-century matchmakers. When one had a general's daughter and a Duke's son, what more did one want? As it happened, Fanny Sébastini and Théobald de Praslin were in love, a rare event among the betrothed of rank. Theirs was to be a *mariage d'inclination*, and not a *mariage de convenance*. But a closer look by the

gritty pundits who were already congratulating themselves on the perfection of such a union might have raised some early doubts.

Despite her youth, Fanny Sébastini was already starting to be a dominating woman. She was fiery and passionate and given to outpourings of emotion which later were to be confined to her remarkable letters and diaries. By contrast, her fair-haired and pallid husband was aristocratically aloof and withdrawn. He rarely spoke — a characteristic which did not hide, as it sometimes does, either a great intellect or an iron will, for he had neither. In fact, one who knew him described him as timid. Despite these contrasts, the girl and the youth were

MAN AND WIFE . . . The beautiful young Duchess (above) and the man (facing page) who first married and then murdered her. It was a major scandal.

— Bibliothèque Nationale

joined together, in October 1824, in a marriage that was the talk of fashionable Paris.

The radiant bride was then 17. Seventeen years later, when she was 34, the mothering of nine children had reduced her dark beauty to pale, careworn wrinkles. The Duchess was now a corpulent, baggy-eyed and singularly unattractive woman. In that year, 1841, the new Duke and Duchess of Praslin moved with their considerable family into the Château Vaux — for Théobald's father had died and left him the title and the vast property.

All this materialism proved to be of little comfort to a marriage which had been going wrong for some time. The Duke and Duchess lived apart in the château, to the evident distress of the Duchess, who poured her pleas, her des-

pair, her anguish into a stream of letters to him: "There are treasures of love in my heart to calm you and to sweeten your bitterness — but you thrust me aside."

What ailed the Duke, it seemed, was his wife's propensity to dominate. Already a withdrawn man, his inclination was to withdraw even further — thereby provoking still greater outbursts from his emotional wife. And then there was the question of the Duchess's guilty secret. Was she a lesbian — did she really have such tendencies? It was evident that the Duke thought so, for, as he withdrew from her affections, he noted that she redirected them towards feminine company.

A certain Mademoiselle Desprez, for example, who was governess to the ducal children for four years, was believed by outsiders to have been a practising female homosexual. The parallel in suggested sexual tastes between the Duchess's own governess when a child, and that of this particular one of the several governesses she employed for her own children, has not escaped historians trying to piece together the jigsaw of emotions that made up the Duchess of Praslin, and which are revealed only by hints and innuendoes in her writings.

Curious decree

For some reason which is not known, Mademoiselle Desprez left the household, and in due course was replaced by an even darker lady. Mademoiselle Henriette Deluzy-Desportes came from a well-born family fallen upon hard times. She was the bastard daughter of a Napoleonic soldier; a pretty, intelligent spinster with artistic tastes and accomplishments, she was in her late twenties when she joined the Duke's household.

Her arrival coincided with a deepening rift in the Duke's marriage. As a result of it, the Duke drew up a curious "decree" forbidding his wife access to their children except in the presence of the new governess. The Duchess, claiming that she would do anything for a restoration of conjugal relations, signed it, and thereby signed away her very rights to motherhood.

What happened next was inevitable. More and more the Duke was attracted to the company of the ebullient, lighthearted governess and the children always about her. Mademoiselle Deluzy, also a copious journal and letter-writer, described the scene that was set for the Duke's evening visits:

"Our gaiety and high spirits gave him pleasure without demanding any effort of him. There was a friendly and open atmosphere in our little circle that the similarity of our tastes and our way of thinking induced. All etiquette and differences of rank were gradually forgotten,

but everything was kept within the bounds of the strictest propriety by the presence of the children."

When the Duchess was excluded by her husband's command from such informal gatherings it was predictably not long before the female supremacy in the château belonged exclusively to Mademoiselle Deluzy. As predictably, perhaps, a new note of insanity entered the Duchess's already mad writings. Besides her husband, she now had a new object for her emotive outpourings: the governess.

Hate, abuse, and poison gushed from her pen, stripping bare the character of her victim. Between it all was interlaced her own torment and suffering. "I am as unhappy as a person can be," and "Think of the torture that you (the Duke) have put me to," were phrases that now began to occur with startling frequency in her journals.

Deadly barbs

Sometimes the bitterness was coloured by an anecdote—as when the Duke, in an icy rage, broke all her umbrellas. Or when, on a seaside holiday, he chased her from their hotel into the night. In any event, the marital crisis could not be contained forever within the walls of the Château Vaux. And, when it was known that the Duke of Praslin had his mistress living with him in a *ménage à trois*, the nineteenth-century wits of Europe—whose barbs were famed for their deadliness—had a lethal time of it.

Curiously, although the whole continent now accepted that Mademoiselle Deluzy, his children's governess, was beyond doubt the Duke's mistress, living and travelling everywhere with his family, none of the principal parties in the drama admitted to it. Mademoiselle Deluzy herself always steadfastly denied it. There was never any direct evidence against either her or the Duke. The Duchess herself did not believe that her husband and the governess ever shared the same bed, and many times said so.

Everyone else, including King Louis-Philippe, did. The King listened anxiously to the gossip, for its ramifications were important to him. The Duchess's military father had been appointed ambassador to London and was now a *maréchal*; the Praslins moved within the inner circle of the court and were close friends of the royal family. It was permissible for a peer to have a mistress, of course; but it was a question of degree. A duke wasn't supposed to ostracize his duchess in order to co-habitate with a servant under his own roof.

And, as far as gossip was concerned, the Duchess was a much wronged lady. She emerged as a mother whose nine children had been torn from her bosom

and placed in the care of a loose woman kept under her roof. What had she done to deserve this? She was religious, charitable, friendly. The public, of course, knew nothing of her dementia, her paranoia, her ungovernable outbursts of temper; to them the only reason why the austere, thin-lipped Duke treated his wife with such barbarity was that he was a "fiend".

The Duchess, however, displayed a guile not usually demonstrated by the innocent. Suddenly, in 1846, she appeared to offer an olive branch to Mademoiselle Deluzy, who for the past six years she had been studiously insulting: "I extend my hand to you, Mademoiselle, and ask you to forget all the painful moments that

STERN-FACED portrait of the Duchess's father (above), a Corsican and one of Napoleon's generals. The Praslin scandal rocked high society at the time.

I may have occasioned you." But even as she wrote those words the Duchess was preparing plans to swap the olive branch for an asp.

The following year she revealed the serpent in her bosom. For the past 12 months she had petitioned her father, the *maréchal*, and elicited the aid of influential prelates, including a bishop, to support her in claiming a divorce from the Duke on the grounds of adultery. Now, on the same June day in 1847, she arranged for both the Duke and Mademoiselle Deluzy to be told separately of her decision.

For the Duke, assuaged by his wife's recent attempts at a rapprochement between herself and the governess, it was a staggering blow. Powerful men, not just an overwrought, temperamental woman, were now ranged against him. He was

bound to lose. His private life would become an open scandal; his children would be taken from him and their prospects ruined; he could expect expulsion from the court and the ridicule of the people. All this when he was innocent of any misdemeanour other than the accepted custom of maintaining a mistress.

For Mademoiselle Deluzy, her position was no longer tenable. Bewildered and distraught, she offered her resignation at once and it was accepted. Some days later, when she had left the château and was living in anguish and resentment in a *pension,* the Duke met her. According to Mademoiselle Deluzy's later testimony, his usual composure was shattered, and he confided to her something that was deeply shocking.

Like the Duchess in her letters, Mademoiselle Deluzy never revealed the exact nature of any distressing happening, but referred to this one as "a most grave event". A few phrases she wrote in allusion were later interpreted by two French historians as no less a thing than that the Duchess had been seducing her own young sons—and that one of them had confessed it to his father the Duke.

Curious contradiction

It has been said that in every man there dwell the seeds of crime; whether they grow or are stifled in their growth by the good that is in him is a chance mysteriously determined. Some men add even greater mystery to that chance: they are those of refinement or studious habits who suddenly burst on the astonished gaze of their fellowmen as murderers. Such a man was the Duke de Choiseul-Praslin.

His crime was to be coldly premeditated. Two weeks before the murder he removed all but one of the screws securing the upper part of the Duchess's fourposter bed in the bedroom of their Paris house. This was in the vain hope that it might crash upon his wife and kill her. He also busied himself in removing bolts from doors and securing others so that the only access to the Duchess's room after she retired would be via his own.

The Duke chose the early hours of August 18 for his crime, knowing that on that night the watchman would leave the house for another appointment at 4 a.m.—thus leaving the house unguarded until the servants were awake soon after 5 a.m. He hoped no doubt to commit the crime rapidly and then open a door on to the park—the Praslin apartments being all on the ground floor, the suggestion would be that an intruder had broken in and murdered the Duchess.

That the Duke failed in all this emphasized the curious contradiction of his character. Both cunning and clumsiness marked everything he did in setting up the crime, yet he later made a determined

Danese-Rapho

Radio Times Hulton

attempt to escape from the horrors of his situation and showed at the same time a curious insensibility to its real gravity.

On the night of August 17 the Duchess went to bed early with a book which she read for a while by candlelight. By her side was a tray of light refreshment and the table knife she was soon so desperately to use in a vain attempt to resist her murderous husband. The Duke arrived at the house soon after the Duchess extinguished her candle. It was then about midnight; probably he did not go to bed at all that night. Four and a half hours later he crept from his room down the corridor that led to his wife's room, and set about his grim errand.

By the time the sun had risen high over Paris the house at No. 55 Rue du Faubourg St. Honoré was swarming with officials and policemen. The Duke at first denied any knowledge of the murder, but his replies to the simplest questions were pathetic. He could give no explanation for the clothing still smouldering in his bedroom hearth, for his pistol being found under his wife's body, for the water daubs

CRUEL CONTRAST . . . The magnificent Château le Vicomte (above) was the home of the Duke and Duchess of Choiseul-Praslin. After the murder, the dying Duke was dragged to the Luxembourg jail (inset), where he died in great pain.

still wet on his *robe de chambre*, for the scratches on his body. If any more proof of guilt was needed it came when, during the afternoon of that same day, the Duke swallowed a dose of arsenic.

In a fever heat of panic to see justice done before the inevitable happened, the Court of Peers—which alone could try a man of Praslin's rank—convened and hastily arrested the Duke. He was taken to prison and questioned remorselessly. At the end of six days of unrelieved suffering, the poison denied the people the verdict for which they clamoured and which the peers dreaded: the Duke died on the day of his wife's funeral.

But all was not yet done. With a ruthlessness for which French justice is celebrated, Mademoiselle Deluzy was arrested and put on trial. The prosecution's object

was to prove that she was an accessory to the crime in that she had provoked the Duke to murder the Duchess in the hope of marrying him herself.

For three months she was interrogated daily. At last her inquisitors, grudgingly admiring her unshakable resolution, gave up the task and freed her. At once she left France, and was next heard of again in the United States. In May 1851, Henriette Deluzy married Henry M. Field, a New England Presbyterian minister ten years her junior. They lived first in Massachusetts and later in New York City—where Henriette Field's social circle became renowned for its wit and elegance.

Mrs. Field was 63 when, in 1875, she died. She was by then so celebrated for her local charitable and social works that American newspapers eulogizing her in their obituary columns found only a sentence to recall that she was once a governess who was involved in the "Duke de Praslin affair" in France. But for Henriette Field, that one sentence—and the bizarre facts behind it—earned her a gruesome place in French history.

63

Murder at the Savoy Hotel

Madame Fahmy

Glamour, wealth, a beautiful woman and one of the greatest lawyers the British courts had ever produced —the trial of Madame Marguerite Fahmy (right) for the murder of her husband (left) in their Savoy Hotel suite had all the ingredients for a sensational trial. No one was disappointed.

THE TRIAL of Marie-Marguerite Fahmy for the murder of her playboy husband Prince Ali Kamel Fahmy Bey, which opened in London's Central Criminal Court on September 10, 1923, had all the elements of a drama of powerful passions. The accused was an attractive and sophisticated 32-year-old Parisienne brunette of slender height and striking beauty.

Her late husband, ten years her junior, was an abnormal and vicious young Egyptian of considerable wealth and worldly possessions, who was widely believed to have treated her with disgusting cruelty. He held the nominal post of attaché at the French Legation in Cairo and had obtained his princely title in return for making gifts to various Egyptian charities.

Prince Fahmy's death, which his wife admitted she had caused by shooting him, had taken place during the night of the previous 9-10 July in the Savoy Hotel in London, where they occupied a luxurious suite of rooms. At the inquest which followed the killing, the coroner's jury returned a verdict of wilful murder against Madame Fahmy.

Mr. Justice Rigby Swift presided at the trial. He was the youngest judge on the High Court bench, having been only 46 at the time of his appointment three years previously, but he had already made his mark by his effective handling of jury cases. The prosecution was led by Mr. Percival Clarke, son of the famous Victorian advocate Sir Edward Clarke. Marguerite Fahmy was represented by two leading King's Counsel, Sir Edward Marshall Hall and Sir Henry Curtis Bennett, though in fact the defence was to be entirely handled by Marshall Hall, who had taken Sir Edward Clarke's place as the most popular and sought after defence lawyer in the country.

Incompatible

Opening the case for the Crown, Mr. Percival Clarke said that Fahmy Bey had inherited great wealth from his father, an engineer. He became infatuated with the accused, then Madame Laurent, a divorcée, whom he first met in Paris in May of the previous year. He followed her to Deauville, where she became his mistress, and they lived there and in Egypt and Paris. In December, Marguerite became a Moslem and there were civil and religious marriage ceremonies. Prince Fahmy returned to Cairo where he was later joined by his wife, who had remained in Paris, but at no time were they happy. Their natures seemed incompatible.

At the beginning of July 1923, the couple came to London and put up at the Savoy Hotel, accompanied by a secretary, valet and maid. On July 9 they had some disagreement because the wife wanted to go to Paris to have an operation which the husband wished to have performed in London. At supper in the hotel restaurant that night there was a violent quarrel during which Madame Fahmy, it was alleged, said to her husband: "You shut up. I will smash this bottle over your head."

When the band leader came to her table and asked if there was any particular tune she would like to be played, she replied, "I don't want any music—my husband has threatened to kill me tonight!" The polite maestro bowed gravely and said, "I hope you will still be here tomorrow, madame." After supper Fahmy twice asked his wife to dance, but she refused, though she danced once with his secretary Seid Ernani.

They went upstairs to their suite about 1.30 a.m. A violent thunderstorm was raging at the time. Shortly afterwards

a luggage porter was passing the door of the suite when Fahmy came out in his pyjamas and said to the porter: "Look at my face! Look at what she has done!" The porter saw a slight red mark on his cheek. Then Madame Fahmy, who was in evening dress, came out and, speaking hurriedly in French, pointed to her eyes; the porter told them to go into their rooms and not create a disturbance in the corridor, and then continued on his way.

Hearing a whistle, the porter looked back and saw Prince Fahmy stooping down, whistling and snapping his fingers at a little dog which had come out of their suite. A few moments later the porter heard three shots in quick succession, and running back to the suite saw Madame Fahmy throw down a pistol. Her husband was lying on the floor bleeding from his head. "Oh, sir," said Madame Fahmy when the manager was summoned, "I have been married six months which has been torture to me. I have suffered terribly."

The police and a doctor were sent for and the wounded man was removed to hospital where he died shortly afterwards. Marguerite was then taken into custody.

Seid Ernani was the first to give evidence for the prosecution, corroborating details of his late master's life and marriage. Cross-examined by Marshall Hall, he denied that he had any influence over Prince Fahmy which would have made his wife jealous.

Sickening flattery

"Was he in the habit of beating women?"

"He would dispute with them," the secretary replied, "but I have never seen him beat them."

"You have known of his intimacies with many women?" Marshall Hall continued.

"Yes," the witness agreed.

"You said that you tried to dissuade the prince from marrying her?"

"Yes."

"Did you say he was an Oriental, and passionate?"

"Yes."

"You were very much attached to Prince Fahmy?"

"Yes."

"Was he infatuated with her at that time?"

"Yes, very much in love with her."

Marshall Hall then quoted a letter written in French from Egypt by the Prince to Marguerite in terms of sickening flattery. The translation read in part:

"Your image pursues me incessantly . . . Torch of my life . . . your head so haughty and majestic, brightly encircled by a crown which I reserve for it here. Yes, this crown I reserve for you on your arrival in this beautiful country of my ancestors."

"Everybody thought he was a prince, then?" Madame Fahmy's counsel asked.

"We always refer to our ancestors," was all the secretary could say.

"But they do not all wear crowns?"

"No."

Divorce condition

Answering further questions, Seid Ernani said that it was in Cairo that the question of marriage first arose. Fahmy first suggested that she live with him, and then suggested marriage. Two of the stipulations in the contract were that Madame Fahmy would not be obliged to wear Egyptian clothes and that she would have the right to divorce her husband. She adopted the Moslem religion because Fahmy's mother had left him a large legacy on condition that he married a woman of that faith.

"When the religious ceremony took place, did Fahmy decline to allow the divorce condition to be inserted?"

"Yes."

"After the religious ceremony, then, he could divorce her, as she was a Moslem, at a moment's notice and she could not divorce him, and he had the power to take three wives if he liked?"

The witness agreed that this was so. Marshall Hall then turned to the prince's treatment of his wife.

"Were people always set to watch her when she went out?"

"They were lately," the witness again agreed.

"On February 21st was there a very serious scene? Do you know that he swore on the Koran to kill her?"

"No."

"Do you know that she was in fear of her life?"

"No, I never knew that."

"On the 23rd, did Fahmy take her on his yacht at Luxor?"

"Yes."

"Were there six black servants on board?"

"Yes."

"I suggest that from that moment Fahmy began to treat her with persistent cruelty?"

"I cannot say cruelty. He was a bit unkind."

Training

"The day he arrived at Luxor, did he smack her face, tell her she must not leave the yacht, and then kick her?"

"I have not seen him kick her. I knew he locked her in." Further pressed by Marshall Hall, the secretary was obliged to admit that he remembered an incident when Fahmy struck his wife a violent blow on the chin and dislocated her jaw.

To drive home his point Marshall Hall went on to read from a letter which Fahmy had written to his wife's younger sister:

THE DAILY MIRROR, Tuesday, September 11, 1923.

GERMANY SEEKING NEW CONFERENCE WITH FRANCE

The Daily Mirror

NET SALE MUCH THE LARGEST OF ANY DAILY PICTURE NEWSPAPER

No. 6,194. | Registered at the G.P.O. as a Newspaper. | TUESDAY, SEPTEMBER 11, 1923 | One Penny.

SAVOY SHOOTING: MME. FAHMY'S TRIAL OPENS

Mme. Said, sister of the dead man, with her husband, Dr. Said (centre), and Abdul Faath Razal Bey, an Egyptian lawyer, representing Mme. Said.

Sir Henry Curtis Bennett, K.C., one of the counsel engaged for the defence.

Mr. Cecil Whiteley, K.C., who held a watching brief, arriving at the Old Bailey.

Said Enani, the dead man's secretary, said the couple were not very happy.

A new portrait, received from Paris last night, of Mme. Fahmy, who is charged with the murder of her husband, Ali Kamel Fahmy Bey (inset), a wealthy young Egyptian.

The large crowd that waited outside the Old Bailey in the hope of gaining admittance for the opening of the trial. Many fashionably-dressed women were present

Passionate letters, descriptions of life in an Egyptian palace, and an account of frequent quarrels between the dead man and his wife, figured in the evidence and examination of Said Enani, secretary to Ali Kamel Fahmy Bey, at the opening yesterday of the trial of Mme. Marie Marguerite Fahmy on a charge of murdering her husband by shooting him at the Savoy Hotel. In his opening address, counsel for the prosecution stated that after marriage Mme. Fahmy always slept with a pistol close at hand.

"Just now I am engaged in training her. Yesterday, to begin with I did not come in to lunch nor to dinner and I also left her at the theatre. This will teach her, I hope, to respect my wishes.

"With women one must act with energy and be severe – no bad habits. We still lead the same life of which you are aware – the opera, theatre, disputes, high words, and perverseness."

"When you came over from Egypt," counsel continued, "his treatment of his wife was the talk of the ship?"

"They were always quarrelling," replied the secretary.

"Do you know that he locked her in her cabin for 24 hours and that the captain had to have her released?"

"I don't know that."

"Was not the Madame Fahmy of 1923 totally different from the Madame Laurent of 1922?"

"Perhaps."

"From a quite entertaining and fascinating woman she became miserable and wretched?"

"They were always quarrelling."

"Did she say that you and Fahmy were always against her, and that it was a case of two to one?"

"Yes."

Notorious relationship

Marshall Hall went on to suggest to the witness that Prince Fahmy was a man of vicious and eccentric sexual appetite, and that he had a homosexual relationship with Seid Ernani which was notorious in Egypt. He showed the witness a coloured cartoon which had appeared in an Egyptian newspaper depicting Prince Fahmy, his secretary and a friend as "The Light, the Shadow of the Light, and the Shadow of the Shadow of the Light".

While agreeing that he and his employer were represented in the cartoon, the witness loyally denied any unfavourable reflection on his or his master's morals. The judge then asked to see the cartoon, and when he had examined it he remarked that it did not reflect on anybody's moral character, except perhaps the artist's.

It was a masterly cross-examination. Marshall Hall did not attack the secretary's character, though he got very near to it at the end. Had he done so, this would have entitled the prosecution to attack that of Madame Fahmy, and it was of vital importance to her counsel's case that she should not be exhibited as an habitually loose woman. As it was, the secretary admitted enough to impress the jury by creating an atmosphere of intense sympathy for the accused woman, who had been in the power of this decadent Oriental millionaire.

The porter, night manager and assistant manager of the Savoy Hotel followed the secretary into the witness box. In cross-examining the assistant manager, Marshall Hall again showed his characteristic skill and incidentally his knowledge of the French language. According to this witness, Madame Fahmy had said to him in French immediately after the shooting, "Monsieur, what have I done? I have lost my head."

The actual words used by Madame Fahmy were, *"J'ai perdu la tête."* Marshall Hall put it to the witness that the real meaning of the phrase was not "I have lost my head", but "I was frightened out of my wits". The witness agreed, and this interpretation was not challenged by the prosecution.

Painful complaint

Robert Churchill, the gunsmith and firearms expert, testified that the weapon used in the killing was a .32 Browning automatic of Belgian manufacture, capable of holding eight cartridges. Prosecuting counsel asked him: "Is it a weapon that continues to fire when the trigger is pressed, or does the trigger require pressure for each shot?"

"The trigger has to be pulled for each shot," the witness replied. "It is automatic loading, but not automatic firing." The gunsmith added that the pull of the trigger was 8¼ pounds. It was not a light pull. The pistol had a safety grip and a safety catch and was not the sort to go off accidentally. Churchill was cross-examined at length about the mechanism of the weapon by Marshall Hall who suggested that, when the pistol was tightly gripped, a very small pressure on the trigger would discharge each shot. The witness agreed that this was so and also explained that after one shot had been discharged through the barrel it would immediately be replaced by another. An inexperienced person might thus easily reload the weapon, believing that in fact he had emptied it.

Dr. Gordon, who had been attending Madame Fahmy and had made arrangements for her to go into a London nursing home for her operation on the day after the killing, testified that he was called to the scene of the tragedy and asked Madame Fahmy what she had done. "I have shot my husband," she replied. She was in a white evening dress trimmed with beads, and was very dazed and frightened.

"Did you see any marks of bruising on her arms?" asked the prosecutor.

"She showed me a scratch on the back of her neck about 1½ inches long, probably caused by a finger nail. She told me her husband had done it."

Asked by Marshall Hall in cross-examination whether the marks on her neck were consistent with a hand clutching her throat, the doctor said they were.

"When you visited Madame Fahmy for her illness, did you see her husband?"

"No. He was in the next room, and a black valet was outside Madame's door."

Questioned about the nature of Madame Fahmy's illness, Dr. Gordon agreed that she was suffering from a painful complaint which might have been caused by the conduct she alleged against her husband. The published accounts of the trial are silent on the nature of this conduct, but it may well be that Prince Fahmy forced his wife to have anal intercourse and may conceivably have communicated a venereal disease to her in the process.

After police evidence of the accused's arrest, the prosecution case was closed and Marshall Hall opened his defence with a speech to the jury, to whom he submitted that it would be impossible justly on the facts to find "this poor unfortunate woman guilty" of either murder or manslaughter. She was "perhaps a woman of not very strict morality", he went on, because they had heard that she had been divorced and had lived with Fahmy before their marriage.

There was no doubt, however, that although they were infatuated with each other at the beginning, she had made a terrible mistake in her estimate of his character.

"We know that women are sometimes very much attracted to men younger than themselves," Marshall Hall told the jury, "and he went out of his way, with all his Eastern cunning, to make himself agreeable and acceptable to her. But this was a man who enjoys the sufferings of women. He was abnormal and a brute. After marriage all restraint ceased and he developed from a plausible lover into a ferocious brute with the vilest of vile tempers and a filthy perverted taste. It makes one shudder to consider the conditions under which this wretched woman lived."

New evidence

Coming to the night of the tragedy, Marshall Hall recounted how Fahmy had called his wife into his bedroom and pointed to a heap of money on the table. She asked him to give her the French money, about 2,000 francs, for her travelling expenses to Paris for her operation. He told her she could not have it unless she agreed to a suggestion he made, apparently for abnormal sexual intercourse. She refused and he spat in her face, telling her to go to the devil. He then followed her outside into the corridor, catching her by the neck and tightening his grip on her so that she feared she would be strangled.

"Thanks to the judge's intervention, Marshall Hall went on, "a new and wonderful piece of evidence" had come into his hands. This was the report of the prison medical officer, who was also the governor of Holloway Prison where the accused was taken after her arrest. He was called

Daily Mirror

The Daily

NET SALE MUCH THE LARGEST OF ANY 1

No. 6,195. Registered at the G.P.O.
as a Newspaper. WEDNESDAY, SEPTEMBER 12,

MME. FAHMY'S SECRET

Mme. Fahmy and, inset, Ali Kamel Fahmy Bey, of whose murder she stands accused.

Dr. E. F. Gordon (on left), who had attended Mme. Fahmy, was one of the principal witnesses yesterday.

Mr. Arthur Mariani, night manager of the Savoy Hotel, who gave evidence.

Remarkable allegations regarding the dead man were made by counsel at the trial of Mme. Fahmy at the Old Bailey yesterday. He declared also that Mme. Fahmy had given her lawyer in Egypt a sealed document not to be opened till after her death.

as the first witness for the defence, and he described how Madame Fahmy, when she was admitted to Holloway, had three abrasions on the back of her neck apparently caused by a man's hand.

Marshall Hall intended to call the accused next, but before he did so he informed the judge that it was necessary to discuss a point of law in the absence of the jury. When the jury had accordingly been sent out, the leading defence counsel said he had been told by the prosecutor, Mr. Percival Clarke, that he proposed to cross-examine Madame Fahmy to show that, as she was a woman who lived an immoral life, she would therefore be a woman of the world well able to look after herself. "The only effect of that," observed Marshall Hall, "would be to prejudice the jury unfavourably towards this woman. We know the effect of these suggestions."

Legal discussion

"Sir Edward has said she was an immoral woman," the judge remarked, "but he has said it in such a way as to give the impression to everyone who listened to his speech that she was an innocent and most respectable lady. It is a difficult thing to do, but Sir Edward, with all that skill we have admired for so long, has done it." Mr. Justice Swift then ruled that the evidence so far did not justify Mr. Clarke in asking Madame Fahmy about her relations with any other men, but with regard to the dead man he might ask anything he liked.

When the jury returned to court, the judge said he did not propose to inform them of the legal discussion which had taken place, and added: "I must now give instructions that you are not to be allowed access to any newspapers until the trial is over. I am sorry to deprive you of them. It must be very boring to be shut up all the evening without even a newspaper, but I am bound to do it."

Then the prisoner was called to testify in her own defence. Slowly and carefully — through the medium of an interpreter, since she knew no English — Marshall Hall took her through the tragedy of her life with Prince Fahmy until the three fatal shots were fired. She said she had married her first husband M. Laurent in April 1919 and had divorced him a few months later for desertion. On the subject of her second husband's treatment of her, she said that his black valet was always following her about and used to enter her room when she was dressing. When she complained to her husband, he replied: "He has the right. He does not count. He is nobody."

She described how one day in Paris, when her young sister Yvonne Alibert was present, he had threatened her with a horsewhip, seizing her by the throat and

69

throwing her backwards. He only stopped when her sister, who had a revolver in her hand, told him to desist. After the scene on the yacht, she described how Ali Fahmy had taken the Koran and sworn on it that he would kill her. Later she wrote to her French lawyer that she had been held literally prisoner on board the yacht for three days and that on her arms were "the marks of my husband's gentleness"

Final scene

In further replies to her counsel, she said that she had never fired a pistol till the night of her husband's death. Fahmy himself had given her the Browning .32 loaded, saying, "It is all ready to fire." She had often seen him unload the pistol by opening the breach and taking out a cartridge. On that dreadful night, when he had tried to strangle her and she had been in an agony of fear, she had tried to do the same thing. But her hands had not been strong enough to pull back the breach cover fully, and she had struggled to extract the bullet by shaking the weapon in front of the window. While she was thus engaged, somehow the first cartridge went off and the bullet spent itself harmlessly out of the window.

"After the cartridge had been fired," she said, "I thought the revolver was not dangerous." However, unknown to her, the second cartridge had automatically come up into position.

"I know nothing about automatic pistols," she said, as her counsel handed the weapon to her. At first she shrank back from it, but eventually she took it in her hands. She tried, but was quite unable to pull back the breach cover.

"Why did you assent to come to London when you were so frightened?" Marshall Hall asked her.

"I had to come to London for family reasons," she replied. "I had always hoped he would change. Every time I threatened to leave him, he cried and promised to mend his ways. I also wished to see my daughter who was at school near London."

With a sob punctuating every phrase, she told the story of the final scene.

"He advanced and had a very threatening expression. He said, 'I will revenge myself.' I had taken the revolver in my hand . . . I went out into the corridor in front of the lift. He seized me suddenly and brutally by the throat with his left hand. His thumb was on my windpipe and his fingers were pressing on my neck.

"I pushed him away, but he crouched to spring on me, and said, 'I will kill you.' I lifted my arm in front of me and without looking pulled the trigger. The next moment I saw him on the ground before me. I do not know how many times the revolver went off. I did not know what had happened.

"I saw Fahmy on the ground and I fell on my knees beside him. I caught hold of his hand and said to him, 'Sweetheart, it is nothing. Speak, oh, please speak to me!' While I was on my knees the porter came up."

Marshall Hall asked her two final questions in his examination-in-chief.

"When the pistol went off, killing your husband, had you any idea that it was in a condition to be fired?"

"None," the witness answered emphatically. "I thought there was no cartridge and that it could not be used."

"When you threw your arm out when the pistol was fired, what were you afraid of?"

"That he was going to jump on to me. It was terrible. I had escaped once. He said, 'I will kill you. I will kill you.' It was so terrible."

Mr. Percival Clarke began his cross-examination by asking if her father was a cab-driver in Paris. Immediately the judge intervened. "Does it matter whether he

Mansell

WORLD'S GREATEST . . . That was the verdict of many people after Sir Edward Marshall Hall's masterly performance in the sensational trial of Mme. Fahmy.

was a cab-driver or a millionaire?" he asked the prosecutor. "I don't want a long inquiry into the lady's ancestry or into circumstances which may not be admissible."

Counsel did not pursue this line. Instead he asked the witness, "Can I correctly describe you as a woman of the world, a woman of experience?"

"I have had experience of life," Madame Fahmy answered sagely.

Asked whether she had not gone to Egypt with the idea of marrying Prince Fahmy, she said that she had arrived at no decision but had merely "accepted to be his *amie*".

"Were you not very ambitious to be-

come his wife?"

"Ambitious, no," replied the witness. "I loved him so very much and wished to be with him."

Asked what she did when her husband was cruel, she said, "Once only I boxed his ears when he had beaten me very much. I was always alternating between hope and despair," she went on. "Some days he would be nice and I had new confidence in him, but the next day he would be bad again, and it was always the same." Their physical relations she described as "being never quite normal". She added that when she went out to buy new dresses, her husband's secretary Seid Ernani was always sent with her and she had to undress before him.

"Why did you not have him to protect you if you feared your husband?"

"He was not my friend. He obeyed my husband's orders, not mine."

"Did you think that he was in league with your husband to ill-treat you?"

"Sometimes I have thought so, because I noticed each time I told him something he immediately went to my husband and told him what I said, and did whatever he could to make matters worse."

On the whole Madame Fahmy stood up well to this cross-examination, particularly when she was asked about the pistol. "I never intended to shoot it out of the window," she said. "I just wanted to get the ball out, and I tried to pull the thing back but I had not the strength to do it. As I was shaking it, it went off and I felt perfectly certain it was safe."

Important letter

"Did you not think that when you got rid of the cartridge you were depriving yourself of the only defence left to you if your husband assaulted you?"

"I never wanted to kill my husband," the prisoner answered between sobs. "I only wanted to prevent him killing me. I thought the sight of the pistol might frighten him. But I never wanted to do him any harm. I never did . . . I never noticed that I had pressed upon the trigger . . . I saw my husband lying on the ground before I could think or see what had happened."

Marshall Hall had kept one important piece of evidence in reserve for re-examination. This was a letter Madame Fahmy had written to her lawyer, accusing her husband of being responsible should she disappear. It read in part:

"Yesterday, January 21, 1923, at three o'clock in the afternoon, he took his Bible or Koran—I do not know how it is called—kissed it, put his hand on it, and swore to avenge himself upon me tomorrow, in eight days, a month, three months, but I must disappear by his hands. This oath was taken without any reason, neither jealousy, nor a scene on my part."

LONDON-MANCHESTER AIR MAIL CRASH: FIVE DEAD

The Daily Mirror

NET SALE MUCH THE LARGEST OF ANY DAILY PICTURE NEWSPAPER

No. 6,198   Registered at the G.P.O. as a Newspaper.   SATURDAY, SEPTEMBER 15, 1923   One Penny.

SUMMING UP IN FAHMY TRIAL: VERDICT TO-DAY

Sir Edward Marshall-Hall, whose dramatic final speech for the defence was in striking contrast to the quiet reply of Mr. Percival Clarke (inset) for the Crown.

Mr. Justice Rigby Swift had not concluded his summing-up when the Court adjourned yesterday, the fifth day of the trial.

Mme. Fahmy, the Frenchwoman charged with the murder of her husband. The verdict...

Daily Mirror

"Is that letter true?" asked Marshall Hall, holding it up.

"It is the exact truth," Madame Fahmy answered with conviction.

After the prisoner's sister, maid, and chauffeur had been called to corroborate the catalogue of Prince Fahmy's cruelties, Marshall Hall began his closing speech to the jury on the fourth day of the trial. "She made one great mistake, possibly the greatest mistake any woman of the West can make," he said of his client, "she married an Oriental. I dare say the Egyptian civilization is, and may be, one of the oldest and most wonderful civilizations in the world. But if you strip off the external civilization of the Oriental, you get the real Oriental underneath. It is common knowledge that the Oriental's treatment of women does not fit in with the way the Western woman considers she should be treated by her husband."

Marguerite Fahmy's defender went on to make the jury's flesh creep with his description of the subtle means by which the prince had enticed her into his "Oriental garden", after which she was constantly watched by his retinue of black servants. "Why was this woman afraid?" he asked the jury and went on to supply the answer. "Was she afraid that some of the hirelings of this man would do her to death? The curse of this case is the atmosphere which we cannot understand — the Eastern feeling of possession of the woman, the Turk in his harem, this man who was entitled to have four wives if he liked for chattels, which to us Western people with our ideas of women is almost unintelligible, something we cannot deal with."

Marshall Hall had not finished when the court adjourned. He resumed his speech next morning with a reference to the storm on the night of the killing. "You know the effect of such a storm when your nerves are normal," he told the jury. "Imagine its effect on a woman of nervous temperament who had been living such a life as she had lived for the past six months — terrified, abused, beaten, degraded."

Theatrical performance

The advocate went on to stage what was perhaps the most remarkable theatrical performance of his professional career when with the pistol in his hand he described the shooting in detail, imitating Fahmy's stealthy crouch as he advanced on his wife. "In sheer desperation — as he crouched for the last time, crouched like an animal, retired for the last time to get a bound forward — she turned the pistol and put it to his face, and to her horror the thing went off."

As he spoke the last words, the great

advocate held up the pistol and pointed it for a moment at the jury. Then he paused and dropped the weapon so that it fell with a clatter on the courtroom floor, just as it had fallen from the prisoner's hands in the corridor of the Savoy Hotel. The effect of this demonstration was chillingly dramatic, yet Marshall Hall always said afterwards that the final touch was an accident and that he had not meant to drop the pistol at all.

He concluded with two references. The first was to what the prosecutor's father Sir Edward Clarke had said in another sensational Old Bailey trial. "To use the words of my learned friend's great father many years ago in the Bartlett case, 'I do not ask you for a verdict—I demand a verdict at your hands.'"

His second reference was to a modern best-selling novel by Robert Hitchens called *Bella Donna*, in the final scene of which a Western woman goes out of the gates of an Oriental garden into the dark night of the desert.

"Members of the jury," he said, "I want you to open the gates where this Western woman can go out, not into the dark night of the desert, but back to her friends, who love her in spite of her weaknesses—back to her friends, who will be glad to receive her—back to her child who will be waiting for her with open arms. I ask you to open the gate and let this Western woman go back into the light of God's great Western sun."

Marshall Hall pointed to the skylight where the bright English September sun was streaming in and suffusing the court with its warmth and brightness. With this final dramatic gesture, he sat down.

Strong protest

In the face of this superb pleading, it took the jury little over an hour to reach their verdict—not guilty of murder, and not guilty of manslaughter. The cheering which greeted the result was so great that the judge immediately ordered the court to be cleared. The prisoner broke down when she was discharged, the climax to an ordeal in which she had not been able to understand a single word of the concluding speeches and the judge's summing up. "Oh, I am so happy, I am so thankful," she sobbed as she stumbled from the dock supported by two wardresses. "It is terrible to have killed Ali, but I spoke the truth. I spoke the truth."

Marshall Hall's oratory in defence of Marguerite Fahmy drew a strong protest to the British Attorney-General from the leader of the Egyptian Bar, who accused the advocate of "allowing himself to generalize and to lash all Egypt and indeed the whole East".

This was unfair, as indeed Marshall Hall himself pointed out. "Any attack I made was on express instructions, re-ceived through Egyptian sources on the man Ali Fahmy, and not on the Egyptians as a nation," he wrote to the Attorney-General. "If my instructions were, as I believe them to be, accurate, anything I said about that person was more than justified. The only thing that I remember saying that might be misunderstood was that it was a mistake for Western woman to marry Eastern man, and his idea of his rights towards a wife were those of possession instead of mutual alliance."

It must be remembered that these were the days of plays like *The Sheik* and *The Garden of Allah* and stories which romanticized the sexual allure of the East. As the English *Daily Mirror* wrote in an editorial at the time, the moral of the Fahmy trial for most people had little to do with the circumstances in which the fatal shot was fired, but bore chiefly if not solely upon the undesirability of marriage which united Oriental husbands and Western wives. The editorial continued:

"Too many of our women novelists, apparently under the spell of the East, have encouraged the belief that there is something very romantic in such unions.

"They are not romantic.

"They are ridiculous and unseemly; and the sensational revelations of the trial which terminated on Saturday will not be without their use if they bring that fact home to the sentimental naive girl."

For Sir Edward Marshall Hall the

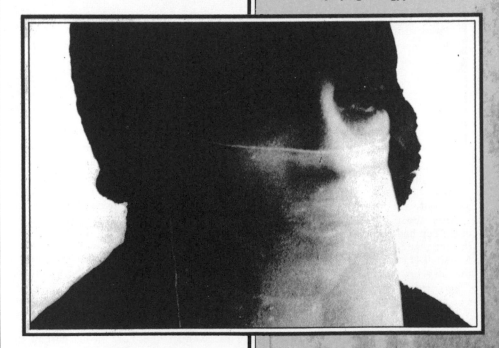

ORIENTAL TWIST . . . Having achieved acquittal on the charge of killing her husband Ali (right), Mme Fahmy broke into films—playing an Egyptian wife!

Fahmy trial remained perhaps his most outstanding and widely known forensic triumph. Letters of congratulations poured in to him from all over the world. One of them was addressed simply to "Marshall Hall, the Greatest Lawyer on Earth". The Post Office delivered it safely to his chambers in the Temple.

Violence in the Sun

Lieutenant Massie

The American population of Honolulu cried for vengeance when a naval officer's wife was raped. It was a cry which brought brutality and killing.

THE PARTY at the Ala Wai Inn had gone on until nearly midnight and showed no sign of ending. There was a lot of dancing, a lot of drinking, and the atmosphere was hot, smoky and noisy. All this—plus the fact that she had just had a tiff with her naval officer husband—was too much for 20-year-old Mrs. Thalia Massie.

Without saying a word to any of the 100 people present, she collected her handbag and slipped out into the warm night air of Honolulu. She decided to walk to her bungalow home a short distance away, and set off along the well-lighted John Ena Road. Being outdoors cleared her head and she felt fresher and livelier than she had done for hours.

Her sense of well being gave her an almost nonchalant confidence, and she paid little attention to the automobile which came slowly up behind her—prowling along the gutter as if its occupants, five dark-skinned men, were looking for something or someone.

She was an attractive figure in her green party dress, and a number of men at the United States Navy base at Hawaii envied her husband, Lieutenant Tommy Massie. She was looking her best on the night of September 12, 1931, and later some people said they were shocked but not surprised at what happened next.

Local boxer

The car came to a halt beside her, four of the men jumped out, grabbed her, threw her onto the back seat and sped to a place she recognized as the Old Animal Quarantine Station. There she was dragged out into the open and one of the men—a famous local boxer called Joe Kahahawi—struck her with his fist and broke her jaw. He and his companions—another Hawaiian, a Chinaman and two Japanese—then flung her to the ground and took turns in raping her.

CENTRAL FIGURE in the Honolulu rape case, Mrs. Thalia Massie, soon discovered that her violent experience had racial and political undertones. Other women had been raped—but they weren't white.

AP

Once they had done with her, they got back into the car—an open tourer—and left her bruised, bloodied and hysterical. Somehow she dragged herself onto the nearest main road, Ala Moana Drive, where she hailed a passing automobile containing a group of white men.

Appalled by the condition she was in, the men rushed her to her home, from where she rang Tommy Massie at the party. Massie arrived at the bungalow to find Thalia with her lips cut and bleeding, her eyes swollen, her mouth and nose red.

Thalia then collapsed into his arms, crying: "It's awful, Tommy—the shame! I just want to die!"

He calmed her as much as he could and then rang the local police station. A police car arrived within minutes, and as it took Thalia to hospital, she repeated her story of abduction, assault and rape. "I even saw the number of the car," she sobbed. "It was 58895."

Savages

By a weird coincidence, the police had already recorded a car bearing that number following another complaint of rape. The previous victim, a Hawaiian woman named Mrs. Peebles, wife of a white man, had told a similar tale to Mrs. Massie's.

An old touring car had pulled up beside her, she had been bundled inside by the occupants, taken to a lonely spot and then ravished. The men had been identified as Horace Ida, a Japanese who owned the car; two Hawaiians, Joe Kahahawi and Ben Anakuelo; a Chinaman, Harry Chang, and another Japanese, David Takai.

The men—two of whom had previously been convicted of sex crimes—were allowed to go at the time due to lack of supporting evidence. On this occasion, however, there would be no generosity on the part of the law. Ida and his gang were going to pay—and pay heavily—for their crime.

The five alleged rapists were rounded up and taken to the hospital—where Thalia, heavily bandaged and under sedation, stated that they were the men who had brutalized her. "I'd know those savages anywhere," she said.

On the face of it there now seemed only one thing for the authorities to do. Have the gang put on trial, and make sure they were sent to where they would not be able to attack and terrorize the white – and coloured – women of the island.

Racial unrest

Hawaii was under United States protection with its own Governor and American-style policemen. But the inhabitants were by no means American or Americanized. The population consisted of an admixture of pure-bred Hawaiians, Japanese, Chinese, Filipinos, Koreans, Portuguese and a leavening of Americans.

Beneath the paradisal surface of the island—with its warm white beaches, rolling surf, palm trees and pineapples—there was a great deal of racial unrest. It was not until 1959 that the Territory of Hawaii became the fiftieth member of the Union (the "Aloha State"), and there were many people opposed to that ever happening.

The police, therefore, found difficulties placed in their way. For one thing, witnesses came forward to swear that Ida, Kahahawi and the other men were with them, on a different part of the island, when the assault on Thalia Massie took place.

Also it was not possible to produce medical evidence positively stating that she had been raped. The hospital doctors would go no further than to testify that she had been attacked. Contrary to popular rumour, she was not pregnant, and no trace of sperm had been found in or on her body.

Added to this there were stories circulating which did not reflect well upon her character and disposition. And there was a strong element of class jealousy and resentment. It was said that Thalia—a member of the American Social Register and the daughter of Long Island socialites — had gone out of her way to flirt with and sexually tease some of her husband's fellow officers.

She led them on and then turned coy and refused to sleep with them. It was they—a bunch of pink-cheeked, clean-cut U.S. sailors—who had raped her, and not the "little swarthy men" she had described to the police.

PROTAGONISTS of the case were Lieutenant Massie (left) and local boxer Joe Kahahawi whom Massie shot dead. It seems certain that Kahahawi committed the rape which led on to his own death.

As these rumours reached the Massies themselves, Thalia became ill and tormented by nightmares in which, she claimed, she relived the "shock and horror" of her midnight ordeal. In turn, Tommie was unable to eat or sleep properly, and they were both relieved when Thalia's mother, Mrs. Grace Glanville-Fortescue, flew to Honolulu.

Indignity to the family

Mrs. Fortescue and her husband, a retired major, had seen their daughter married at the age of sixteen. They both approved of the man of her choice—a newly-commissioned ensign from Annapolis Naval Academy, whose Kentucky parents were both well-born and wealthy.

Mrs. Fortescue came from distinguished stock herself—she was the niece of Alexander Graham Bell, the inventor of the telephone—and she was bitterly distressed that such an indignity as rape should be attached to her family. She threw in her energies with the socially-acceptable white people who were pressing for a trial, and dismissed the fact that some 40 native women had been attacked and hospitalized over the past year without causing more than a legal ripple.

Admiral Yates Stirling, Commander of the U.S. Naval Base, was quick to side with her, and blustered: "Our first inclination is to seize these brutes and string them up on trees. But we must give the authorities a chance to carry out the law. It will be slow and exasperating, but we must be patient."

In an attempt to end the pressure upon them, and generally ease the tension, the much maligned authorities set the accused men's trial for November 19. The jury consisted of seven coloured men and five white, and after listening to fifteen days of conflicting evidence they could not reach a verdict.

The five defendants were released on bail pending a new trial, and the island came dangerously close to an open war between the Americans and the brown- and yellow-skinned races. Mrs. Fortescue and Admiral Stirling were disgusted by the action of the court, and in his memoirs the admiral later wrote:

"The criminal assault of a white woman by the five dark-skinned citizens had gone unpunished by the Courts. Sympathies have been aroused in favour of the accused men. Conviction was thus impossible."

Pistol matches

In the days that followed, the whites and the coloureds split themselves into two completely irreconcilable groups. The coloured people started a Defence Fund for the five near martyrs, and the American women set about defending themselves and their honour.

"Stores did a thriving business selling miniature automatics," recorded Admiral Stirling, "and it was no uncommon sight to see these ordinarily timid women proudly displaying their weapons and challenging each other to pistol matches on the beach . . . I felt it in my bones that something must break. Tension was mounting higher and higher."

Not enough

The break came on Saturday, December 13, when a party of Navy officers seized Horace Ida on the street, threatened him with a gun, and drove him to an isolated plot of ground. There they beat and pistol-whipped him and left him to make his own way back to civilization—the same, they believed, as he had done to Thalia Massie.

No legal action was taken against the men by either the civil or naval authorities—"Honolulu must be made safe for women," declared the Chief of Naval Personnel—although a number of riots broke out and some natives were arrested "for their own good".

But the beating up of Ida—who had not inflicted the major injury upon Thalia—was not enough for Tommy Massie and Mrs. Fortescue. They wanted to get back at Joe Kahahawi—and get back at him they did. They learnt that he had to report each day to the courthouse as a condition

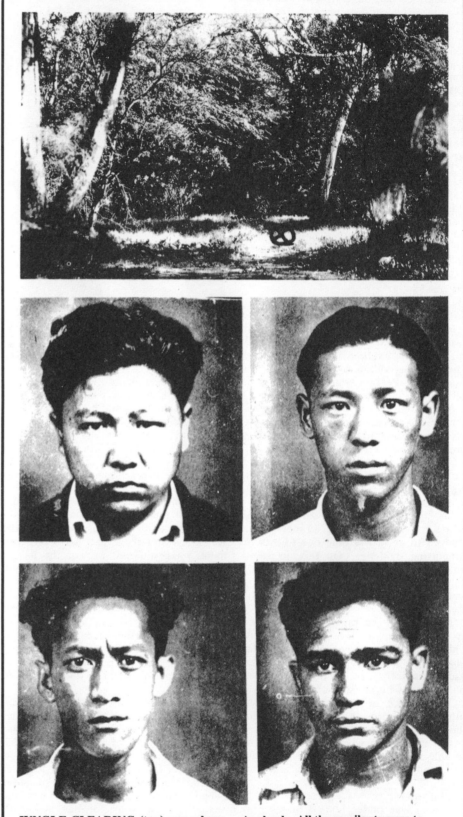

JUNGLE CLEARING (top) was where Thalia Massie was taken and assaulted. The exact spot is marked with an X. The four men who assisted Joe Kahahawi are (left to right, top) Horace Ida and David Takai; (bottom) Harry Chang and Ben Anakuelo. All the assailants were to some extent protected by anti-American feeling on the island which made their trial a confused and tension-racked affair and undoubtedly contributed to the jury's inability to reach a verdict.

UPI

76

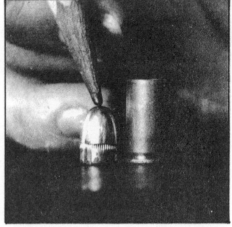

X MARKS the spot where Thalia was picked up and bundled into the rapists' car. The bullet (right) is the one removed from Joe Kahahawi's body after police found him dumped in the Buick.

of his bail, and at 8.30 on the morning of January 8 they were waiting for him outside the Honolulu Hall of Justice.

Together with two enlisted sailors — Edward Lord and Albert Jones — they pounced upon him, forced him into a waiting car, a hired Buick, and drove him to Mrs. Fortescue's rented bungalow in the Ala Moana valley. The car was driven by Tommy Massie, disguised as a chauffeur, and the incident was witnessed by Kahahawi's cousin, who immediately informed the police.

Cocked revolver

Once at the bungalow, Massie took off his peaked cap and dark glasses and confronted the for once frightened and cringing athlete. With a cocked service revolver in his hand, and with the two seamen guarding the door and windows, Massie gave Kahahawi a taste of the third degree.

"Okay," he said toughly. "We're here to get the truth out of you, and to beat it out of you if necessary. If you don't talk before the police get here we'll beat you to ribbons. Now then — who kicked my wife, broke her jaw, and raped her?"

At first, Kahahawi protested his innocence. Tommy, however, persisted. "You're a prizefighter," he rasped. "Of course it was you who hit her. Be a man and admit it!"

Finally, worn down and dispirited, Kahahawi gave in. "Yeah," he mumbled, "I did it all right. We all did it. We attacked your wife."

The picture of the scene on the night of September 12 — with his wife being kicked on the ground and pleading for mercy — flooded Massie's mind like a red-lit, waking nightmare. The next second the gun in his hand exploded and Kahahawi fell to the carpet, mortally wounded. When the police arrived at the bungalow, they found the boxer's dead body, with a .32 calibre bullet in it, wrapped in a piece of canvas and dumped in the back seat of the Buick.

Massie, Mrs. Fortescue, and the two sailors were arrested and taken into custody. Massie claimed that the gun had gone off accidentally, and the four abductors were held awaiting trial on a charge of second degree murder.

Meanwhile, the case became a worldwide *cause célèbre* as everyone involved in the affair — and the newspapers of most nations — had their say in the matter. Thalia Massie was reported as saying: "I'm sorry this man has been shot. But it was no more than he asked for and deserved."

Admiral Stirling, indignant that the Americans had even been arrested for the offence, wrote: "An Hawaiian rapist had been killed by the family of the tortured girl because they felt that legal justice was impossible."

In Washington, Admiral William Lee Pratt, Chief of Naval Operations, cancelled a scheduled visit to Honolulu of the Pacific Battle Fleet, and stated: "American men will not stand for the violation of their women under any circumstances. For this crime they have taken the matter into their own hands repeatedly when they have felt that the law has failed to do justice."

The august *Washington Post* thundered that: "If the strong arm of Uncle Sam is needed to clean out the hot-bed of vice in Honolulu, Congress should not hesitate to use it."

Civil trial

Only the *Honolulu Advertiser*, and the *Honolulu Star Bulletin*, sided with the natives of the island, declaring respectively that: "Vengeance which takes the form of private execution cannot be condoned." And: "People who take the law into their own hands always make a mess of it . . . There is no justification in civilized society for lynch law methods or premeditated killing of any kind."

The civil trial of the defendants was set for April 5, 1932, and the main concern of their friends and families was the obtaining of the right man to argue their case in court. Logically, there was only one man for the job: Clarence Darrow, the brilliant and unconventional "attorney for the damned", who had defended Leopold and Loeb, the young Chicago "thrill-killers", and had appeared with dramatic effect in the Dayton Monkey Trial Case.

There was one snag, however — 75-year-old Darrow had retired from the legal arena. When approached he did not even like the "smell" of the case, but a $25,000 fee (he was in serious financial trouble), and the knowledge that only he could possibly gain an acquittal, made him accept the challenge.

By now the rape and murder sensation was vying with the kidnapping of aviator Charles A. Lindbergh's baby son for the world's front-page headlines, and Darrow was in his element as one of the star actors on the stage. He made his own investigation of the background to the murder, and decided that the only defence open to him was one of "mental illness brought on by extreme provocation". This was what he told Judge Charles Davis, before whom the trial opened.

Mental torment

People had been queueing for entrance to the courtroom since before dawn, and they gazed with naked curiosity at Mrs. Fortescue, wearing a deep red dress, her aristocratic head held proud and high. At Lieutenant Tommy Massie, who nervously chewed his lips. At the two sombre and white-faced sailors. At Joe Kahahawi's parents, dark-eyed and accusing in the well of the court.

Hands thrust down his trouser tops, hair dangling defiantly over his forehead, Darrow recapitulated everything that had happened to the Massie family from the party at Ala Wai Inn onwards. He vividly described the lieutenant's mental torment . . . the pain and humiliation endured by Thalia . . . the natural outrage and indignation expressed by her mother.

But it did not affect the outcome. All four were found guilty as charged and were sentenced to ten years' imprisonment. It was only when the trial was over and Darrow—who said he represented "100 million jurors on the mainland"— had returned to his hotel that he won the battle he seemed to have lost.

Shabby business

He was visited by the prosecuting lawyers who told him they were "embarrassed" by the verdict. There could be no peace on the island until the sentence had been reduced to "one hour's detention", and the Massie family and the two sailors had left Hawaii for good.

Darrow agreed to this on one condition —that no evidence be offered against the alleged rapists when their second trial was eventually heard. "It will do no good to anyone to keep this issue alive," he said. "Set them free and let's bury this whole shabby business."

His condition was met and a few days later Darrow, the Massies, Mrs. Fortescue and the two sailors boarded a ship taking them to the mainland and a life free from anger and hostility. "I felt as we went away," Darrow said, "that we were leaving the island more peaceful and happy than I had found it, for which I was very glad."

A Bungled Attempt

Monsieur Demon

To his neighbours, this cool, arrogant businessman was "the best boss in town". But his private life was less successful. Poor Henri Demon. Even his alleged mistress was a virgin. And when he tried to murder his wife . . .

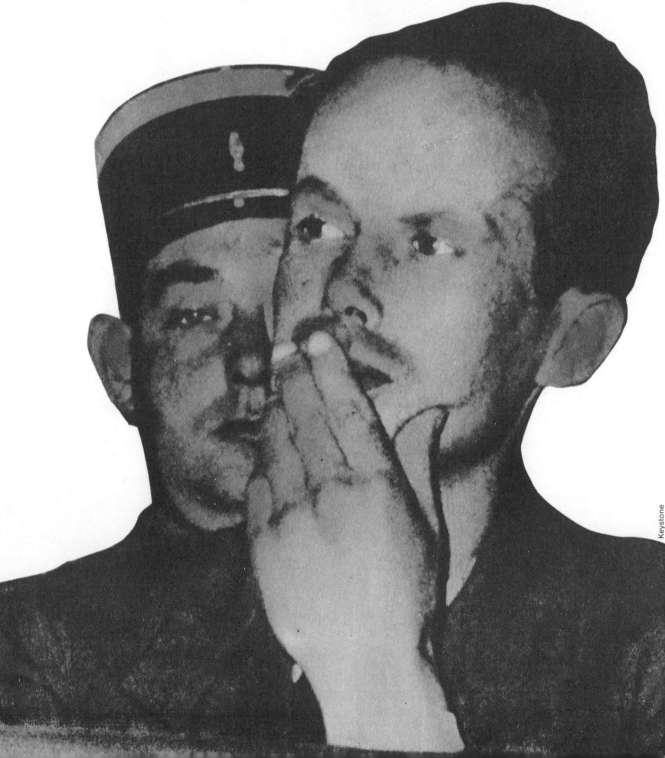

Keystone

AGIP

HENRI DEMON was not the kind of man to try to kill his wife. Anybody in the little town of Phalempin, near Lille, in the north of France, would have told you that. Henri had too much going for him —a flourishing business, a pleasant home, two fine sons.

Things were not, of course, quite right between himself and his wife, Alice. It was not entirely her fault. She was one of those women with an unhappy tendency to become pregnant almost as soon as her husband put his hand on the bedroom doorknob. At the same time, she was a strict Roman Catholic, opposed to birth control. She had turned off sex after having their two sons very quickly after marriage. When she retired at night she put the bulky bolster down the middle of the double bed to discourage any amorous advances from her husband.

It was not much fun for Henri, still only 26. Still, it wasn't an insoluble problem, particularly for someone with his kind of money. He had already sought an outlet for his passions in the brothels of Lille. Every Frenchman would understand that. It was, however, rather regrettable—because it reflected on Alice's

A NASTY SCENE over the "affair" with his secretary Francoise (in witness stand) triggered the ill-fated attempt of Monsieur Demon to kill his wife Alice (opposite page). They'd been childhood friends, but "it's a mistake to marry memories," said Henri.

position as his wife—that he should be so obviously infatuated with his new secretary, Françoise Lejaune. What he should do was set himself up with a discreet and permanent mistress in a flat. Then nobody could complain about propriety.

One other thing they would have told you in Phalempin. If, for some inexplicable reason, Henri *did* decide to kill Alice, he would not fail—and he would not be found out. He was that kind of man. He had a cool, precise, scientific mind. He knew about guns—he had been in the Resistance movement when still in his teens—and he was well up on the finer points of murder. Books and novels about crime were his favourite reading.

Anyone who told you all those things would have been wrong. Henri Demon *did* try to murder his wife. He *did* fail in the attempt. And he bungled the job so badly that the only real question was not whether he was guilty, but whether he would go to the guillotine for his efforts. (In France, even if the victim survives, a would-be killer can be charged with murder, rather than attempted murder, if there is evidence of premeditation or lying-in-wait.)

Forging ahead . . . at 15

Henri and Alice had been childhood friends. He was the son of a blacksmith, she the daughter of a coal merchant with a small business. Henri left school at 15 to go to work for his father. He was bright and industrious, and by the time he was 20, he had transformed the family business. The forge had been built up into a factory with 55 workers, busy manufacturing and servicing agricultural machinery.

At this point his father handed the whole business over to him. He also suggested it was time Henri married. "A man in your position should have a wife

and a home," he said. "And you should also be thinking about sons *you* can hand the business on to one day." Henri saw the point. At the same time, it wasn't going to be easy to fall in with his father's wishes. He had been too busy with the forge to bother about girls. He was there when the workmen arrived in the morning, and he stayed long after they had left.

Then he thought of Alice. He hadn't seen her for some time, but he had always rather liked her and felt sorry for her. With her family business too poor to afford employees, he had sometimes watched her heaving heavy sacks of coal around the streets. It was no work for such an attractive girl.

Accordingly they married in 1945. Henri was still only 20, Alice 23. It did not take long for either of them to realize that childhood friendship plus convenience are not a very sound basis for marriage. As early as the morning after the ceremony, a pensive Henri told a friend: "It's a mistake to marry memories." Things went from discontented to miserable when, having had her two sons in quick succession, Alice began refusing Henri his marital rights.

She, too, found—not surprisingly—that she had cause for complaint. "I can no longer be happy with him," she wrote in a letter to one of her friends. "He leaves me alone to go with other women and he even boasts to me of his successes with them. I don't know whether he does it to annoy me or to make me leave him . . ."

She did not leave, however. Their marriage, with its occasional outbursts of irritation and frustration, stumbled on for another four years. As far as Henri was concerned, his chief love in life was his factory. In the circumstances, his decision to kill Alice seems to have been motiveless. There were so many simpler ways of resolving the problem. That Henri chose murder suggests a streak of hidden instability—or even insanity—in the make-up of the man his workers called "the best boss in town".

It was a nasty scene over his secretary Françoise, a slim, 20-year-old blonde, that almost certainly sparked off Henri's decision to murder Alice. It seems likely that his relationship with Françoise did not progress beyond flirtation and a few stolen kisses in the office. Indeed, later, when her name was being bandied about in court and at café tables throughout France, Françoise paid a visit to her doctor and emerged triumphantly waving a certificate which declared that she was a virgin.

Alice didn't know that, however, when she found a passionate love letter from Françoise in a pocket of a suit which Henri had left out to be sent to the cleaners. Alice, long-suffering by habit, responded to this classic discovery with what was, for her, unusual violence. She took the evidence straight to her father-in-law and told him: "Henri is having an affair with his secretary. I want her fired." M. Demon senior, who shared Alice's devout Roman Catholic views, agreed that it was the respectable course to take.

"Going to divorce Alice"

Henri, who had been away in Lille on business, returned home to find that Françoise had been summarily dismissed and that Alice had moved into the spare bedroom. The next morning, in a fury, he, too, went to see his father. "I want Françoise reinstated," he said, "and I'm going to divorce Alice." "If you divorce Alice," was the response, "I shall be forced to take on the responsibility for her and the children. I shall take the factory away from you as well."

In the face of his father's opposition, Henri could only appeal to his wife's sense of Christian charity. "There was nothing between Françoise and me," he told her. "We never slept together. The letter is just a note from a foolish

Keystone

girl—and now, because of your false suspicions, you have had her sacked with an undeserved slur on her name. Nobody else here will give her a job and she's penniless."

Alice, who had a basically generous nature, responded to her husband's appeal. "All right," she said. "I will accept your word that there is nothing between you. She can have her job back. But I will tell her the news myself." Alice put on her coat and hat and went round to Françoise's home to let her know that all was forgiven, and that she could report for work as usual the following morning. Onto the announcement she tacked a short lecture on the nature and responsibilities of Christian marriage.

The next significant event occurred a month later. One evening when they were walking around the factory, Henri noticed that the power had been left running. "Go and turn it off," he told Alice. She looked at the sign under the switch which said *Attention—Danger of Death,* and replied, hardly surprisingly: "Turn it off yourself." She noticed that, before doing so, Henri put on a pair of thick rubber gloves. It wasn't a precaution he had suggested to her.

Later, after the shooting of Alice, an electricity board expert certified "in no circumstances could there be any danger to the person manipulating the switch in question". Whether Henri had tampered with it on that night in May is not known. With hindsight, however, it seems beyond doubt that Alice had a premonition as to what lay at the back of her husband's mind, yet said nothing about it to anyone.

That premonition hardened a few days

ALICE DEMON was permanently crippled after a 6.35 mm bullet had penetrated her spine. Two different Mausers were used in this clumsy murder attempt.

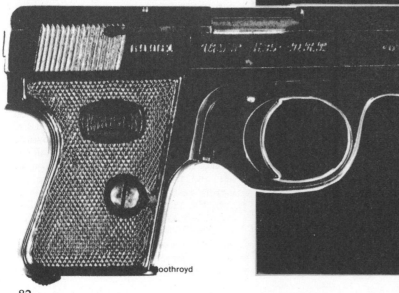
Boothroyd

later when Henri drew her attention to a newspaper item. "Very clever," he exclaimed. "This shopkeeper fixed up a trip-wire that fired a cartridge when it was fouled. He shot a burglar with it." The next day Alice found her husband experimenting with a similar device in his workshop.

Henri was in no hurry to execute the crime that had now taken firm shape in his mind. He waited nearly a month – until the night of June 12, 1951 – before staging the events designed to be the overture to his "perfect murder". In the middle of that night he woke Alice and told her: "I think I hear someone prowling about in the yard between the house and the factory. I'm going outside to take a look."

He took a 6·35 mm. Mauser automatic – one of two he owned – with him. Alice heard a shout. Then came the sound of some half-a-dozen shots. When Henri returned, he stated: "There was someone there. He fired at me twice. I fired back but missed him in the darkness." In the morning Henri went down to the local police station to report the events.

The stage was now set. Henri waited nearly another month – until the night of July 9-10 – to commit his "perfect crime". In the event, it turned out to be a pathetic combination of blunders, inconsistencies, and patent lies which doomed him from the outset.

Earlier in the day Henri excused himself from a business meeting in Lille. "I have a terrible headache," he said. "I'm going home to bed." That, even if a minor one, was his first mistake. It was Alice who went to bed early while Henri, despite his "headache", sat up in the kitchen until 1 a.m., reading. This was his account of what happened next:

"A bullet whistled by. . . ."

"I heard the sound of a gate opening and closing and a noise in the courtyard. I seized my automatic pistol and cried out to Alice upstairs: 'Come down! There is somebody in the yard.' I went outside without waiting for her. There was a shot and a bullet whistled by my ear. I fired in the direction I thought the bullet came from. Then another bullet hit my left arm. I dropped my torch. I fired again, but I had to give up because of my wound and the darkness."

Back at the house, he found Alice lying wounded on the floor, her two small sons in her arms. Her legs were bent at the knees in a position from which they would never change as long as she lived. A 6.35 mm. bullet had penetrated her spine just below the heart, injuring permanently the nerves of the spinal cord and paralyzing her from the waist down.

Neighbours arrived, attracted by the shooting. A Doctor Plane was called.

Police appeared, followed by a police ambulance which rushed the crippled Alice to hospital. Henri stayed behind to have his wounded arm dressed. Then he went to see his father.

The police were suspicious from the start. Neighbours testified that, apparently in a daze immediately after the shooting, Henri had kept repeating: "If they succeed in extracting the bullet from my wife, the ballistics experts will prove it did not come from *my* gun." Then, Henri claimed he had only one gun: his wife and other relatives said he had two. Why, too, had his dog not barked if there was an intruder in the yard?

In the kitchen, where Alice had slumped to the floor after the shooting, the curtains had been pulled back and a vase of flowers moved from the windowsill, apparently to give someone out in the yard – Henri? – a clear field of fire.

The most telling factor of all, however, was a blunder which an intelligent child would have avoided. All the ballistics evidence from the bullets and cartridge cases found at the scene indicated that two guns had been used to wound Alice and Henri. But if an intruder had shot both of them, the bullets should have come from *the same gun*.

Lastly, there was the evidence of Dr. Plane. While he had been giving first aid to Alice in the kitchen, she whispered to him when Henri was out of earshot: "It was he who shot me?" The doctor asked whom she meant. At that moment, however, Henri had come back into the room and she had said nothing more.

"I no longer loved her"

Henri was arrested on July 11 at Lille Hospital, where he had been receiving attention for his wounded arm. The police claimed that he finally broke down under repeated questioning and confessed: "I no longer loved my wife. I no longer loved her even on the day we married. I wanted to get rid of her so I tried to murder her."

He went on to explain that he had hidden his second gun – a 6.35 mm. Mauser like the first – by throwing it behind a bush as he drove to tell his father about the shooting. Police took him to the spot and found the gun easily. On the way back to Lille, the whole party stopped for a drink at a café. Henri, said the police, was quite calm and asked: "Do you think

EVEN A CHILD would have avoided such a blunder. How could Monsieur Demon, gun expert and avid reader of detective stories, plan a murder, yet reckon without the science of ballistics?

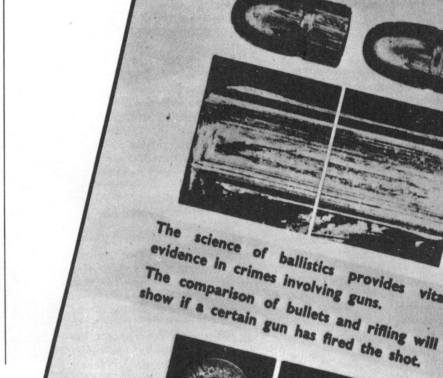

EVERY FIREARM AND BULL LEAVES ITS MARK

The science of ballistics provides vital evidence in crimes involving guns. The comparison of bullets and rifling will show if a certain gun has fired the shot.

Scotland Yard

I would be excused my crime if I volunteered for the war in Indo-China?"

Back at police headquarters, Henri explained how the crime had been committed. "I went out into the yard and fractured the locks on the gate from the outside with a cold chisel," he said. "Then I collected the two automatics from the kitchen and called out to Alice to come down. I had to sound really agitated so that she would come down quickly.

"I rushed out into the yard to wait for her to appear. I had removed the vase of flowers from the window ledge and opened the kitchen curtains so I would be able to see her clearly. When she appeared, it was a whole minute before I had the courage to shoot. Then, as she turned to go upstairs, I fired twice at her back. One bullet struck her and she fell to the ground.

"I rushed to a shed in the corner of the yard where I had fixed up a simple gadget for wounding myself. The second gun was fixed to a board and I pulled the trigger with a wire. The first shot missed, but the second wounded me in the arm. I dismantled the apparatus and hid the second gun in the glove compartment of my Renault standing in the yard. Then I went back to the kitchen."

The police, well pleased with the night's work, locked Henri up in a cell. Unfortunately, the cell already contained an experienced criminal. "How did you get on?" he asked. "They trapped me into confessing everything," said Henri. "You must be mad," said the criminal. "If you don't withdraw the confession you'll lose your head for sure."

Before the Examining Magistrate next morning, Henri denied everything. He claimed he had confessed to a crime of passion of which he was innocent only because he had been under the influence of drugs administered to him in hospital, and because the police had beaten him up.

Some sign of regret . . .

Despite the attack which had crippled her for life, Alice still felt some loyalty to the father of her two sons. In hospital she refused to talk frankly about events on the night of the shooting. She might have continued to keep her mouth shut—and Henri might conceivably have gone free—had he shown some sign of regret for what he had done.

When the Examining Magistrate called on her with a stenographer on July 17, she asked: "What does my husband say?" The magistrate, M. Vuilliet, then read Henri's confession, followed by his denial and a second statement in which he reverted to his original claim that the shooting had been done by a would-be burglar.

"Has he said he is sorry?" Alice inquired at the end. "Obviously not," said M. Vuilliet, "since he's denying every-

thing." Alice thought for a long time. Then she spat out the words: "He's a liar. I'll tell you everything. Crime must be punished. I did not speak the truth before because a lot of pressure was put on me. My father-in-law has a bad heart. He warned me that it would kill him if I accused Henri."

She then told the story she would repeat after being pushed into court in her wheelchair—when, after the customary French cooling off period, Henri was tried for murder 17 months later. Henri's words to bring her downstairs had not been: "Come down, there is somebody in the yard," but: "Come down, Alice, there is somebody here who wants to see you."

"I fell but I felt nothing"

"I went down," she said, "but I was frightened. I knew instinctively what was in Henri's mind. I felt suddenly it was imperative to get back to my bedroom. I turned to climb the stairs and at that moment it happened. I fell but I felt nothing. I thought I had not been hit, but when I tried to get up it was impossible. I called to my children, Alain and Bernard. I said to them: 'Mummy can't get up.' They put their arms around me and tried to pull me up but they were not strong enough.

"I was holding both boys in my arms when my husband came back. He came down on one knee beside me and said: 'We have been attacked, both of us.' I

said to him: 'No, Henri, it was you who fired at me. You called me down to kill me. I understand it all now.' At first he denied it. Then he said: 'I was mad. I should never have done it.' Those were his exact words.

"I could feel the paralysis creeping up my body. My legs were already inert. Then it reached my thighs and my buttocks. When it reached my waist I was frightened. I could feel myself suffocating. I begged Henri to lift me up. I groaned on the floor, telling him he could not leave me to die there without attention, without a priest . . ."

At the court hearing she explained why it had taken her so long to give her version. "He no longer exists for me, but he is still the father of my children," she said. "I wanted to try to save him despite everything. For the rest of their lives, my little boys . . ." Uncontrollable sobs prevented her from finishing the sentence.

The father of her children

And, in the end, she did save Henri from the guillotine. As the jury rose some days later to consider their verdict, she cried out: "Have pity on him, I beg you, have pity on him. If I have been able to find the strength to be present throughout this case, it was only so that I might be able to beg you to be indulgent with the man who is the father of my children. I have remained here so that I might save him. Think of my children . . ."

Judge Romerio commented before the jury left the courtroom: "I don't think, gentlemen, that you will ever see a more noble example of greatness of the soul."

It took the jurors only 20 minutes to find Henri guilty, but they recommended he should be sentenced to penal servitude for life rather than death. The judge concurred. As the prisoner was led from the court between two gendarmes he looked, as he had throughout the trial, arrogant and self-assured. For his crippled wife he did not even spare the glance that would have said: "I'm sorry—and grateful."

In the police van outside, the news was brought to him that, in the civil action which accompanies the criminal action in French law, the judge had ordered him to pay 15 million francs ($50,000) damages to Alice. Henri shrugged. "I do not mind being sentenced now that my business will have to be sold to pay the damages," he said calmly. "The business was my whole life. Now they can do what they like with me." Then he added with typical panache: "The jury were not logical. If they considered me guilty, they ought to have sentenced me to death."

"HAVE PITY ON HIM!" cried Madame Demon. Hers was a "greatness of soul", said the judge—but her bungling husband spared not a glance for his crippled wife.

Ian Howes

The Red Barn Murder

Maria Marten and William Corder

Georgian England turned
Maria Marten into an innocent
murder victim, defiled by
a cruel landowner who met
justice on the gallows.
Her half-naked body was
found rotting in a shallow
grave, with a sack as a
shroud. After his execution,
killer William Corder's scalp
(far left) was preserved and
his skin was used to bind
the book, pictured left with
the gun he used to kill Maria.
But was Corder the villain
he was made out to be? Or was
he a weak-natured man,
driven to kill . . . ?

SHOOTING Maria Marten (below) was William Corder's desperate way of escaping marriage. The Red Barn (left) became famous as the murder scene.

THE FIRST night that middle-aged Mrs. Anne Marten awoke screaming in her east of England cottage was printed indelibly on the memory of her farm labourer husband Thomas. "I dreamed of our Maria," sobbed Mrs. Marten when her husband had done his best to soothe her. "I dreamed she was murdered and buried underneath the right-hand bay of the Red Barn."

Thomas Marten, who all his life had been a realist and had never gained marks for imagination, then settled for the first thing that came into his head. "I'll make you a warm drink," he said. "You'll probably sleep better after that."

For the remainder of that night Anne Marten did sleep. But each successive night throughout the rest of that week, in April 1828, she woke violently, shaking her husband and forcing him to sit up and listen to her. "For God's sake, Tom, go to the Red Barn and look. She's there; I saw the ground open and show her body before it closed again."

Thomas Marten went to the small window of the bedroom. In the distance he could see the Corders' barn, outlined against a dawn sky where the last stars blinked. A year had passed since their daughter Maria had gone off with Corder's son William—a year noteworthy for the complete absence of letters or news from either of them.

Had something terrible happened to his daughter? Or was his wife, driven by despair, now teetering on the brink of madness?

In the next few days Thomas Marten made up his mind about these two things. Unless he went to Corder's barn and looked around for himself, his wife would know no peace. And if he did that, he would have to do it surreptitiously, for if the villagers learned the reason for his inquiries, they would surely declare Anne Marten insane.

Eerie scene

Thomas did not have far to go. Although the farm stretched across 300 prosperous Suffolk acres, his farmhouse, a large black and white Tudor-style building, was in the centre of the tiny village of Polstead, not far from the village pond.

In the grounds immediately behind it was a collection of agricultural outbuildings, one of them a barn so positioned that, when the evening sun lit the meadows around Corder Farm, it cast upon the barn a vivid reddish hue which, according to an onlooker's disposition, might be described as romantic or eerie.

The reason he wanted to look inside the Red Barn, Thomas told Mr. Pryke, the Corders' bailiff, was that he thought his daughter might have left some of her clothes there on the day she went off with young William Corder. When Pryke

opened the barn door, Thomas went straight towards the right hand bay and scratched in desultory fashion with a stick at the loose hay. Suddenly the stick sank into soft earth.

"There may be something buried here," Thomas said. "I'm going to dig."

Feverishly now, he thrust his spade into the earth. At the second strike the spade hit something in a sack. Helped by Mr. Pryke and the light of the lantern they had brought, he scraped back the earth and the sacking. There, gazing up at him ghoulishly in the half light, was the putrifying, half-clothed body of a girl, bent almost double like an embryo.

If Thomas Marten had any doubts about identity they were dismissed at once on sight of a pair of earrings adhering to the rotted, shrunken skin. They belonged to his missing daughter Maria, and this corpse, lying in a hole a foot below the ground, was all that was left of her. Thomas dropped his spade and started back in horror. Pryke, who had shrunk mutely from the opened hole, was the first to recover his wits. Followed by the distraught Marten, he hurried out of the barn and ran across the fields to the constable's cottage.

Small-time thieving

Then, as soon as the primitive communications system of Georgian England permitted it, the hunt was on for William Corder, third son of Farmer John Corder, sometime farm manager, sometime writer, and altogether something of a mystery man. Indeed, while history has been at pains to take affectionate care of the female star of the Red Barn murder, Corder could justifiably complain that he, who dreamed of fame, has been virtually forgotten.

At the Polstead village school which he attended, William's thin talent for writing had served only to isolate him from his fellow pupils, the local sons of the land, who called him "Foxy". It had the same effect on his father, who had made William the butt of his ill will almost from the day the boy was born.

For his other three sons, Thomas, John, and James, Mr. Corder had made it clear that there would be a substantial inheritance; for William there would be nothing. Also there was no question of William becoming a teacher or a writer. He would be a farmer, working for, and not with his three brothers.

William had bitten his lip and retired to his room with his dreams and his collection of books. Later, when he was older and his duties on the farm allowed it, he would take the coach to London and join the disciples of some of the capital's literary lions—including the artist, forger and murderer Thomas Griffiths Wainewright. Sometimes, to get his own back, he

would do a bit of small-time thieving from the family. Once he sold one of his father's pigs and pocketed the cash. Certainly he looked more like a petty thief than the notorious murderer he was to become. He was short and thin, and the hours of midnight reading had made him myopic. He walked habitually with a stoop and according to a friend was given to making "Napoleonic gestures".

Despite all this, William had a way with him. His big eyes and high cheekbones helped with the illusion, noted by Polstead folk, that he was always smiling. This was the smile that one day caught the attention of Maria Marten.

To examine the real facts about Maria Marten and compare them with the Victorian heroine of the Red Barn murder melodrama, it is difficult to believe that they are the same woman. To the Victorians, Maria was rustic innocence brutally defiled – an innocent maiden, peach-skinned, blue-eyed and beautiful, robbed of her cherished virginity by a vicious seducer who then, tiring of her, savagely slew her and buried her pathetic, lifeless body in the Red Barn grave.

In fact, by the age of 24, when she caught the eye of William Corder, who was two years her junior in age and light years her inferior in experience, Maria Marten was already the unmarried mother of three bastard children. She was currently being sought by the police on an immorality charge, and was known by half the adventurous young men of Suffolk as one of the "easiest" girls in the county, as long as you had the money to pay.

Among the lovers whose child she had borne was Thomas Corder, brother of William. And when she finally disappeared from Polstead village, the only people living there who thought she had not gone off to her one true calling as a London whore, were her own devoted parents.

Notable attraction

For Maria, the farm labourer's teenage daughter, the four Corder sons of the village's most prosperous farmer were a notable attraction. Not long after she produced a child by Thomas, the eldest, the unfortunate father was drowned in an accident in Polstead village pond.

Two more of the brothers, James and John, then rapidly succumbed to the dreaded twin killers of nineteenth-century England, typhus and tuberculosis. When they had joined Mr. Corder senior in the village graveyard, the fortunes of William took a sudden turn for the better.

William, however, was unable to rise to his inheritance. It irritated him, for it curtailed his "literary" excursions to London. He sought solace in the company of Maria, whom he had met through his brothers, and fathered her next child.

STILL standing
the Corder
farmhouse (right) and
Marten cottage (below),
with William
and Maria
inset.

ensnared and lacked the courage to get out?

The questions are relevant in the light of the remarkable events that happened on Friday, May 18, 1827. At eleven o'clock that morning William had a date with Maria; he was to call for her at her parents' cottage. He arrived an hour late, but that didn't matter to Maria, for his very arrival annulled some fleeting thoughts in her mind: there had been some bad quarrels lately and she was so much in love . . .

Unmoved

She rushed to the door to greet him as he walked up the garden path. "Bill!" she cried, embracing him tightly about the neck. "You're here at last!" Nothing seemed to matter, the time or the waiting, now that he was with her, now that he still cared.

Unmoved, William detached her slim white arms from his neck. "We're going to get married," he said. "This morning. Get ready—we haven't much time."

Maria recoiled as if she had been hit. "But they'll arrest me!" she said. She was referring to the charge of immorality pending against her.

"I've brought you some clothes—men's clothes," William replied. "They belonged to my brother James. You can put them on as a disguise. I'll take you up to the Red Barn; you can wait there till it gets dark, then I'll come for you."

He thrust a jacket and a pair of trousers at her. "It's what you've always wanted, to get married," he said.

Suspicions

A little while later, when Maria came down from her bedroom wearing the odd outfit, she might, at a short distance, have been mistaken for a man.

What is certain is that Mrs. Marten was in her kitchen a few minutes after she heard the front door close behind her daughter and William. Looking out of the window she saw, some hundred yards away, two figures dressed in male clothing, one of whom she recognized as Corder. They were walking along the path that led to the Red Barn. That was the last time that Maria Marten was ever seen alive.

In the next few weeks William Corder made no attempt to absent himself from Polstead. When Mrs. Marten asked him about Maria he was never evasive. "She is in Ipswich, waiting for the marriage licence to come through and doing some shopping meanwhile . . . She says to tell you she's well and she sends you her love."

Somehow Corder maintained his plausibility throughout that summer of 1827. Significantly, though, Mrs. Marten was beginning to find flaws in the flow of

The baby, born in the spring of 1827, lived for only two weeks. Its burial was a mystery, for there was no funeral, and it was believed that William and Maria secretly buried the little corpse in a field outside the village. If that were so, it gives rise to speculation on how the baby died. Was its death accelerated by one or both of its parents, to whom it was clearly an embarrassment?

The question, which was to be frequently asked in Polstead village during the next two years, was never answered. What everyone was soon to know, however, was that both William and Maria were people little affected by qualms of conscience.

Certainly the disappearance of the baby's body had no adverse effect on William's acceptibility by the Marten family. While the child was still warm in its makeshift grave, old Thomas Marten and his wife eagerly discussed plans with William for his wedding to their daughter. Sometimes Maria would join in and there would be an argument. The Martens began to notice that the arguments between the lovers were becoming more frequent.

By the middle of May a pattern of disagreement was emerging. William had already put off one suggested wedding day that month, and Maria was now siding with her parents and fretting for a quick marriage. Perhaps her enthusiasm could be interpreted as nagging, and perhaps it made William anxious. Did he begin to see his dreams of a literary life receding under the onslaught of a shrewish wife? Did he feel that he was already gossip and information that Corder supplied her about Maria. She began to notice things—like the time Corder turned up at a funeral carrying Maria's green umbrella—and she pigeon-holed them in her memory.

It was this talent for observation that later was to make Mrs. Marten the principal and highly effective witness against Corder.

By harvest time that year Corder was beginning to realize that he had started something bigger than he could maintain. He would go to Ipswich, he said, get married to Maria, and return to the village. He packed his bags and, as soon as he was out of sight of Polstead, he turned towards London.

There, in fact, he did get married. His bride, however, was not the turbulent Maria but Miss Kathleen Moore, who was as different in upbringing and character from Maria as is iron from water.

They had met some time previously when Corder made a trip to the Sussex coast, and in London Corder lost no time in renewing the friendship. Miss Moore, a schoolmistress of great virtue, gentleness, and intelligence, returned his ardour and married him at St. Andrew's Church in Holborn.

A century and a half ago the London suburb of Ealing was "in the country", and it was in this rural village that the newly-wed Corders set up Kathleen's new school. For William, it was paradise attained. Each day he came into the classroom, wearing glasses and carrying books.

Fearful urge

Thus went winter, and when spring's blossom covered the Suffolk countryside in the following year, 1828, William Corder and Maria Marten had, as far as Polstead villagers were concerned, passed into history. Except, that is, in the mind of one villager—Mrs. Anne Marten.

Each night, as she busied herself in her cottage, Mrs. Marten gazed out of her little window at the vivid reddish hue which fell from the setting sun upon Farmer Corder's barn. The restless, fearful urge to cry out that something was wrong, that Maria was horribly dead, that her daughter's blood demanded vengeance, swelled within her. Finally, in April, in her nightmare, she saw it all, and told her husband where to find the body.

Tracking down the suspect in his old "literary" haunts in London fell to the lot of Police Constable Jonas Lea, of

TRUTH AND FICTION: A handsome and dashing Corder according to a film of the tragedy made in 1928, but, inset, a drawing made while the landowner was in Bury jail. Opposite page, plays such as this gave a twisted idea of the tragedy.

Lambeth, who diligently followed the trail to the Ealing school. When he knocked on the Corder's door one April morning William Corder was half way through his breakfast.

"I've never heard of a girl called Maria Marten," he said, peering bookishly over his spectacles at the policeman.

Nearly four months went by before Corder entered the dock at Bury St. Edmunds Assizes, Suffolk, to face a murder charge—and the damning evidence of the lynx-eyed Mrs. Marten. Those four months saw the genesis of the Maria Marten myth—the fiction of the innocent maid ravished and then slain by a wealthy, unprincipled scoundrel— that the Victorians were to turn into their favourite after-dinner melodrama.

The plot began to take shape in church pulpits, where ministers ranted against loose girls who met their "dark end" at the hands of people like Corder. Impressed by this hell-raising, travelling showmen demonstrated puppets that re-enacted the murder in the Red Barn. In fairground booths the grisly details quickly became a permanent sideshow. And with each new development in the story line, Maria became more and more pure and Corder more and more vile.

The reason why is not difficult to understand. As every nineteenth-century novelist and dramatist knew, the Georgians and Victorians simply preferred stories about the despoilation of an innocent virgin to stories about hardened female seducers—particularly when the heroine

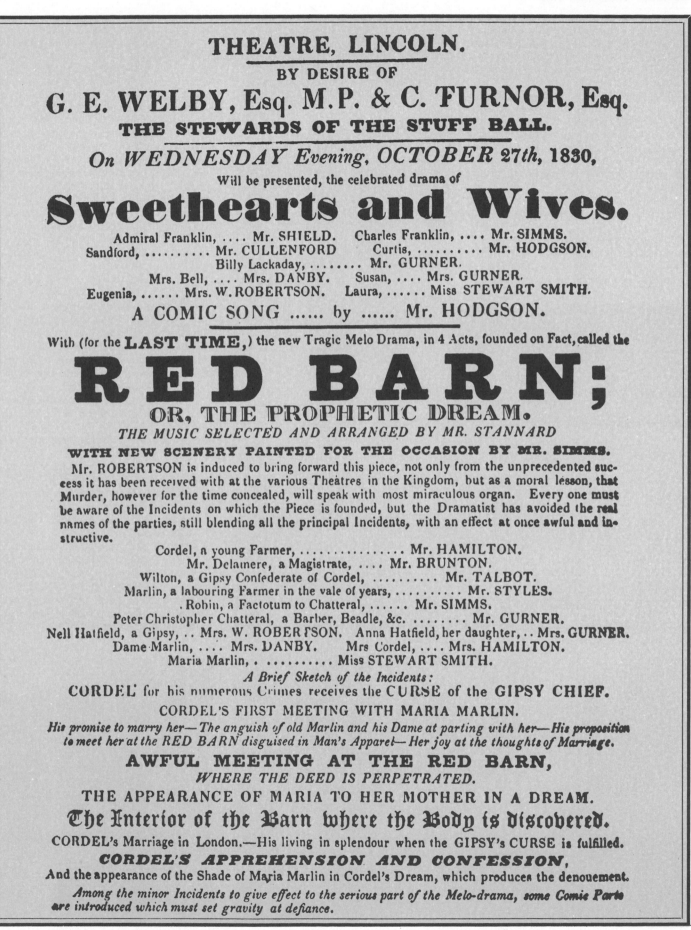

THEATRE, LINCOLN.

BY DESIRE OF

G. E. WELBY, Esq. M.P. & C. TURNOR, Esq.

THE STEWARDS OF THE STUFF BALL.

On WEDNESDAY Evening, OCTOBER 27th, 1830,

Will be presented, the celebrated drama of

Sweethearts and Wives.

Admiral Franklin, ... Mr. SHIELD.   Charles Franklin, ... Mr. SIMMS.
Sandford, ... Mr. CULLENFORD   Curtis, ... Mr. HODGSON.
Billy Lackaday, ... Mr. GURNER.
Mrs. Bell, ... Mrs. DANBY.   Susan, ... Mrs. GURNER.
Eugenia, ... Mrs. W. ROBERTSON.   Laura, ... Miss STEWART SMITH.

A COMIC SONG ...... by ...... Mr. HODGSON.

With (for the **LAST TIME,**) the new Tragic Melo Drama, in 4 Acts, founded on Fact, called the

RED BARN;

OR, THE PROPHETIC DREAM.

THE MUSIC SELECTED AND ARRANGED BY MR. STANNARD

WITH NEW SCENERY PAINTED FOR THE OCCASION BY MR. SIMMS.

Mr. ROBERTSON is induced to bring forward this piece, not only from the unprecedented success it has been received with at the various Theatres in the Kingdom, but as a moral lesson, that Murder, however for the time concealed, will speak with most miraculous organ.   Every one must be aware of the Incidents on which the Piece is founded, but the Dramatist has avoided the real names of the parties, still blending all the principal Incidents, with an effect at once awful and instructive.

Cordel, a young Farmer, ... Mr. HAMILTON.
Mr. Delamere, a Magistrate, ... Mr. BRUNTON.
Wilton, a Gipsy Confederate of Cordel, ... Mr. TALBOT.
Marlin, a labouring Farmer in the vale of years, ... Mr. STYLES.
Robin, a Factotum to Chatteral, ... Mr. SIMMS.
Peter Christopher Chatteral, a Barber, Beadle, &c. .... Mr. GURNER.
Nell Hatfield, a Gipsy, .. Mrs. W. ROBERTSON.   Anna Hatfield, her daughter, .. Mrs. GURNER.
Dame Marlin, ... Mrs. DANBY.   Mrs Cordel, ... Mrs. HAMILTON.
Maria Marlin, ... Miss STEWART SMITH.

A Brief Sketch of the Incidents :

CORDEL for his numerous Crimes receives the CURSE of the GIPSY CHIEF.

CORDEL'S FIRST MEETING WITH MARIA MARLIN.

His promise to marry her—The anguish of old Marlin and his Dame at parting with her—His proposition to meet her at the RED BARN disguised in Man's Apparel—Her joy at the thoughts of Marriage.

AWFUL MEETING AT THE RED BARN,

WHERE THE DEED IS PERPETRATED.

THE APPEARANCE OF MARIA TO HER MOTHER IN A DREAM.

𝕿𝖍𝖊 𝕴𝖓𝖙𝖊𝖗𝖎𝖔𝖗 𝖔𝖋 𝖙𝖍𝖊 𝕭𝖆𝖗𝖓 𝖜𝖍𝖊𝖗𝖊 𝖙𝖍𝖊 𝕭𝖔𝖉𝖞 𝖎𝖘 𝖉𝖎𝖘𝖈𝖔𝖛𝖊𝖗𝖊𝖉.

CORDEL's Marriage in London.—His living in splendour when the GIPSY's CURSE is fulfilled.

CORDEL'S APPREHENSION AND CONFESSION,

And the appearance of the Shade of Maria Marlin in Cordel's Dream, which produces the denouement.

Among the minor Incidents to give effect to the serious part of the Melo-drama, some Comic Parts are introduced which must set gravity at defiance.

was as pretty as Maria Marten. It was an age of high emotions and grand gestures, and given the stuff of the Red Barn murder, dramatists and showmen projected an ideal image of Maria that no mortal woman could live up to.

Against this kind of pantomime played out at fever pitch up and down the land, what possible chance, William Corder's defence counsel demanded to know, had the prisoner of getting a fair trial? Mr. Justice Alexander concurred; he deplored the goings-on, but declined to halt the trial.

Testifying against Corder, a witness remembered seeing him walking towards

EVEN in her final grave (right) Maria could not escape the Red Barn. Below, Corder's death mask, and the crowd that turned out for his execution.

the Red Barn during the late afternoon on the day of Maria's disappearance carrying a pick-axe. Another witness revealed that Corder had borrowed a spade from him about the same time and returned it later the same day. A long knife and a pair of pistols were produced; one of these was the murder weapon.

Corder's defence was pathetically weak. There had been a quarrel in the barn, he said, and he had walked off in a pique, leaving Maria there. He had gone only a yard or two when he heard a shot; hurrying back, he found Maria lying dead on the barn floor. There was a pistol beside her and picking it up he realized with horror that it was his own.

"She must have taken it from my bedroom," Corder said. "I decided to bury her in the best way I could, thinking that suspicion would surely fall upon me."

His story, however, failed to allay that suspicion, for the jury took only 30 minutes to find him guilty. Corder accepted the verdict philosophically and had nothing more to say until a few hours before his execution. Then, in a rush of words, he decided to tell all.

What had happened, he said, was that there had been a quarrel in the Red Barn and then a scuffle. In the struggle he took his pistol from his pocket and shot Maria in the side.

On the scaffold, nineteenth-century murderers died hard. As a crowd of thousands watched, Corder stepped on to the platform erected outside Bury St. Edmunds' Jail and declared contritely, "I deserve my fate."

A mask was put over his head and the body dropped. The hangman then increased the weight on the rope by pulling on the twitching victim. Despite this primitive act of "mercy", it took nearly ten minutes for the Polstead farmer, and would-be man of letters, to die.

WILLIAM
EXECUTED AT BURY ST. EDMUNDS

An Arsenic Mystery

Madeleine Smith

Was it the coffee and chocolate nightcaps served up by his mistress that made Pierre L'Angelier feel so ill? Or was it his own peculiar vice that killed him . . . and brought the elegant Madeleine Smith to trial for murder?

SUCH an excited, jostling mob had never before been seen in the precincts of the High Court of Justiciary in Edinburgh as gathered that morning of June 30, 1857. Shouting, laughing, they pressed against the closed doors eager to be allowed in and to commandeer the best seats in the public gallery, from which they could observe 21-year-old Madeleine Smith undergo the ordeal of trial for murder.

Already the mob had formed itself into factions, some for young Madeleine, some against; others, the equivalent of the modern pollsters' "don't knows", had come just to see a life and death spectacle and cared little for either the girl's guilt or innocence.

On the stroke of eight o'clock the doors swung open and the crowd surged forward into the moderate-sized courtroom, rushing blindly to the few available seats. In moments all the seats were taken and the less nimble and those too far towards the back of the crowd were turned out of the court building, cursing and protesting against their ill luck. Many had travelled from all over Scotland, buoyed up with the thought that even if they caught no more than a glimpse of this beautiful girl, accused of poisoning her lover with arsenic, they could return home happily.

Sherlock Holmes

Most of those who had gained admittance immediately took out packages of bread and cheese, or pieces of pie wrapped in flowing handkerchiefs, and began to eat breakfast; they had two hours to wait before the proceedings would begin. As they munched they looked down from their gallery upon the more privileged, constantly arriving spectators in the well of the court. Among those were leading Scottish churchmen, lawyers and famous journalists of the day. Notable newspapers and magazines had sent some of their best artists to sketch Madeleine Smith and the legal protagonists in the case. The artist from the *Illustrated Times* was Charles Doyle, father of Conan Doyle who was later to achieve international fame as the creator of Sherlock Holmes.

At 10.20 the packed courtroom fell into a sudden silence as a bull-lunged official bellowed the one word "Court!" and there entered in slow bewigged procession the Right Honourable Lord John Hope, the Lord Justice-Clerk, and his two brother judges, the Lords Handyside and Ivory. All in the courtroom leapt to their feet and as the judges took their places on the Bench every eye was riveted upon a small area of floor immediately in front of the prisoner's dock.

Slowly that square of floor rose, revealing itself to be a trap-door beyond which those in the well of the court could see a flight of stairs leading down to the cells below the building. From the dim interior

ALMOST NONCHALANT, the tall and elegant Miss Smith transfixed a courtroom filled with goggling spectators as she swept gracefully into the dock.

there arose first a policeman and then, close behind him, veiled and clasping a handkerchief in her right hand, came the central figure in the drama whom all had come to see: Madeleine Smith, spinster, of Blythswood Square, in the City of Glasgow, the accused, or, in the legal terminology of Scotland, "the panel".

She was tall and graceful and elegantly dressed in brown with a mass of rich, dark brown hair partly covered by a trim and fashionable bonnet. She moved towards the dock almost nonchalantly, pausing to whisk away a spot of dust on her shoes with a quick flourish of her handkerchief. As she raised her veil the goggling spectators saw that her features were impressive rather than startlingly beautiful, as newspaper readers had been led to believe. Her face was just a little too long, her nose a shade too prominent to meet the requirements of classic beauty; but her mouth was full and sensuous and her dark grey eyes shone with a lustre that was unforgettably compelling.

The charge was read to her that she "did wickedly and feloniously administer

to (or cause to be taken by) Pierre Emile L'Angelier, now deceased, a quantity or quantities of arsenic" with intent to murder him in February 1857, and in fact to murder him in March of that same year. Quietly but clearly and without a tremor in her voice she pleaded not guilty.

Since under Scottish law there was no opening speech by the prosecution, the jury of 15 men and the spectators had to build their own picture of the allegedly murdered man from the jig-saw pieces provided by the individual witnesses. L'Angelier, they learned, was 31, born of French extraction in Jersey in the Channel Islands, had drifted around the Continent and finally found his penniless way to Glasgow, in Scotland.

There he obtained a £50 a year job as a packing-clerk and became the secret lover of Madeleine Smith, daughter of a wealthy architect. But, in the courtroom, he was as yet a shadowy figure, and the jury were first to hear of his departure from life before they discovered much about the time he spent living it. Nervous Mrs. Ann Jenkins, wife of joiner David Jenkins, was the first and one of the most important prosecution witnesses. L'Angelier had lodged at the Jenkins' house, 11, Franklin Place, Glasgow, until his death.

Crucial evidence

Mrs. Jenkins remembered him as a gentleman "who was in the habit of receiving a great many letters" — about which the jury were later to hear some other, crucial evidence — and he kept "a photograph of a lady lying about his room". Ann Jenkins well recalled the day when she had asked the young man: "Is that your intended, sir?" L'Angelier had sighed: "Perhaps — some day."

But then there were the times, which Mrs. Jenkins braced herself to tell about, when L'Angelier began to suffer mysterious illnesses. Gently, the leader of the prosecution, James Moncrieff, the Lord Advocate, took her through the series of frightening events. There was one day in February, 1857, for example, when she found him in bed one morning, almost green with sickness.

"I said," Mrs. Jenkins told the court, " 'Why did you not call on me?' He said, 'On the road coming home I was seized with a violent pain in my bowels and stomach and when I was taking off my clothes I lay down upon the carpet. I thought I would have died and no human eye would have seen me. I was not able to ring the bell.' "

Subsequently, L'Angelier had been

taken ill again and, that time, a doctor was summoned. Pressing her hands together, Mrs. Jenkins told of how she had now become both alarmed and mystified. She explained to the jury: "I remarked to the doctor, 'It is strange; this is the second time he has gone out well and returned very ill. I must speak to him and ask the cause.'" But she had no chance to ask. L'Angelier lay in his bed, listless, his eyes glazed, and on Monday, March 23, 1857, he died.

What, Mrs. Jenkins was asked, had she known about his background, where he went, whom he saw? They were not questions the joiner's wife could answer. She shook her head. "I did not ask him where he had been," she said. "He had said he was going to be married and I knew from that time there was a private correspondence. But I did not know who the lady was or where she lived. That was the reason why I did not ask where he had been at nights."

The clinical details

But the poisoner—if there was a poisoner—could not expect that such a mysterious death would be allowed to pass without investigation and Dr. Frederick Penny, Glasgow professor of chemistry, came to the witness box to report upon his post-mortem examination of young L'Angelier. This was to be key evidence and the court stirred with the restlessness of anticipation. Madeleine Smith, seated unmoving in the dock, showed no sign of emotion as Dr. Penny unfolded the clinical details. She seemed to be listening with completely detached interest.

Summed up, Dr. Penny's evidence centred on one basic fact: L'Angelier's body exhibited traces of very large doses of arsenic—82 grains in the stomach alone. How much arsenic, the Lord Advocate asked, would be required to destroy life? Dr. Penny adopted the medical profession's necessary caution.

"It is not easy to give a precise answer to that question," he replied. "Cases are on record in which life was destroyed by two and four grains. Four or six grains are generally regarded as sufficient to destroy life." In an understatement, in view of the 82 grains in L'Angelier's stomach, the doctor added that the quantity of arsenic in this case "was considerably more than sufficient to destroy life".

Had Madeleine Smith, the accused, actually purchased any arsenic? John Currie, a druggist of Sauchiehall Street, Glasgow, swore that she had. He did not know her by sight at the time, he said,

"STRANGE," said Mrs. Jenkins. "This is the second time he has gone out well and returned very ill." L'Angelier died in her house before she could ask why.

but a Miss Smith had indeed been to his shop and bought arsenic. The 15-man jury followed Mr. Currie's testimony with obvious care, for it seemed that, if she were the murderess, she had laid her plans in a rather reckless and easily-traceable way.

For, as Mr. Currie explained, his attention had been particularly drawn to the young lady when she visited his shop. His assistant had told him that she wished to "buy poison to kill rats" and was asking for arsenic. "I said to Miss Smith we would rather give her something other than arsenic," Mr. Currie recalled.

"She did not insist on having it, but she said she would prefer it. I then objected that we never sold arsenic to anyone without entering it in a book and that she must sign her name and state the purpose to which it was to be applied. She said she had no objection and from her apparent respectability and frankness I had no suspicion." She bought one ounce of coloured arsenic and signed the book "M. H. Smith".

On the third day of trial, still the scene of daily battles by spectators to fight their way into the courtroom, that excitement rose to a new peak. It was touched off by the calling of the name of William Harper Minnoch—for this was the second man in Madeleine Smith's life. L'Angelier had been her lover but this was her officially betrothed. If, by now, L'Angelier had acquired a certain amount of glamour—possibly because all young Frenchmen, even a "Jersey Frenchman", were thought by the British to be glamorous—William Minnoch was a notable contrast.

Slim and short, he looked, as he took his place in the witness box, exactly what he was: a successful young businessman, in his thirties, respectable but unexciting.

Yes, he told the court, he had "paid his addresses to Miss Smith" and she had accepted his proposal of marriage. The wedding, sadly, had been set for this very month, June. Mr. Minnoch spoke briskly. He was unaware when he proposed, he said, of any "attachment or peculiar intimacy between Miss Smith and any other man".

A flock of birds

But later he "heard a rumour that something was wrong" and also, for the first time, heard from her the name of L'Angelier. "She told me she had written a letter to M. L'Angelier, the object of which was to get back some letters which she had written to him previously."

At the mention of letters to L'Angelier the normally subdued chatter of the crowd in the public gallery rose in volume until it sounded like a flock of birds suddenly taking wing, for there had been much gossip of letters that Madeleine was said to have written to her "Frenchman" lover; letters, some said, that were of a

particularly "indelicate" nature.

The fondest hopes of the mob were realized. The Lord Advocate proposed that Madeleine's letters, secured by the authorities after L'Angelier's death, should be read to the court. They would, in the prosecution's view, have a most important bearing on the supposedly innocent character which Madeleine Smith wished to present in this case.

The aged clerk of the court was handed a large package containing the letters and, opening it and bracing himself as though to an embarrassing task, he began to read in a thin monotone. Madeleine Smith watched, leaning forward on to the railings in front of the dock and resting her left cheek on her hand. Once or twice, during the readings, she stirred with obvious relief when the Lord Advocate intervened and suggested that occasional "objectionable" passages in the letters should be omitted.

The style of the letters alone showed how close Madeleine Smith's liaison with L'Angelier had been, even when she was considering another man's proposal of marriage. Many times she conferred upon her lover the term "husband". One letter began: "Beloved husband, this time last night you were with me. Tonight I am all alone. Would we had not to part. . . . Emile, my only love, my sweet dear husband . . . I love you more this night than ever. Do, beloved, stay near me, my only friend, my only love. You are the only being I love—on this earth "

Breathtaking intimacies

"Beloved and best of husbands," she wrote on another occasion, "a fond embrace for thy letter of this evening. Oh, how glad I am to get such letters from you, the man I love and adore. My love, my own darling, Emile, my husband ever dear. . . ." But the breathtaking intimacies appeared to lose their savour after Mr. Minnoch began "paying his addresses" to her in earnest and when, it seemed, she had decided that an ardent young packing-clerk might be exciting as a lover but marriage to a well-endowed businessman would offer greater security.

For after she had written to L'Angelier —as she told Minnoch she had—to break off their secret attachment, her lover seemed to be threatening her in some way. In a final letter read out by the clerk she pleaded with him: "On my bended knees I write to you and ask you, as you hope for mercy at the judgment day, do not inform on me . . . Write to no one, Papa, or any other . . . Do not make me a public shame."

As they listened to the sequence of the "illicit correspondence" the jury could see that after that letter the breach between the two, Madeleine and her Emile, seemed to have been repaired. Yet, they had already

been told that it was then that Madeleine began buying arsenic. The dry, official voice read to the hushed court a significant letter, written by Madeleine after L'Angelier's first attack of sickness. "You did look bad, Sunday night and Monday morning," it said. "I think you got sick with walking home so late—and the long want of food, so the next time we meet I shall make you eat a loaf of bread before you go out."

But it was a small, elderly spinster, Mary Perry, demure in brown dress and black bonnet, who offered some of the most damaging evidence against Madeleine. She had attended the same chapel as L'Angelier and acted as go-between for the lovers. And, according to the story that she had to tell, she was the one person to whom L'Angelier had communicated his personal suspicions that Madeleine had been trying to poison him. During their secret meetings at the Smith home Madeleine had apparently refreshed her lover with cups of coffee and chocolate.

Coffee and chocolate

"He told me," Miss Perry declared, "'I can't think why I was so unwell after getting that coffee and chocolate from her.' He said, 'It's a perfect fascination, my attachment to that girl. If she were to poison me I would forgive her.' I said, 'You ought not to allow such thoughts to pass through your mind. What motive could she have for giving you anything to hurt you?' He said, 'I don't know; perhaps she might not be sorry to be rid of me.'"

As Miss Perry gave her evidence, all eyes once again focused upon Madeleine,

PREPOSTEROUS, said Lord Advocate Moncrieff (above), prosecuting. "She told the druggist one story, the police another." But for the defence the Dean of Faculty (right) was no less eloquent. And at no time did Madeleine lose her nerve . . .

watching carefully to see how she reacted. But, as ever, her face conveyed no hint of her thoughts. And there was no question of the spectators enjoying the high entertainment of hearing her story from her own lips, for there was then no provision in the law for an accused person to go into the witness box and testify. Jury and onlookers had to make do with a reading of Madeleine's "declaration" taken down when she was arrested.

Once more the wearied clerk arose and read out the lengthy document. In it Madeleine Smith insisted: "I had not seen M. L'Angelier for about three weeks before his death and the last time I saw him was about half-past ten one night. On that occasion he tapped at my bedroom window, which is on the ground floor . . . I talked to him from the window, which is stanchioned outside, and I did not go out to him, nor did he come in to me . . . This was the last time I saw him."

On a previous occasion, the statement said, she remembered "giving him some cocoa from my window one night . . . He took the cup in his hand and barely tasted the contents. I was making some cocoa at the time and had prepared it myself." As to buying the arsenic, the statement had a pert explanation for that: "I had bought it on various occasions . . . I used it all as a cosmetic and applied it to my face, neck and arms, diluted with water. . . . I had been advised to the use of the arsenic in the way I have mentioned by a young lady, the daughter of an actress, and I had also seen the use of it recommended in the newspapers. The young lady's name was Guibilei, and I had met her at school at Clapton, near London."

The prosecution, as was to be expected, had seized on Madeleine's explanation of her use of arsenic and they now produced Miss Augusta Guibilei, who had been a pupil-teacher at the Clapton school during Madeleine's stay there in 1852. But the

bustling schoolmistress was emphatic in her evidence. "I never advised her to use arsenic as a cosmetic, or to apply it to her face, neck, or arms, mixed with water, nor to use it in any way," she rapped. "I had no conversation with her, that I recollect of, about the use of arsenic."

On the seventh day of the trial the Lord Advocate, Moncrieff, at last had the opportunity of summing up the prosecution's case against Madeleine Smith. At 46 he had already won fame as a brilliant lawyer and he was noted in the courts for the quiet, analytical skill which he brought to his work. He studiously avoided courtroom histrionics, and this occasion was no exception.

But he was in no doubt about the weight of evidence, as the Crown saw it, against Madeleine Smith. Occasionally patting his ample side-whiskers, he told the jury: "While a prisoner in the position of this unfortunate lady is entitled—justly entitled —to say that such a crime shall not be lightly presumed or proved against her, yet, gentlemen, if the charges in the indictment be true, if the tale which I have to tell be a true one, you are trying a case of as cool, premeditated, deliberate homicide as ever justly brought its perpetrator within the compass and penalty of the law."

Sexual encounters

In essence his case was this: unknown to her parents, Madeleine had taken L'Angelier as her lover, admitted him secretly to the family home in Blythswood Square for sexual encounters, had eventually grown tired of him and, since he then constituted a nuisance and possible impediment to a "respectable" marriage, had killed him.

The motive was clear, the Lord Advocate suggested: "She knew what letters she had written to L'Angelier, she knew what he could reveal. She knew that if those letters were sent to her father, not only would her marriage with Mr. Minnoch be broken off but she could not hold up her head again." The means were there. The evidence of her buying arsenic was beyond doubt and how could the jury, the Lord Advocate asked, with a dismissing wave of his right hand, accept "her preposterous story" of using the poison as a cosmetic? She had told the druggist one story, that she wanted the arsenic to dispose of rats, and told the police, in her statement, that she wanted it as a cosmetic.

"I fear, gentlemen, there is but one conclusion," the Lord Advocate told the jury, "and that is, that there is not a word of truth in the excuse. And if, therefore, you think there are two falsehoods about the poisoning, I fear the conclusion is inevitable that the purpose for which she purchased the arsenic was a criminal one. . . . I see no outlet for this unhappy prisoner, and if you come to the same result as I have done, there is but one course open to you, and that is to return a verdict of guilty."

It was an eloquent address to the jury but one of greater eloquence was to come —from the tall and dignified, 47-year-old Dean of the Faculty of Advocates, Madeleine's defence counsel. He spoke at length and with passion and attempted to show L'Angelier in a new light, as an adventurer, as a man who was "depressed and melancholy beyond description". He had threatened, "whether he intended it or not", to commit suicide on more than one occasion. He was the seducer.

Corrupting influence

"Think you," the Dean demanded, "that, without temptation, without evil teaching, a poor girl falls into such depths of degradation? No! Influence from without—most corrupting influence—can alone account for such a fall." There was evidence, the Dean declared, that at one time in his life L'Angelier had boasted of being an arsenic eater and there was evidence that he had been a frequent sufferer from severe stomach ailments. But, most important of all, there was no positive proof produced by the Crown that Madeleine had met him on any of the occasions of his final bouts of illness.

The Dean pressed the acceptance of her explanation that she had used the arsenic for cosmetic purposes. Whatever the prosecution might think, he said, many women had made such experiments encouraged by articles in a number of reputable magazines.

The Lord Justice-Clerk delivered his charge in a hoarse voice—he was suffering from laryngitis—and, at the end of the trial, on its ninth day, the jury filed out into their room. Twenty-five minutes later they returned and delivered their verdict: not guilty on the first charge of attempted murder, not proven on the second charge of attempted murder, not proven on the third charge of murder.

A wave of hysteria swept the courtroom. The crowds in the public gallery broke into a frenzy of clapping and cheering, punctuated by some cat-calls. And a fresh howl of excitement was heard from outside the building as the news was passed to those who had been denied a personal view of the drama. Madeleine herself said nothing. As people in the courtroom came forward to offer their congratulations she merely smiled briefly before she disappeared down through the trap-door, to collect her belongings from the cells, and escape from the crowds through a side exit of the court building.

The Dean of Faculty, who had fought so hard on her behalf, sat at his table, holding his head in his hands. This peculiarly Scottish verdict, "not proven", was not the one for which he had striven. It was not the same as not guilty. There were many ways of interpreting it and the most generally accepted was: "We are reasonably sure she did it but some parts of the evidence were just a little too doubtful to risk a conviction."

Despite her incredibly strong nerves, Madeleine, too, felt that the verdict had deprived her of a true sense of freedom. She left Scotland for London where she married an artist and bore him three children. After he died she lived in the United States until her death aged 91. She protested her innocence to the end.

THE MYSTERY of Madeleine Smith has intrigued every generation since. Books and films have sought for a solution Ann Todd portrayed the role in a 1949 movie.

The Dominant Woman

Snyder and Gray

It had been a passionate affair. "You are my Queen, my Momsie, my Mommie," he told her. "And you are my Baby, my 'Bud,' my Lover Boy." Ruth Snyder was a powerful woman, and she dominated the weak Judd Gray. They loved together and died together . . . when Ruth Snyder finally got the meanness off her ample chest.

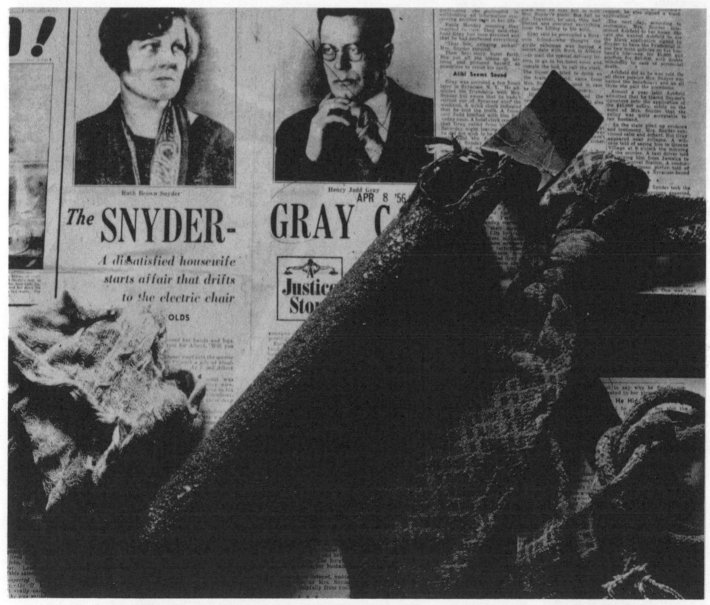

A DEADLY DUO: They strangled their victim with picture wire . . . and bludgeoned him with a sash weight

HOUSE OF DEATH:
The three-storey clapboard home in Queens, New York State, where Ruth Snyder tried half a dozen times to arrange fatal "accidents" for her husband. Cheerful Albert Snyder, a "good, solid, silent man", apparently suspected nothing, even when she gave him poisoned whiskey (below).

DOUBLE INDEMNITY:
"Mommie" Ruth Snyder used daughter Lorraine to ensure respectability when she had hotel assignations with her lover. She was keen on insurance . . . and took out a policy worth the best part of $100,000 (left) on her husband's precarious life.

She wanted a slave, he wanted a mother . . . and they met on a blind date

HE WAS nothing to look at as he entered the little Swedish restaurant, peered myopically around, and went nervously up to a booth at the back of the room. With his cleft chin, round wire-rimmed glasses, slight build, and eyes that were constantly blinking, he resembled nothing more than what he was—a drummer (or commercial traveller) who would never earn more than his current salary of some $5000 a year. But to his blind date in the booth —gum-chewing Mrs. Ruth May Snyder— he represented everything she had looked for in life and marriage and so far failed to find: an adoring, full-time slave.

It was in June 1925—the fifth year of Prohibition in the United States, the year in which Charlie Chaplin appeared in *The Gold Rush,* and the year when Anita Loos published her "gold-diggers" novel, *Gentlemen Prefer Blondes*—that Judd Gray and Ruth Snyder formed a liaison that was to bring about the murder of Mrs. Snyder's husband, Albert, and eventually take her and Gray to the electric chair in Sing Sing prison. But on that hot summer's afternoon in Henry's restaurant in New York City they were too busy sizing each other up, eating *smörgasbord* and drinking bootleg gin to sense that fate—and mutual friends—had done them a tragic disservice in bringing them together.

Ignoring the couple with them in the booth, they took turns to relate the sad and hopeless stories of their marriages; the fact that neither of them had the spouse that he or she had yearned for; the atmosphere of bitterness and tension that pervades a home with no love, respect or understanding in it. It was Ruth —her thick blonde hair set-off by a grey fox fur draped over her shoulders, her wrists clanking with the cheap copper trinkets she habitually wore, her firm thrusting jaw aimed at Judd like a pistol —who, first of all, as she put it, "got the meanness" off her ample chest. What she had to say was not novel, but it made Gray—whose job was selling ladies' corsets—lean sympathetically forward.

According to herself, Ruth Snyder— then aged 30 and of Swedish-Norwegian stock—had been the victim of a man, Albert Snyder, who ten years earlier had taken advantage of her youth, innocence and naïvety and manoeuvred her into a marriage she did not really want. "He was so mean, that guy," she told Judd, taking his hand in hers beneath the table.

"He took me out dining and dancing, then got real angry when I wouldn't come across and get into the sack with him. I was a self-respecting girl then and so he changed his line. He bought me a box of chocolates with a diamond solitaire in them. Picture that! I was all of 19 then— 13 years younger than him. He had this good job as art editor of *Motor Boating*— that's a Hearst magazine, you know—and the day we got married I was too weak and faint to go to bed with him. He had to wait till I was better before he got his way. But to him I was never any better than the ex-switchboard operator who worked in the typing pool."

A quiet, honest man

As he listened to this lament—which could have come straight from one of the silent picture melodramas of the time— Judd Gray felt nothing wrong, nothing false about her words. Even at 19 Ruth must have been a strapping, full-figured girl, and the thought of anyone pushing her around—let alone pushing her into marriage—was more than somewhat absurd. Albert Snyder—curly-haired, cheerful, and wind- and suntanned from long solitary hours of boating and fishing—was just not the sort of man to bully anyone, and certainly not an inexperienced girl who claimed to be religious, God-fearing, and a virgin. Later, after Albert's death, his editor and publisher, C. F. Chapman, was to say of him: "He was a man's man . . . a quiet, honest, upright man, ready to play his part in the drama of life without seeking the spotlight or trying to fill the leading role. Our world is made up of good, solid, silent men like this."

Gray, however, knew and cared nothing for this as the lunch-hour wore on and three and then four o'clock passed. In comparison with Ruth's marriage—a relationship that alternated between blazing rows and frozen silences—his own domestic background was of peace, tranquility and eternal boredom. His wife, Isabel, was so seldom seen or heard by anyone that she had taken on the aspect of an "invisible woman". Few of Gray's colleagues at the Bien Jolie Corset Company had ever met or spoken to her, and some of them did not even know that the 32-year-old salesman had a wife at all. In his autobiography written in the Death House, Gray said frankly:

"Isabel, I suppose, one would call a home girl; she had never trained for a career of any kind, she was learning to cook and was a careful and exceptionally exact housekeeper. As I think it over searchingly I am not sure, and we were married these many years, of her ambitions, hopes, her fears or her ideals— we made our home, drove our car, played bridge with our friends, danced, raised our child—ostensibly together—married.

Never could I seem to attain with her the comradeship that formed the bond between my mother and myself . . ."

It took nearly four hours for Snyder and Gray to exchange marital and emotional histories. They said goodbye to their mutual friends in the booth at Henry's and arranged to meet again in August—after Ruth, Albert, and their seven-year-old daughter Lorraine had returned from a boating holiday on Shelter Island. Although Judd Gray did not then know it, he was the latest in a string of "men friends" with whom Ruth had gone dancing, beer-drinking, and who had helped her to devour plates of her favourite pretzels. On the evening of August 4 Gray rang the Snyder residence—a three-story clapboard house in Queens Village, New York City—and asked Ruth to have dinner with him at "their place"—Henry's Swedish restaurant.

After the meal and drinks Gray— with a daring that came more from the rye than any personal quality—invited Ruth to come back to his office on 34th Street and Fifth Avenue. "I have to collect a case of samples," he said lamely. "The latest thing in 'corselets'." Ruth smiled at his modesty—the word "corset" never crossed his lips—and agreed to his suggestion. Once inside the office she took off her scarf, ostensibly because she was suffering from holiday sunburn. "I've some camphor oil in my desk," said Gray solicitously. "Let me get it for you." He did so and proceeded to dab the oil over Ruth's blistered neck and shoulders. "Oh, that's so good!" she exclaimed. "No one is ever kind to me like this!" Gray flushed at her words. "I've something else for you," he murmured. "A new corselet. Please let me fit it on for you." Ruth shrugged. "Okay," she said, "you can do that. And from now you can call me 'Momsie'."

Lust and indiscretion

So in the deserted offices of the Bien Jolie Corset Company Ruth Snyder and Judd Gray began their affair—which was to burn with increasing ardour until March 1927, when they were trapped, arrested, and then turned on each other like warring rats. In the meantime, however, their lust and their indiscretion knew few limits. As often as they could they spent the night—or part of the night —in Manhattan hotel bedrooms, when Gray would sink to his knees and caress Ruth's feet and ankles. "You are my queen, my Momsie, my Mommie!" he declared, looking up at her imperious face. "And you are my baby, my 'Bud', my Lover Boy," she replied. Sometimes, by way of "respectability", little Lorraine Snyder would be taken along and left in the lobby while her "parents" retired upstairs. It was at this stage that Mrs.

Snyder first told Gray of the strange series of "accidents" that had befallen her husband in the summer of 1925—shortly after she and Gray had first met.

The first incident occurred when Albert Snyder was jacking up the family Buick in order to change a tire. Suddenly, as he lay by the hub, the jack slipped, the car toppled sideways, and he only just missed being badly injured. A few evenings later he had a mishap with the crank, struck himself on the forehead and fell down unconscious. Some men might have felt that two such near escapes were enough, and that it might be a case of third time unlucky. But not Snyder. Later that August he again entered the garage of his salmon-painted house at 9327, 222nd Street, Queens, and stretched beneath the car with the engine running. Like a dutiful wife Ruth brought him a glass of whiskey to keep out the cold and praised his skill as a mechanic. She went back into the house and within a few minutes of drinking the whiskey Albert felt strangely sleepy. Just in time he noticed that the garage doors had somehow swung shut and that he was inhaling carbon monoxide fumes. He just managed to wriggle from under the car and reach the fresh air before being poisoned.

Ruth was desperate

If Snyder saw nothing ominous or significant in these happenings, then Judd Gray certainly did. "What are you trying to do?" he gasped, as Ruth ended her story. "Kill the poor guy?" She hesitated. "Momsie can't do it alone," she answered. "She needs help. Lover Boy will have to help her." At the time it is doubtful if Gray took her seriously. After all, they had both been drinking more than they should and had spouted more "big talk" than was wise. He only realized she was in earnest when she next met him and said triumphantly: "We'll be okay for money. I've just tricked Albert into taking out some hefty life insurance. He thinks it's only for 1000 dollars, but it's really for 96 thousand—if he dies by accident. I put three different policies in front of him, only let him see the space where you sign, and told him it was the thousand buck policy in triplicate. He's covered for 1000, 5000, and 45 thousand with a double indemnity accident clause!"

After this Snyder had three more close shaves with death—in July 1926 when he fell asleep on the living room couch and was almost gassed; in January 1927 when he was taken violently ill after Ruth had given him bichloride of mercury to "cure" an attack of hiccoughs; and in February when Ruth "unwittingly" turned on the gas tap in the living room. More by good luck than caution or commonsense Snyder survived all these attempts on his life. Ruth was now desperate and was determined there would be no "miraculous escape" from her seventh attempt.

"My husband's turned into a brute—a killer!" she claimed. "He's even bought a gun and says he'll shoot me with it!" This time, she continued sternly, there would be no slip-up—Albert would die and she and Judd would live richly ever after. One night in February 1927 they booked into the Waldorf-Astoria Hotel and there Ruth gave Judd his instructions. He was to buy some chloroform on his next trip out of town—to Kingston, New York—and also purchase a sash weight and some picture wire. "That way," she explained, "we have three means of killing him. One of them must surely work!" For a moment Gray raised objections to her plan, but he became obediently silent when she threatened: "If you don't do as I say then that's the end of us in the bed. You can find yourself another 'Momsie' to sleep with—only nobody else would have you but me!"

To prepare him for his coming role, she invited him round to Queens one night when Albert and Lorraine were away. She got drunk with him and then—as Gray later testified—"We went upstairs to her daughter's room, where we had intercourse." After that—encouraged by erotic love-play and fearful that it would abruptly end—Gray agreed to everything Ruth said as, stage by stage, she masterminded the "accidental" death of her still unsuspecting husband. One such "planning meeting" took place over lunch at Henry's, with Lorraine as an inquisitive witness as slips of paper outlining the imminent death of her father were handed back and forth across the table. She overheard some of the guarded conversation, but not enough for her to warn her father about what to expect in the early hours of Sunday, March 20.

At a bridge party

It was then that Gray—reinforcing his resolution with sips of whiskey from a flask—took a bus from downtown Manhattan to Queens Village and let himself into the Snyder house through an unlocked side door. The time was just after midnight and Ruth, Albert, and Lorraine were out at a bridge party in the home of one of their neighbours, Mrs. Milton Fidgeon. They returned tired but as happy as they ever were at about two o'clock—with Gray then hidden in the upstairs spare bedroom. The chloroform, sash weight, and picture wire were already concealed under the pillow of the bed, and he sat steadily drinking and staring at the blue "immigrants's" handkerchief and Italian newspaper which he had brought with him as false "clues".

Gray was not the only person who had been drinking that night. Albert Snyder had consumed more alcohol than he was used to, and after putting the car away he lurched upstairs, seconds after a snatched conversation between his wife, in the corridor, and Gray in the middle bedroom. With Lorraine put to bed and Albert lying in their room in a drunken haze, Ruth slipped along the hall and rejoined her lover. She was wearing slippers, a nightgown and negligee, and after kissing Gray she hissed: "Have you found the sash weight?" "Sure," he nodded. "Keep quiet, then. I'll be back as quick as I can."

Whispered consultation

Half-an-hour later Ruth left the master bedroom and held another whispered consultation with Gray. Together they finished the last of the whiskey and at three o'clock they were ready to act. There was no sound in the house, nor in the street outside, and apart from being tight Albert Snyder was also deaf in one ear. It is debatable if he would have heard the conspirators had they resorted to shouting at each other. "Okay," breathed Ruth. "This is it." Taking Gray by the hand she led him out of the spare bedroom and along the darkened corridor. He was wearing long rubber gloves so as to leave no fingerprints on the sash weight. It was she who carried the chloroform, wire, handkerchief, and some cotton waste.

They entered the front bedroom quietly, furtively. There, for the first and last time, Gray saw Albert Snyder—the man he had been ordered to kill. He paused for a moment, as if appalled by the reason for his being there. Then as Ruth opened her mouth to say something, he raised the weight with both hands and brought it crashing down on Snyder's exposed head. The blow was a strong one—but not strong enough to kill the sleeping man. Snyder awoke, sat up, and began to fight for his life. He clenched his hands and struck out at the half-seen intruder. Again Gray smashed the weight against Snyder's skull—this time drawing blood. The injured man caught hold of Gray's necktie and as he did so the weight fell to the floor. "Help, Momsie!" cried Albert pitifully. "For God's sake help me!" Whether or not he saw his wife in the room was never established. But Ruth answered him by retrieving the weight, lifting it with her strong and muscular arms and battering him on the top of the head with it.

Incredibly, Albert was still alive. He remained so until Grey clambered over his twitching body . . . until Ruth stuffed the chloroform-soaked cotton waste into his mouth and nostrils . . . until finally she tied his hands and feet and then methodically strangled him with the picture wire. There was blood everywhere—but mostly

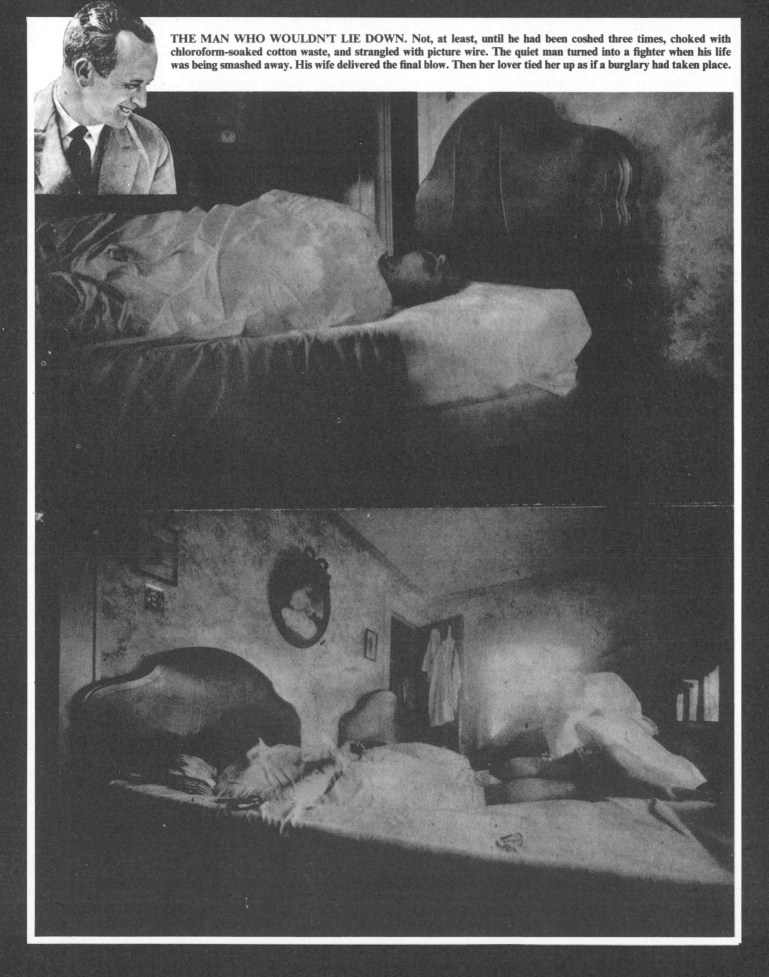

THE MAN WHO WOULDN'T LIE DOWN. Not, at least, until he had been coshed three times, choked with chloroform-soaked cotton waste, and strangled with picture wire. The quiet man turned into a fighter when his life was being smashed away. His wife delivered the final blow. Then her lover tied her up as if a burglary had taken place.

on Ruth's nightgown and the buckskin gloves she had borrowed from Gray, and on the salesman's freshly laundered shirt. For the next hour they washed themselves, sponged or changed their clothes (Gray put on a clean blue shirt of Albert's), hid the sash weight in the cellar, removed her jewellery and furs, and disarranged the ground floor furniture and cushions to make it seem as if a burglary had taken place. Only then did Gray tie his mistress up, fasten cheesecloth over her mouth and leave her lying in the spare bedroom, together with the Italian newspaper. He was ready to travel to the Onondaga Hotel in Syracuse, Kansas, and resume his corset selling activities first thing on Monday morning. As he left he looked back at Ruth Snyder—possibly for the first time with disgust and loathing—and said: "It may be two months, it may be a year, and it may be never before you'll see me again." One thing was sure: he and Snyder were never to drink, dance, make love, or even speak to each other again.

Curious tapping

Dawn broke gently in Queens Village on the morning of March 20. Young Lorraine Snyder was tired after her late night at the grown-ups' party and would have slept in had it not been for the curious tapping she heard at her bedroom door. Puzzled, she called out to her father and then her mother. Getting no reply she jumped out of bed and ran bare-footed to open the door—from where she saw her mother lying gagged and bound in the corridor. Lorraine bent and untied the cheesecloth and her mother told her to run and get help. The girl did so and a few minutes later Ruth was babbling out her story to her neighbours, Harriet and Louis Mulhauser. "It was dreadful, just dreadful!" she cried hysterically. "I was attacked by a prowler . . . He tied me up . . . He must have been after my jewels . . . Is Albert all right?" Mr. Mulhauser went to the main bedroom and came back white-faced with the news that Albert had two gaping head wounds and was dead.

Twice more that morning Mrs. Snyder repeated her thin and preposterous story of being attacked by "a big, rough-looking guy of about 35 with a black moustache. He was a foreigner, I guess. Some kind of Eyetalian." She gasped this out to Dr. Harry Hansen of Queens, who was called to the house to examine the body and check Ruth for any sign of assault. He found none and was convinced that her account was "a fabrication of lies". This opinion was shared by Police Commissioner George McLaughlin, who headed the 60 policemen who converged on the Snyder house before breakfast. Ruth—pale and trembling and far from being

"The Granite Woman" she was to be dubbed by the press—was grilled for 12 hours by McLaughlin and Inspector Arthur Carey.

Their suspicions had first been aroused by the frantic disorder of the downstairs rooms. "This doesn't look like a professional burglary to me," growled Carey. Ruth looked resentfully at him. "What do you mean?" He indicated to the turned over chairs and cushions. "It just doesn't look right." "How do you mean?" "I've seen lots of burglaries," he replied. "And they are not done this way. Not with killing." A search of the house soon revealed Ruth's rings and necklaces stuffed beneath a mattress, and a fur coat hanging in a closet. No one then had any doubts about it being an "inside" job.

After examining an address book containing the names of 28 men—including that of Judd Gray—and on discovering a cancelled check made out to Gray for $200, Ruth Snyder was taken to the Jamaica precinct police station, where she was tricked into making a partial confession. Told that Gray had already been arrested and had "told all", she admitted that she and the corset salesman had plotted to kill her husband and fake a break in. "But I didn't aim a single blow at Albert," she protested. "That was all Judd's doing. At the last moment I tried to stop him—but it was too late!"

Terrified, snivelling

By then detectives had found the bloodstained sash weight in the basement and had come across the insurance policies which made Albert Snyder a rich man—once he was dead. The next move—acting on information provided by Ruth—was to arrest the terrified and snivelling Judd Gray at his Syracuse hotel. The officers who brought him to New York City intimated that Snyder had not, in fact, died of his head wounds. He had been doped with chloroform and then strangled while unconscious. By the time the train pulled into 125th Street station, and Gray was taken from the private compartment to a waiting police car, he, too, had given his version of the night's deed. Faced with a murder charge he unexpectedly showed more courage than his "Granite Woman" lover and freely admitted to his part in the slaying of Snyder. He did not, however, cover up for Ruth and recounted everything she had said and done in the house in Queens. "I would never have killed Snyder but for her," he wept when he had completed his statement. "She had this power over me. She told me what to do and I just did it."

From then on the case against Gray and Snyder proceeded with all the implacability of the law. On April 18, 1927, their trial opened in Queens County

Courthouse and continued there for the next 18 days. Ruth appeared dressed in a black coat and hat, with a black rosary and crucifix conspicuously dangling at her throat—while Gray wore a double-breasted blue pinstripe suit with knife-edged creases in the trousers. Among the many star reporters and sob sisters who packed the press box was Peggy Hopkins Joyce, who gushed in the New York *Daily Mirror*: "Poor Judd Gray! He hasn't IT, he hasn't anything. He is just a sap who kissed and was told on! . . ."

Passionate vampire

"This putty man was wonderful modeling material for the Swedish-Norwegian vampire . . . She was passionate and she was cold-blooded, if anybody can imagine such a combination. Her passion was for Gray; her cold-bloodedness for her husband . . . You know women can do things to men that make men crazy. I mean, they can exert their influence over them in such a way that men will do almost anything for them. And I guess that is what Ruth did to Judd."

On May 9 Snyder and Gray were duly found guilty as charged. Both their subsequent appeals were refused and they were sentenced to die in the electric chair in Sing Sing at 11 o'clock on the night of January 12, 1928. While in the Death House they both wrote their autobiographies, and Ruth received 164 offers of marriage from men who—in the event of her being reprieved—were eager to exist humbly beneath her dominance. But there was no reprieve, and "Momsie" and "Lover Boy" perished within four minutes of each other. They kept their last rendezvous when they were laid out in the prison's autopsy room on a pair of stone slabs. However, if Ruth's religious convictions were anything to go by, it was not quite the end of their relationship—or of their triangle with Albert. In a poem published shortly before her death, and apparently addressed to all those of the police, press, and public who had "sullied" her name as a loving wife and mother, she said:

"You've blackened and besmeared a
    mother,
Once a man's plaything—A Toy—
What have you gained by all you've
    said,
And has it—brought you Joy?

And the hours when 'Babe' needed my
    love,
You've seen fit to send me away—
I'm going to God's home in heaven,
Ne'er more my feet to stray.

Someday—we'll all meet together,
Happy and smiling again,
Far above this earthly span
Everlastingly—in His reign."

IN THE CHAIR:
The last seconds
of Ruth Snyder's
life . . . a unique
last picture, shot
by a newsman
with a hidden
camera.
In court, her
lover said he
would never have
killed but for
her. "She had
this power
over me."

Passionate Letters

Thompson and Bywaters

She died for her vanity . . . and a nation's morals. But did she really persuade her masterful lover to kill her "cad" of a husband? The fatal passion of Edith Thompson and Frederick Bywaters was writ large in love letters. They caused a sensation in court . . . a story of love and murder in the suburbs.

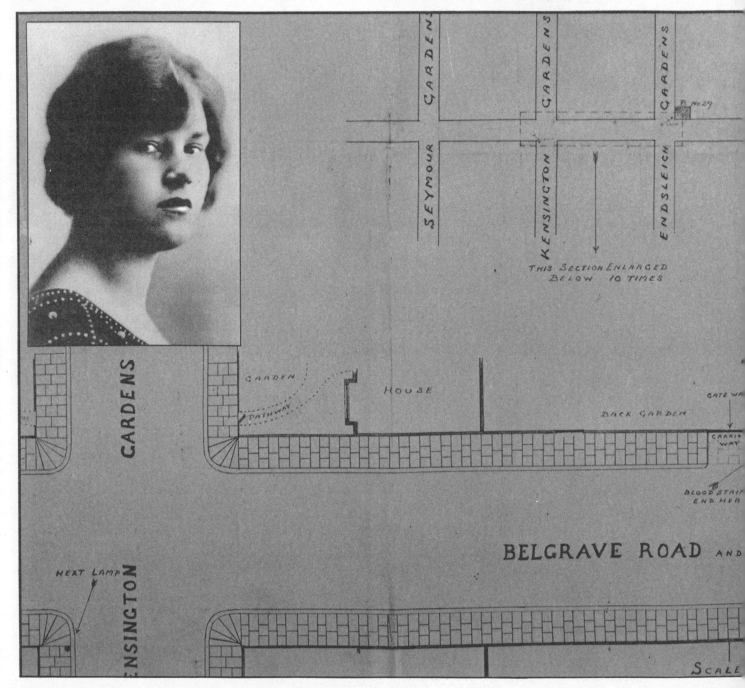

THE TRIAL which began in No. 1 Court at the Old Bailey in London on the morning of December 6, 1922, before a jury of eleven men and one woman was unquestionably the most sensational one of the year in England if not for the whole period between the two World Wars. It aroused nationwide interest, so much so that when the court doors were opened there was a line outside of more than 50 people which had formed during the previous afternoon and throughout the night for the few seats available in the public gallery.

The accused were Frederick ("Freddy") Bywaters, a 20-year-old laundry steward on an ocean liner, and his mistress Edith ("Edie") Thompson, a married woman, who worked as manageress-bookkeeper in a firm of wholesale milliners in the City of London and was eight years older than her lover. Just over two months previously, Edith's husband Percy Thompson, a 32-year-old shipping clerk, had been killed near his home at Ilford, a small town in London's commuter belt, when returning late one night with his wife. Bywaters was charged with his murder, while Edith Thompson was charged with inciting her lover to carry out the killing after she had unsuccessfully tried to kill him herself by giving him poison and mixing powdered glass with his food.

As soon as the judge, the venerable-looking Mr. Justice Shearman, had taken his place on the Bench in the historic wood-panelled courtroom, the accused were brought up by a policeman and a female wardress from the cells below where they had been anxiously waiting. As they took their places in the dock, Bywaters, a good-looking youth with curly dark hair, gave the impression of being a virile almost animal type, essentially a

MURDERER: Youthful seaman Frederick Bywaters was a man of action. His mistress's life was being "made hell" by her husband. So Bywaters stabbed the husband, while Edith cried, "Oh, don't, oh, don't!" In the death cell, Bywaters insisted: "She never planned it. She's innocent."

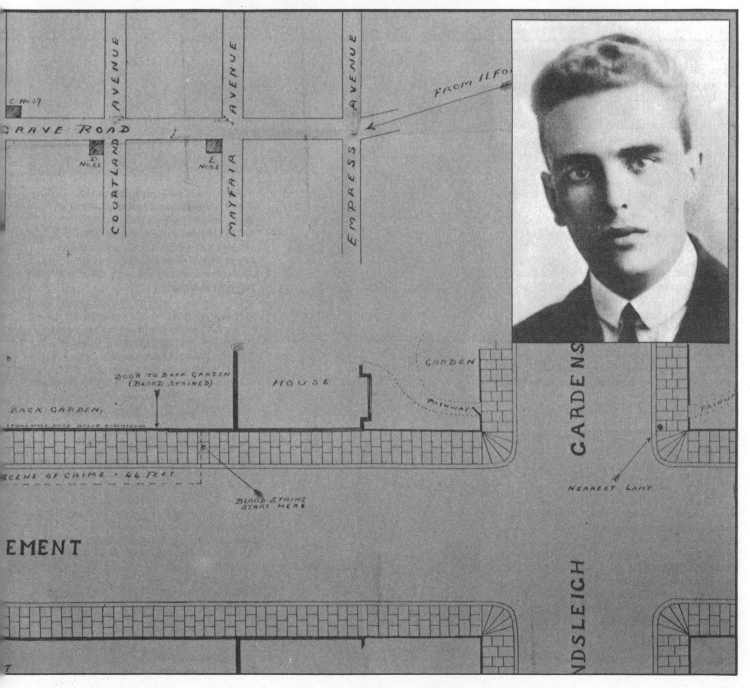

man of action, determined and masterful, His companion, however, looked pale, and she trembled slightly as she followed Bywaters and gave her plea to the Clerk of the Court as he had done: "Not guilty".

Edith Thompson's defence was in the hands of Sir Henry Curtis-Bennett, King's Counsel, who was a fashionable leading advocate of the day in criminal cases. As his counsel Bywaters had Mr. Cecil Whiteley, another eminent K.C. and a prominent criminal lawyer. The prosecuting team was led by the Solicitor-General, Sir Thomas Inskip, since it was customary for a Law Officer of the Crown to prosecute in any case involving a poison charge. Sir Thomas was a stern Sabbatarian and no criminal could expect any mercy at his hands.

Enough for an elephant

On the table in front of the Solicitor-General was a large bundle of letters, 62 in all, which Edith Thompson had written to Bywaters in the course of their love affair and which had been recovered by the police, some in the house in London where Bywaters had lived with his mother and others in his locker on his ship. Some of them were to be described by the judge as "gush". Certainly Edith analyzed her feelings and emotions in remarkable detail. Her favourite term of endearment for her lover was "Darlingest", contracted to "Darlint". The letters breathed a curious passion, in which the writer depicted herself as half mother and half slave-mistress. She also described how she had tried to do away with her husband on several occasions.

"You said it was enough for an elephant," she wrote in one letter. "Perhaps it was. But you don't allow for the taste making it possible for only a small quantity to be taken." And again: "I'm going to try the glass again occasionally — when it's safe. I've got an electric light globe this time." In fact, according to her, she used the light bulb three times in his food, "but the third time he found a piece — so I've given it up — until you come home."

Be jealous, darling

They were foolish letters to write and even more foolish to keep. Incidentally Edith Thompson never referred to her husband in them by his Christian name, but always as "he" or "him". In one letter she wrote:

"Yes, darlint, you are jealous of *him* — but I want you to be — he has the right by law to all that you have the right by nature and love — yes, darlint, be jealous, so much that you will do something desperàte."

In this letter she enclosed a cutting from a newspaper which described how a

VICTIM (left and above) with wife. Percy Thompson was making his wife's life a hell; he beat her and criticised her but refused to separate from her. He was stabbed while walking home with her one night down Belgrave Road; the knife was found in a grating by the roadside (far right).

woman's death had been caused by taking a bowl of broth made from the carcase of a chicken which had been killed by rat poison. Other cuttings enclosed in Edith's letters contained headings like "Patient Killed by an Overdose", "The Poisoner Curate", "Poisoned Chocolates", "Masterful Men", and "Woman the Consoler".

Compromising passages

Edith Thompson's counsel had been shown these highly compromising letters before the trial opened, since under the rules of criminal procedure the prosecution was bound to disclose them to the defence if it was intended to introduce them as evidence against her. Not only did they contain passages suggesting on the face of them that Edith had tried to kill her husband with poison and powdered glass, but they also plainly indicated that that on at least one occasion she had aborted herself and had a miscarriage after becoming pregnant by her lover.

Thus Sir Henry Curtis-Bennett had to reckon with the prosecution showing that she was not merely an adulteress but also

a self-abortionist as well as a potential murderess. The nature of her relations with her husband were also reflected in certain passages in the letters describing how, after Bywaters first went to sea, she rejected her husband's sexual approaches. Eventually, however, she yielded to him and became "the dutiful wife" which she thought was the best way to allay his suspicions if she and Bywaters had to take what she called "drastic measures"

Realizing that the letters were dynamite, Sir Henry did his best to persuade the judge to rule that they were inadmissible as evidence against his client. Therefore, as soon as the jury had been sworn, Sir Henry jumped to his feet and with a glance in the direction of the bundle of letters informed the judge that he had an objection to make to certain evidence which he understood the Solicitor-General proposed to put before the jury. The jury were then sent out of the court room while Curtis-Bennett and Inskip argued the point with the judge.

Admissible evidence

Briefly Curtis-Bennett's argument was that the letters could not and should not be admitted until the prosecution had shown that Mrs. Thompson took some active part in the murder—if it was murder—of her husband. The Solicitor-General replied by submitting that they were admissible because she was being charged as a principal in the second degree, although she did not strike the fatal blow. "The crime is one where one hand struck the blow," said Inskip, "and we want to show by these letters that her mind conceived it and incited it—the evidence of that is the letters that Mrs. Thompson wrote to the man who struck the blow."

After listening patiently to the argument, the judge then gave his ruling. "I think these letters are admissible as evidence of intention and motive," he said, "and I shall admit them." Turning towards Edith Thompson's counsel, he added: "I do not think you can contest the letters, showing the affectionate relations between the parties, are not evidence of motive in so far as they show affection."

Sir Henry was overruled. He had done everything he could to exclude the damning letters; now he knew that the task before him was all the more difficult. He glanced at his client in the dock. Her face, almost hidden by the brim of her black velour hat, looked anxious and drawn.

The jury were then brought back to court, and the Solicitor-General proceeded to open the case for the Crown. "May it please your lordship, members of the jury," he began, "on October 4, a little after midnight, Percy Thompson was stabbed to death on his way home from Ilford station. He was in a dark part of the road, not over-well lit at the best of times, when he was struck, first of all, apparently from behind, and then in front, by some assailant. The only person present was his wife, Mrs. Thompson who is now in the dock. She is charged with Bywaters, who is said by the prosecution to have been the assailant, with the murder of Percy Thompson."

It was a sombre tale which the Solicitor-General went on to relate. Husband and wife had been to the theatre, and as they were walking along the road from Ilford station to the terraced row of suburban houses in Kensington Gardens where they lived, a man suddenly jumped out of the shadows. Seizing Percy Thompson by the arm, he said, "Why don't you get a divorce from your wife, you cad?"

Thompson, who appeared to recognize the man, replied, "I've got her, I'll keep her, and I'll shoot you."

Strange attacker

The assailant then pulled out a knife from his coat pocket. With it he stabbed Thompson several times, while Edith Thompson shouted, "Oh, don't! Oh, don't!" The attacker turned, ran off, and disappeared into the darkness. Meanwhile Percy Thompson fell to the ground, blood pouring from his mouth. He was dead before a doctor, who had been summoned, arrived on the scene followed by the police.

Edith Thompson was still in too hysterical a condition to tell the police very much except that her husband had been "attacked by a strange man". However, a woman named Mrs. Fanny Lester, who lived in the same house with the Thomp-

**NATIONWIDE INTEREST was aroused
by the trial and crowds gathered
to hear the verdict. Mrs. Bywaters,
the accused's mother, gave evidence.**

sons was also questioned, and it was Mrs. Lester who put the police on the track of the killer. She stated that about 18 months previously Frederick Bywaters had lodged in the house for some weeks. He had left due to a row he had had with Percy Thompson caused by the attentions Bywaters had apparently been paying Edith. The police also learned that Bywaters was a steward with the P. & O. line. In turn this led the officers to find the letters Edith had written to him and which he picked up at the various ports at which his ship called.

Stifled sobbing

Bywaters was eventually traced to the home of Edith Thompson's parents who lived at Manor Park, near Ilford. There he was arrested and taken to Ilford police station where he was formally charged with the murder. Later that day Edith Thompson was picked up and taken to the same police station where she was likewise charged on the basis of the letters with being a principal in the murder; or, alternatively, with being an accessory to it.

At this time neither she nor Freddy Bywaters knew that the other had been arrested. As she was being led past a window of the police station, she looked in and saw her lover sitting there obviously in police custody. The sight shook her extremely. "Oh, God, why did he do it?" she cried, the words coming out involuntarily between stifled sobs. "I didn't want him to do it."

Under police interrogation, Bywaters agreed with what his mistress had said. At the same time he did his best to shield her and insisted that she knew nothing of his intention to waylay Percy Thompson on their homeward journey from the theatre. Both prisoners signed statements confirming what they had told the police when they were arrested, and they were put in evidence by the prosecution in

addition to Edith Thompson's letters.

The story of the fatal encounter which Bywaters told in his statement was as follows:

"I waited for Mrs. Thompson and her husband. I pushed her to one side, also pushing him up the street . . . We struggled. I took my knife from my pocket and we fought and he got the worst of it . . .

"The reason I fought with Thompson was because he never acted like a man to his wife. He always seemed several degrees lower than a snake. I loved her and I could not go on seeing her leading that life. I did not intend to kill him. I only meant to injure him. I gave him an opportunity of standing up to me as a man but he wouldn't."

Bywaters stuck to this story when he went into the witness-box on the third day of the trial, although he did qualify his admission, "I only meant to injure him," by saying that what he really intended was "to stop him from killing me."

Nor could the Solicitor-General shake him in cross-examination about his mistress's compromising letters, for which the witness had a ready explanation.

"As far as you could tell, reading these letters," Sir Thomas Inskip asked, looking sternly at the man on the witness stand, "did you ever believe in your own mind that she herself had given any poison to her husband?"

"No," replied Bywaters with an air of self-confidence, "it never entered my mind at all. She had been reading books. She had a vivid way of declaring herself. She would read a book and imagine herself as the character in the book."

He also stated in reply to the Solicitor-General that it was Percy Thompson who attacked him first. The expression on Sir Thomas Inskip's face clearly showed that he did not believe the witness. "Do you mean to suggest that he made the first assault upon you?" he asked incredulously.

"Yes, he did."

"And that you then drew your knife?"

"I did."

"Is it the fact that you never saw any revolver or any gun at that moment?"

"I never saw it, no," Bywaters had to admit.

Mr. Cecil Whiteley, K.C., did something to repair the damage caused by this admission when he re-examined his client about the possibility of Percy Thompson having a gun. "Although I never saw a revolver," said Bywaters, "I believed that he had one, otherwise I would not have drawn my knife. I was in fear of my life."

"At any time have you had any intention to murder Mr. Thompson?" defence counsel asked in conclusion.

Tension mounted

"I have not," replied Bywaters firmly and unhesitatingly. He added that he had met Mrs. Thompson in a teashop near her place of work on the afternoon of the killing, but he strongly repudiated the prosecution's suggestion that the purpose of the meeting was to plot her husband's death.

The atmosphere of tension mounted when the usher called out "Edith Jessie Thompson", and the prisoner left the dock to follow her lover on to the witness stand. There was no need for her to testify. Had she remained silent, the prosecution could not have commented upon the fact. The only evidence against her consisted of the letters, and Curtis-Bennett would have preferred to have dealt with them himself in his speech to the jury, rather than risk his client being cross-examined by the ruthless Solicitor-General and probably convicting herself out of her own mouth.

However, Edith Thompson brushed aside all her counsel's objections, determined as she was on getting the limelight. She realized the enormous public interest in the case, her counsel said afterwards, and decided to play up to it by entering the witness box.

The story of her relations with Freddy Bywaters, which she told in her examination-in-chief, was a curious one. She and her husband had known the Bywaters family for some years, she said, the acquaintance going back to the days when her brother and Bywaters were school-mates. In June 1921, Bywaters was on extended leave from his ship, and he accompanied her husband and herself on a holiday to the Isle of Wight in the south of England. At that time she and Freddy, she went on, were no more than friends. The friendship continued after Freddy went to live with the Thompsons as a paying guest until his ship was ready to sail.

"How did you become lovers?" her counsel asked her.

"Well," said Edith, "it started on the August Bank Holiday. I had some trouble with my husband on that day—over a pin!"

Kissed on lips

It was a fine sunny afternoon and all three were in the garden at the back of the house. Edith Thompson was sewing. Suddenly she looked up and said, "I want a pin."

"I will go and get you one," said Bywaters.

When he returned with the pin, husband and wife were arguing, Percy Thompson saying she should have got the pin herself. Edith Thompson then went into the house to prepare tea. Her husband followed her and a further argument ensued as she was laying the table in the sitting room. Her sister Avis Graydon was expected, but she was a little late and, unlike his wife, Percy Thompson did not want to wait for her. He went on to make some uncomplimentary remarks about Edith's family and then began to beat her. Finally he threw her across the room and she collided with a chair which overturned. Hearing the noise from the garden, Bywaters rushed in and told Thompson to stop.

"Why don't you come to an amicable agreement?" said Bywaters. "Either you can have a separation or you can get a divorce."

Thompson hesitated before replying. "Yes—No—I don't see it concerns you."

"You are making Edie's life a hell," said Bywaters. "You know she is not happy with you."

"Well, I have got her and I will keep her."

Edith went upstairs and Bywaters returned to his room. After a short while she joined him there, when he comforted her and for the first time kissed her on the lips. When he came back to the sitting room, he extracted a promise from her husband that he would not knock her about or beat her any more. But Thompson flatly refused to take any steps towards obtaining a legal separation or a divorce from his wife. Shortly afterwards, Bywaters left the house and went to stay with his mother.

During the next few weeks—he was due to embark early in September—he and Edith met secretly from time to time. Most of these meetings took place in tea shops or municipal parks such as Wanstead or Epping Forest near Ilford. There

THE DETECTIVES who handled the case. Who made the first assault? Did Percy Thompson have a gun? Was the crime planned over tea that afternoon?

were not many opportunities for more than hand holding at dance teas and an occasional embrace on a bench. It was the age of the *thé dansant,* and at one of these occasions the orchestra played *One Little Hour,* which became "their tune". However, just before Bywaters' ship sailed on September 9 the two became lovers, apparently going to a small hotel for the purpose and registering under assumed names.

Poison letters

Questioned by her counsel about the letters and the news cuttings, she explained that she had deliberately deceived her lover into thinking that she wished to poison her husband, but that she had no intention of acting upon what she had written. She had sent the letters with their suggestive enclosures, so she said, because she was anxious to keep Freddy's love. Occasionally he would go out with other girls, one of whom was Edith's unmarried sister Avis, and Edith thought that he might be tiring of her.

When the Solicitor-General rose to cross-examine, it was not difficult for him to entrap her as Curtis-Bennett had feared he would. Inskip held up one letter in which she had written to her lover:

"Why aren't you sending me something? I wanted you to . . . If I don't

Syndication International

mind the risk, why should you?"

"What was it?" the Solicitor-General asked sternly.

"I've no idea," Edith replied as non-chalantly as she could.

"Have you no idea?"

"Except what he told me."

"What did he lead you to think it was?"

"That it was something for me to give my husband."

"With a view to poisoning your husband?"

Edith paused before answering, not knowing exactly what to say and looking distinctly uncomfortable. "That was not the idea," she said at last, "that was not what I expected."

"Something to give your husband that would hurt him?" the Solicitor-General went on.

"To make him ill," she blurted out.

Replying to further questions, Edith Thompson admitted that she had urged Bywaters to send the "something to make him ill", instead of bringing it. "I wrote that," she added, "in order to make him think I was willing to do anything he might suggest, to enable me to retain his affections."

Frank explanation

Again the Solicitor-General eyed her severely. "Mrs. Thompson, is that quite a frank explanation of this urging him to send instead of to bring?"

"It is, absolutely," was the unconvincing reply. "I wanted him to think I was eager to help him."

At this point, the judge leaned forward in the direction of the witness. "That does not answer the question, you know," he remarked.

There was little that Curtis-Bennett could do in re-examining his client to repair the damage caused by her replies to the Solicitor-General's questioning. But he did his best. For example, the phrase, "He is still well", which she had used in one letter, he was able to show referred not to her husband but to a bronze monkey that Bywaters had bought in some foreign port and given her as a souvenir. Her defence counsel also made the most of her conduct on the night of the killing.

Extraordinary life

"As far as you could," he asked her, "from the moment you got to your husband, did you do everything you could for him?"

"Everything I possibly could," echoed Edith Thompson.

Curtis-Bennett came back to this point in her favour when he made his closing speech to the jury. "The letters provide the only evidence upon which the charge of murder is framed against Mrs. Thompson," he stressed his words deliberately. "Everything that was done and said by her on that night shows as strongly as it can that not only did she not know the murder was going to be committed, but that she was horrified when she found her husband was killed."

His client was no ordinary woman, he continued. "She reads a book and then imagines herself one of the characters in the book. She is always living an extraordinary life of novels." So far as her relations with Freddy Bywaters went, Sir Henry made it clear that for his part he did not care whether they were described as "an amazing passion" or "an adulterous

intercourse" or whatever. "Thank God, this is not a court of morals," he told the eleven men and one woman in the jury box, "because if everybody immoral was brought here I should never be out of it, nor would you. Whatever name you give it, it was certainly a great love that existed between these two people."

Mr. Justice Shearman began his summing-up of the evidence to the jury with the ominous words: "You should not forget you are trying a vulgar, common crime!" Edith Thompson's letters to her lover the judge proceeded to describe as "full of the outpourings of a silly but at the same time a wicked affection".

"Members of the jury, if that nonsense means anything," he went on to say, "it means that the love of a husband for his wife is something improper because marriage is acknowledged by the law, and that the love of a woman for her lover — illicit and clandestine — is something great and noble. I am certain that you, like any other right-minded persons, will be filled with disgust at such a notion. Let us get rid of all that atmosphere and try this case in an ordinary common sense way."

Strongly hostile

The summing-up was strongly hostile to both prisoners. The red-robed and bewigged figure on the judicial bench left little doubt in the jury's minds that "these two by arrangement between each other agreed to murder this man Thompson, and the murder was effected by the man Bywaters". The impression was heightened by the sense of moral indignation expressed by the judge at the prisoners' sexual morals. In the event it took the jury just over two hours to find both prisoners guilty of murder.

"I say the verdict of the jury is wrong," exclaimed Bywaters when he heard it. "Edith Thompson is not guilty. I am no murderer. I am no assassin." These words were echoed by the woman who stood beside him in the dock. "I am not guilty," she cried. And again, after both had been sentenced to death by hanging, she repeated, "I am not guilty. Oh, God, I am not guilty!"

Both prisoners appealed on the grounds that the verdict was against the weight of the evidence and that the judge had misdirected the jury. Each of the appeals was dismissed by the Court of Criminal Appeal, which saw no grounds for quashing the conviction or ordering a new trial, the President of the Court describing it as a "squalid and rather indecent case of lust and adultery" and one which

MERCY MAIL: Petitions (left) for Edith Thompson's reprieve failed. She was hanged at London's Holloway Prison on January 9, 1923, at 9.00 a.m. (right).

Radio Times Hulton Picture Library

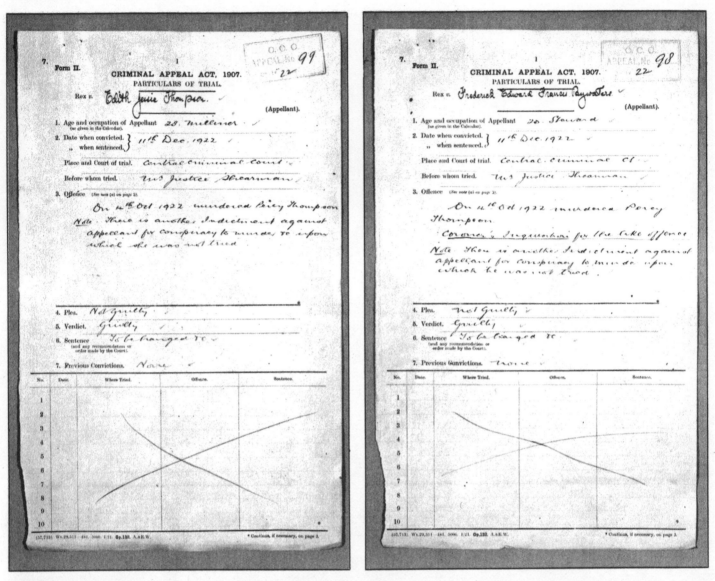

"exhibits from the beginning to the end no redeeming feature".

At the time no woman had been hanged in England for 15 years. Largely for this reason there was considerable public agitation that Edith Thompson should be reprieved, and a petition for reprieve containing many thousands of signatures was sent to the Home Secretary, with whom the final decision rested.

Lawyer's last dash

Three days before the date set for the execution, Bywaters had a meeting with his mother in the condemned cell in Pentonville Prison, where he was being held. He told his mother that he had no grievance against the law so far as he himself was concerned, and that execution had no terrors for him. "I killed him and I must pay for it," he said. "The judge's summing-up was just, if you like, but it was cruel. It never gave me a chance. I did it, though, and I can't complain."

His mistress's case was quite different, he stressed. "I swear she is completely

DEATH DOCUMENTS: They died at the same moment, in places a quarter of a mile apart. Even Bywaters' confession had not swayed the Home Secretary.

innocent. She never knew that I was going to meet them that night . . . For her to be hanged as a criminal is too awful. She didn't commit the murder. I did. She never planned it. She never knew about it. She is innocent, absolutely innocent. I can't believe that they will hang her."

When this was reported to Edith Thompson's solicitor, the lawyer dashed through the night to make a last minute appeal to the Home Secretary who had gone off to spend the weekend at his country house some two hundred miles from London. When he had read Bywater's "confession", the Home Secretary promised to give the solicitor his decision next day, the eve of the execution. He did so, but it was that there could be no reprieve for either prisoner and the law must take its course.

They were both hanged at the same

hour, 9.0 a.m. on January 9, 1923 — she at Holloway and he a quarter of a mile away at Pentonville. Freddy Bywaters met his end "like a gentleman", as he told his mother he would, protesting his mistress's innocence to the last. Edith Thompson, however, had to be carried from the condemned cell to the scaffold by two wardresses as she was in a state of complete collapse during her last moments.

Spoiled her chances

Edith Thompson's leading counsel was greatly upset by the verdict and its outcome, which he felt would have been different if she had taken his advice. "She spoiled her chances by her evidence and demeanour," he said afterwards. "I had a perfect answer to everything, which I am sure would have won an acquittal if she had not been a witness. She was a vain woman and an obstinate one. Also her imagination was highly developed, but it failed to show her the mistake she was making . . . In short, Mrs. Thompson was hanged for immorality."

A Suggestion of Suicide?

Sergeant Emmett-Dunne

Syndication International

THE TALL, powerfully built British army sergeant, cutting an impressive figure in his crisply pressed uniform, snapped smartly to attention before the members of the court martial in Düsseldorf, Germany. He stared ahead, with expressionless eyes which seemed to be focussing far beyond the array of officers at the long table, as an official read the charge.

Murder, on November 30, 1953, in Duisburg, Germany, a civil offence, under section 41 of the Army Act, committed while on active service. He was asked for his answer to the charge. Firmly and loudly he replied: "Not guilty, sir."

Behind the apparently unemotional eyes of Sergeant Frederick Emmett-Dunne, Royal Electrical and Mechanical Engineers, there was a ferment of shock and disbelief. For, nearly two years before his trial, in June 1955, the fellow sergeant he was alleged to have murdered, Reginald Watters, had been found hanging in the army's Glamorgan Barracks, in Duisburg, and declared a suicide.

Emmett-Dunne, it had seemed at that time, was merely the unfortunate friend who had found the corpse—and, along with others, mourned the untimely death of a comrade. But, soon afterwards, Emmett-Dunne had married Watters' German-born widow and settled down with her in England. The suspicions aroused by the surprisingly swift romance set Emmett-Dunne upon the road back to Germany and a charge of murder.

Single man

In the British courtroom in what was once enemy territory were gathered some of the sharpest and most notable minds of the English Bar. The doors were closed and the rustling of army dossiers and pink ribbon-bound files of evidence ceased as the formidable counsel for the prosecution, Mr. Mervyn Griffith-Jones, rose to outline the case.

In matter-of-fact tones, he carried the members of the court martial back to the evening of November 30, 1953, and to the two principal characters in the drama: Emmett-Dunne, then Company-Sergeant-Major in the Fourth Infantry Duisburg workshops, "a single man living in barracks", and Reginald Watters, a sergeant in the technical training school.

"The dead man," said counsel, "married some time ago a German girl and, at the time of his death, was living in a flat a mile and a half away from the barracks. It is important in this case to note that he was a small, thickset man, only 5 ft. 1 in. high. The defendant . . ." Mr. Griffith-Jones briefly pointed in the direc-

UNDER ESCORT (previous page), Emmett-Dunne goes to the courtroom. The woman in the case was Mia, pictured (right) as the wife of the accused man.

tion of Emmett-Dunne, by now sitting stiffly upright on a straight-backed chair, ". . . the defendant, you will appreciate, is a very tall and powerful man.

"Sergeant Watters was found about three o'clock in the early hours of December 1 hanging from the banisters in Block Two of the barracks, by a rope which was loose around his neck, by Quartermaster-Sergeant Fry, the orderly officer on duty, and by Emmett-Dunne who was accompanying Fry in searching the barracks. . . .

"At about seven o'clock the same morning Emmett-Dunne made a statement to the Criminal Investigation Department in which he said he had brought Watters back to barracks about 7 p.m. and had dropped him outside the gates. That was the last he had seen of him until, with Quartermaster-Sergeant Fry, he found him hanging by the neck."

Inexperienced

A Dr. Alan Womack had been called to examine the dead man—and at a later court of inquiry had testified that Watters died from shock, due to strangulation. Largely as a result of that testimony it was concluded that Watters had committed suicide. But here Mr. Griffith-Jones paused for a moment and then, as he resumed, it was clear that what he had next to say caused him some regret.

"Dr. Womack," he told the court, "will not, I am sure, mind my saying that at that time he was a very young and in-

experienced pathologist. He conducted a most careful post-mortem, finding a number of facts, and apparently observing everything there was to observe. But he drew from those findings of fact the wrong conclusion."

Severe blow

The conclusion would have gone permanently undisputed had not Watters' body been exhumed in February 1955. The exhumation, Mr. Griffith-Jones explained simply, was undertaken "for various reasons". But there were a handful of people in that courtroom who knew the main reason among those "various reasons": a former army special investigator, who had subsequently joined the civil police back in England, had learned of Emmett-Dunne's marriage to Sergeant Watters' widow on June 3, 1954—only six months after the "suicide"—and communicated his suspicions to his superiors.

But, Mr. Griffith-Jones went on, an examination of the exhumed body by Dr. Francis Camps, one of Britain's leading forensic scientists, brought to light evidence very different from that produced by Dr. Womack; evidence, said counsel,

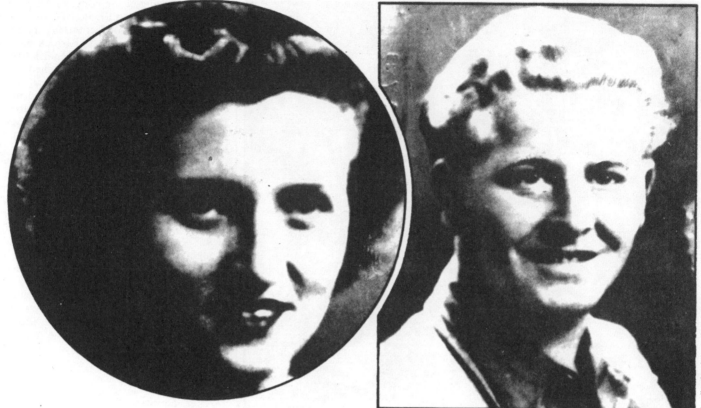

"that this man never died from hanging, but that he died as a result of a severe blow across the front of the throat. As a result of that, and of other evidence not known at the time, the defendant stands charged before you with murdering Watters on that night."

As the details of the exhumation were unfolded Emmett-Dunne still showed no hint of emotion. But the question to which the court now required an answer was: if there *was* murder, was there a motive? Mr. Griffith-Jones sought the answer.

Fishy business

From the end of 1952 right up to the day of Sergeant Watters' death, the defendant, counsel proceeded to allege, "had been carrying on a clandestine affair or association with Watters' wife. You will hear that Emmett-Dunne and Sergeant Watters' wife were secretly meeting, that he was paying overdue attention to her at sergeants' mess parties, that he was in the habit of telephoning to the next-door house frequently, and often just after lunch when Watters had returned to the barracks and would not know."

It was this alleged "association" between the defendant and the dead man's wife on which the prosecution pinned the main burden of its case. As soon as he had concluded his opening statement, Mr. Griffith-Jones concentrated upon witnesses who would testify to the popular knowledge that Emmett-Dunne had been "carrying on" with young Mrs. Watters.

Amid a barrage of stamping feet and wrist-trembling salutes, the defendant's former comrades came forward to the long table to tell what they remembered of those past days. Staff Sergeant Frederick Cracknell recalled the time when Watters "told me he suspected there was some fishy business going on between his wife and Emmett-Dunne. I told him I knew nothing about it. Watters asked me to tackle the company-sergeant-major about the matter. I asked him if he had any facts but he said no, it was just suspicion . . . He was not upset but very inquisitive and he wanted to get to the bottom of the matter. He was jealous as far as his wife was concerned."

Warrant Officer James Henry Ivens provided even more direct evidence than Sergeant Cracknell. "I noticed," he told the court, in a formal army-reporting voice, "that there was a very familiar attitude between Mrs. Watters and Sergeant Emmett-Dunne. I said he would be well advised to leave Mrs. Watters alone."

Casual remark

Mr. Griffith-Jones leapt upon that statement. "What did he say to that?" he demanded. "He gave," replied Ivens, "a very negative answer. I cannot recall what it was. I said it was obvious to most of us who lived in the mess, and more so to those who lived in the quarters, that the association between the two of them was liable to cause embarrassment."

From another sergeant came evidence

POPULAR Sergeant Reginald Watters was not the kind of man to commit suicide, as his fellows pointed out. His wife (left), however, seemed unconcerned.

of a casual remark by Emmett-Dunne that the prosecution saw as part of the preparation for the "suicide" scene that was to be set for Watters. "In just ordinary conversation," said the sergeant, "the defendant told me there was a certain person in our mess who would commit suicide if his wife did not behave herself."

Mr. Charles Cahn, the Judge Advocate, the legal authority appointed to guide the court martial members on facts of law, carefully noted the questions and answers on his notepad. It now seemed to the court that the prosecution's case was taking shape: defendant wants another man's wife; his liaison with the wife has become common knowledge; the husband is known to be jealous; if the husband dies what is most likely but that his friends will think he killed himself out of despair? That, the prosecution was saying, was how Emmett-Dunne had *hoped* the chain of events would go.

But the Judge Advocate and the court had not failed to notice one other most significant fact. Witnesses had testified that Watters was a "hail-fellow-well-met type of man and popular in the sergeants' mess". Nothing that was said of him indicated that he was the kind of man who would take his own life.

As with the rest of the testimony in this

trial, the finding of the body, by Sergeant Fry in company with Emmett-Dunne, was described in matter-of-fact terms. Fry and the defendant entered the barrack block and there was Watters, suspended from the noose, "the head rather hunched into the shoulders". On the floor near the slowly gyrating corpse was an upturned bucket which, so it had seemed, Watters had stood upon while adjusting the rope and then kicked away as the final and fatal action of his life.

It was Emmett-Dunne, Sergeant Fry stated, who had cut the body down and then reeled against the wall as though attempting to be sick. "I asked him 'What's up?' And he replied 'As I took the body down it gurgled and it has made me feel sick.'" Sergeant Fry was shocked at the thought of a fellow-soldier taking his own life, although there was one thing that seemed to him a little odd.

"I thought the arms were in a peculiar position," he told the court. "They were raised two or three inches above what I thought would have been the normal position for the arms to settle in. The body was stiff."

Message

After Sergeant Fry's departure from the witness-stand there came a tightening sense of expectation in the court as the prosecution called its main witness, army private Ronald Emmett — the defendant's half-brother — who had served with Emmett-Dunne and lived in the same barracks at the time of Watters' death. As he stepped up, clearly in a state of tension, the court president, Brigadier D. L. Betts, leaned forward and told him, quietly: "You are free to answer any questions if you are prepared to do so. There is no danger of your being tried by court martial." Emmett swallowed hard, as if with relief, and replied: "Thank you, sir."

Emmett's story was that his half-brother had sent him a message asking that the two should meet, sometime just before 8 p.m. on November 30, outside the sergeants' mess. There Emmett-Dunne said: "Remember you are my brother, and I said 'Yes.' So he said, 'I have killed a man.' I asked him how and he said he had had an argument and either struck or pushed this man. He had fallen and he was dead."

Sergeant Emmett-Dunne led the way and Private Emmett followed him into entrance number four of the barracks block. Now, with Mr. Griffith-Jones leading the way with his questions, Emmett re-lived the most frightening moments of his life.

THE FORCES of Justice were present in strength: Griffith-Jones (far left), Judge Advocate Charles Cahn (left) and Defence Counsel Curtis-Bennett (above).

"We went down the corridor and there was a cape covering a body. My brother removed the cape and the body was lying with the knees up towards the chest and the head sloping down. The face was showing. My brother said he wanted to make it look as though it was suicide, sir. There was a rope fastened to the banisters and the other end was around the neck. The man was not hanging up and my brother asked me to hold this man. So we both lifted the man up and I held him. My brother stepped on the bucket and fastened the knots at the top."

As the evidence unfolded Emmett-Dunne paid no attention to his brother, his eyes still searching beyond the court. Mr. Griffith-Jones pressed ahead with his interrogation. "After the body had been secured in that way, what was done?" — "The bucket was turned on its side." —

army to which he had committed his life.

Emmett-Dunne gave his evidence briskly, clearly and without anxiety. He had met Watters outside the barrack block, he said, and they had talked together in Emmett-Dunne's car. "He was accusing me of having lived with his wife in Cologne during an army exercise period in September. I told him he was talking out of the side of his hat, or words to that effect. He said, 'I know what I'm talking about and I have got proof.'

Loaded gun

"I said not to be so ridiculous. Mia and I are good friends but I am not such a . . . . as to break up a friendship. I listened and argued and implored him. I had never seen Reg like this before. He seemed strange. If I had not known him well I should have thought he was a madman."

Griffith-Jones then launched a fusillade of questions that increased in velocity. "Did you look at Sergeant Watters?" counsel barked. "Yes." — "What did you see?" — "He had a pistol in his hand. I gathered he took it from a coat pocket. It was covered with a piece of cloth and he removed it." — "What did you see then?" — "The pistol was pointing at me, right between my eyes. It was loaded. I could see there were three 'or four rounds in it. The next compartment to fire was loaded, I could see. I raised my arm slowly."

What, Mr. Griffith-Jones demanded, was Emmett-Dunne intending to do? "I was going to gain possession of the pistol, I was going to stun Sergeant Watters," the defendant replied. "I was going to hit him across the jawbone. I expected the blow to land *there*." Emmett-Dunne touched his own jawbone to illustrate the

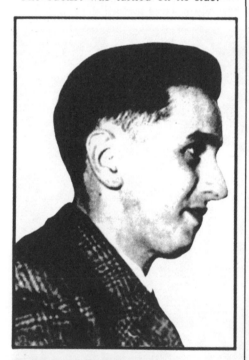

TOP Home Office pathologist Francis Camps (centre) and the less experienced Dr. Alan Womack (above). Far right: court president Brig. Betts.

"Who did that?" — "I did." — "On your own initiative, or at somebody else's request?" — "I am not sure, but to make it look as though the man had kicked the bucket over. That was the object."

So, at last and after the court had heard medical and technical evidence, Emmett-Dunne left his seat and came forward to give his version of events and support his plea of not guilty. His counsel, Mr. Derek Curtis-Bennett, Q.C., at once made it clear that the defendant's case would be that he had killed Watters in self-defence — and that, in staging the suicide charade, he had acted foolishly and out of fright lest he should be discharged from the round. There was a noise from him. I took him through the first doorway and he passed out. I continued carrying him into the building and I fell over. Instinctively I released my grip. He fell to the ground. A rope had tripped me. I realised he was dead and I propped him against the wall and put my coat on him."

There was total silence in the courtroom, apart from the to-and-fro of questions and answers. But there was no doubt that the officers of the court martial were waiting for *the* one essential point: if it had been an accident why hadn't Emmett-Dunne immediately reported it and cleared himself of all personal danger? Yes, he said, he had tried. He had gone to

LITTLE seemed to escape the eager attention of Frau Kruger and Fraulein Dislich, who had seen Emmett-Dunne and Mia together and testified so in court.

HALF-BROTHER Ronald Emmett (above and right) gave the most damning and persuasive evidence of all: proof that Emmett-Dunne had lied about his actions.

action. But Mr. Curtis-Bennett sprang to the defence, seizing the opportunity to disprove any murder motive.

"Did you intend to kill him?" he asked. Loudly, Emmett-Dunne responded: "No, sir. The purpose of the blow was to stun him to get possession of the pistol. It was not intentional to do any bodily harm or even to hurt him, other than to gain possession of the pistol."

But, purely by accident, Emmett-Dunne asserted, the blow had been fatal. "He sort of slumped against the car door. I went around the front of the car to help him to his feet. I did so to take him to his office. I put my arm around him to support him and I thought he was coming the nearby medical inspection room to announce what had happened and seek assistance. "But," he added, "when I got there the door would not open." Because he was "frightened" he had staged the suicide scene helped by his half-brother.

On the surface, it sounded as though Emmett-Dunne's story might stand up to scrutiny. Panic, and the play-acting of the hanging, could have been something that a man might do—even if afterwards he saw it to have been a stupidly perilous reaction. But the moment had come for the court to put the verbal explanation to practical test. With a crashing of feet, soldiers and witnesses sprang to attention as the court's officers rose and, with Emmett-Dunne in the rear, trooped outside to examine the black B.M.W. car in which the "accident" was supposed to have happened.

Confined space

As the officers grouped themselves around, a soldier of similar build to Watters slid into the passenger seat and Emmett-Dunne eased his bulk in behind the steering wheel. "Now," Mr. Griffith-Jones instructed the defendant, "will you please indicate to the court how you managed to strike him across the front of the neck?" As Emmett-Dunne raised his arm, counsel hurriedly added: "Show us . . . just show us . . . Don't hit him hard!" Among those closely watching was the one man whose conclusions from the demonstration would carry great weight: Dr. Francis Camps, the pathologist.

However, soon after the hearing resumed inside the courthouse it became clear that the practical demonstration had gone a long way towards sealing the sergeant's fate. In the confined space in the small car it would not have been possible for Emmett-Dunne to have struck and killed Watters in the way he had described, Dr. Camps insisted. The death blow had been powerful and would have required a "rhythmical swing" behind it.

In the car, and in the manner demonstrated by Emmett-Dunne, there was not room enough to swing the arm in a wide arc. The blow that Emmett-Dunne had shown to the court would not have landed on the victim's Adam's apple—as the fatal blow to Watters had, indeed, landed—and it would not have had a lethal force.

From that moment on there was little hope for Emmett-Dunne. A crucial piece of evidence came from a medical orderly who swore that the medical inspection room was not locked at the time when Emmett-Dunne said he had tried to get help for Watters. That appeared to demolish the plea of self-defence. It seemed certain that Emmett-Dunne had struck the fatal blow, and that his intention had been to commit murder.

Pale and attractive, Mrs. Mia Emmett-Dunne—the young woman for whose love the sergeant was said to have killed a man—gave softly-spoken evidence that there had been no affair between herself and Emmett-Dunne during her former husband's lifetime. For her, what had been a brief but happy marriage in England to her second husband was now coming to an end. Its conclusion was drawn by the court when, on July 7, the members retired for 76 minutes and returned a verdict of guilty. The sentence was death by hanging.

On July 19, the Commander-in-Chief, General Sir Richard Gale, confirmed the court martial's verdict. But Sergeant Frederick Emmett-Dunne was not to die —even though capital punishment was still then in force in Britain. For, on May 26, 1952, Britain had signed a convention in Bonn, the Federal German capital, containing an article prohibiting the enforcement of the death penalty on Federal territory by armed forces' authorities.

Emmett-Dunne, who might have committed and got away with the perfect murder, was sentenced to life imprisonment. Released after ten years in England, he disappeared into private life.

HOME TO JAIL . . . Emmett-Dunne, now convicted and stripped of his military stripes, is brought ashore in England. He was lucky to have escaped execution.

A Hypochondriac Husband

Mrs. Maybrick

JAMES MAYBRICK was a strange man. He had a hypochondriac's passion for the strongest medicines and liked to take a little arsenic with his breakfast. But why did his wife buy arsenic too — enough to kill fifty people . . . ?

Radio Times Hulton and Mary Evans/Quartet

SHREWD only in appearance, James Maybrick was neither a wholly successful businessman nor a sensible family man. The mansion he lived in with Florence (above) was far beyond his means. But he hardly deserved to be murdered . . . !

FLORENCE MAYBRICK perfectly fitted the role of the ambitious businessman's ideal wife: attractive, vivacious, an excellent hostess, subtly skilled at choosing breathtaking gowns that matched her shining violet eyes and emphasized her well-rounded figure. Moreover, the American-born beauty was 23 years younger than her English husband and that, in itself, made James Maybrick the envy of many men in the Liverpool "society" in which the couple lived and entertained. For the fact that this plain cotton broker had, at the age of 42, been able to captivate and marry this desirable creature in her 18th year spoke well of his virile masculinity.

That was how it seemed to friends and neighbours receiving the Maybricks in their gaslit Victorian drawing rooms, or visiting the couple's 20-room, heavily furnished Battlecrease House in the Liverpool suburb of Aigburth, four and a half miles from the city centre. Clearly, not only had James Maybrick married well, but he was a self-possessed, impeccably mannered, shrewdly successful man. In every way, it seemed, he was the head-of-the-family who so precisely fitted the British middle class image.

Hysterical type

In fact, with the guests gone and the gas mantles turned low, James Maybrick presented a very different spectacle. In the first place, he was by no means a supremely successful businessman. Battlecrease House, with its five servants and that ultra-modern adornment, a flush toilet, was the regulation outward show of opulence. But he could not properly afford it, and clung to it only by restricting Florence to a £7-a-week allowance on which to cope with all the food and domestic bills, including the servants' wages.

In the second place, he secretly maintained a mistress, as Florence had discovered after the birth of their second child. And, most crucial of all, he was a hypochondriac of an acutely hysterical type. Hypochondria was not uncommon in the 19th century when virulent diseases were all around, and even childbirth was a notoriously hazardous event. Maybrick, however, suffered the condition to the point of severe psychological disturbance. Not only did he go in dread of every ailment, but he settled all hopes on one last-ditch remedy: arsenic.

Strong medicine

Maybrick was an eccentric among eccentrics, an arsenic addict. The habit had started in 1877 when he was on a cotton-buying visit to Norfolk, Virginia, and went down with a bad dose of malaria. A doctor treated him with arsenic and strychnine; when he recovered he continued to take both drugs, especially a daily dose of arsenic.

By the time Florence entered his life he was "topping up" the arsenic with every kind of patent medicine he could find. An American friend, who knew of his hypochondria, remarked: "Maybrick's got a dozen drug stores in his stomach!" But astonishingly, apart from a somewhat florid complexion, there was little outward sign of his regular "treatment". When Florence Elizabeth Chandler, from Mobile, Alabama, met him on board the White Star liner *Baltic*, while sailing for a tour of Europe in March 1880, she fell in love with him at once.

Maybrick and Florence were married at St. James's, Piccadilly, in London, on July 27, 1881, and spent the next three years living for half of each year in Liverpool and the other half, during the cotton season, in Virginia. In 1884 they settled permanently in Liverpool, moving finally to Battlecrease House in 1888. Their son, James Chandler, was born in 1882 and their daughter, Gladys Evelyn, in 1886.

Strangely, for a wife, it took Florence longer to realize the extent of Maybrick's hypochondria than to discover that he kept a mistress. It was not until the summer of 1888 that she told his doctor: "James is taking some very strong medicine which has had a bad influence on him." She also informed her own doctor, Dr. Richard Humphreys, that her husband was taking a "white powder". Humphreys frowned and replied: "Well, if he should ever die suddenly, call me and I can say that you had some conversation with me about it."

By this time, through a combination of Maybrick's mistress, his drug-taking, and shaky business affairs, the enviable marriage had begun to go sour. A fateful moment in Florence's life occurred when a handsome young bachelor, named Alfred Brierley, turned up as a guest at a Battlecrease House dance. At six feet he was

FRIENDS would cast envious glances at James Maybrick's pretty, young wife, little suspecting that her apparently youthful innocence concealed a mind capable of hatching a plot to poison her husband. Only his own eccentricity with strong medicines saved her from the hangman. No one could be quite sure that she gave the fatal dose.

Radio Times Hulton/Quartet

127

nearly three inches taller than James. He was also 15 years his junior, and where James made do with a rather mousy, drooping moustache, Brierley sported an eye-catching pointed beard.

Florence was infatuated, Brierley rather more hesitant. The strong-willed Florence, however, had no intention of waiting upon hesitancy and on March 22, 1889, she took action which, in the end, would help place her on the path to disaster. She sent a telegram to the manager of Flatman's Hotel, Henrietta Street, London, reserving a two-room suite in the name of "Mr. and Mrs. Thomas Maybrick, of Manchester".

Of all the extravagant things that Florence Maybrick ever did, this remains one of the most reckless and inexplicable. For not only had she used her married name, but she had chosen a central hotel (perhaps because it was the only one she knew in London) frequently used by Liverpool cotton men on their trips to the capital.

Furious row

She told her husband the unlikely-sounding story that she was going to visit a sick aunt, met Brierley at the hotel in Covent Garden, and spent two nights with him. It was not a wholly satisfactory escapade. For later Florence disclosed: "Before we parted he gave me to understand that he cared for somebody else and could not marry me and that rather than face the disgrace of discovery he would blow his brains out. I then had such a revulsion of feeling I said we must end our intimacy at once."

Maybrick either heard about the affair or suspected it, for, a few days later, after their return home from the Grand National at Aintree race course near Liverpool, there was a furious row between James and Florence, overheard by the children's nanny, Alice Yapp. He had observed Florence talking to her lover at the race track and felt publicly humiliated. "This scandal will be all over town tomorrow," he shouted, tearing her dress and blacking her eye. For a week tension between them remained high. Gradually it eased and the normal domestic state of disquiet was resumed.

Flypapers

Towards the end of April, Florence—at odds with both her husband and her lover—went to a local chemist's and bought a dozen flypapers. Two days later she bought two dozen more at another shop. One of the housemaids, tidying Florence's bedroom, saw the papers soaking in a basin of water and subsequently Florence explained that the resulting solution formed a kind of face lotion she had often used back home in the States. All the flypapers had one thing in common: they contained arsenic.

Radio Times Hulton

On the morning of Saturday, April 27, James complained of feeling ill. He experienced a numbness in his limbs and vomiting but, all the same, he insisted on keeping an appointment at the Wirral races in Cheshire. There he was caught in a heavy rainstorm and returned home apparently suffering from a severe chill. The following day he was worse and Dr. Humphreys diagnosed chronic dyspepsia, a much-favoured Victorian description for a wide range of baffling disorders. Again Florence mentioned the mysterious "white powder", but when the doctor put that to Maybrick he made the untrue and rather odd reply: "I can't stand strychnine or nux vomica at all."

Common remedy

On April 29 he seemed much better and Florence left him resting comfortably in bed while she went out—to buy two dozen more flypapers. The next day he was well enough to return to his office. The day after that, however, he again felt unwell, shortly after eating a meal prepared for him by Florence from a patent food called Du Barry's Revaleta Arabica. The jug containing the meal was later found to contain traces of arsenic.

Over the next few days the returned illness rose and fell in intensity. Dr. Humphreys, still working on the dyspepsia theory, prescribed a commonly used remedy comprising a mixture of white arsenic and carbonate of potash. James Maybrick's condition, which was now mainly one of constant vomiting, showed no improvement.

Lucrative career

Meanwhile, Florence and Brierley, despite their "parting" after the hotel affair, had begun writing to each other. On May 8, as Maybrick's illness significantly worsened, she wrote addressing him as "Dearest" and including a sentence that was to have dire consequences for her: "Since my return I have been nursing M day and night. *He is sick unto death.*" The letter, openly addressed to "A. Brierley", care of a local post office, was given to Alice Yapp to deliver. It was never received. Miss Yapp, already involved in servants' gossip about the "meaning" of the flypapers soaked in the basin, opened the letter, read it, and handed it to Edwin Maybrick, James's brother. Edwin immediately telegraphed

THE TRIAL took place in St. George's Hall, Liverpool (top) on July 31, 1889. Sir Charles Russell (left) appeared for the defence but was able to do very little against the damning evidence produced by the prosecution. Most damning of all was the letter (far left) that Florence wrote to her lover, anticipating her husband's death.

another brother, Michael, to come at once from London.

Michael Maybrick was a forceful personality who had "got on" in life and made a highly lucrative career as a singer and a composer (under the name of Stephen Adams) of such Victorian hymns as *The Holy City* and *Star of Bethlehem*. Now, as soon as he arrived at Battlecrease House, he learned of the below-stairs tittle-tattle that centred around Florence. Passing these rumours on to Dr. William Carter, a specialist who had taken over the case, he said rhetorically: "God forbid that I should unjustly suspect anyone. But do you not think, if I have serious grounds for fearing that all may not be right, that it is my duty to say so to you?"

From then on the whole household, brothers, doctor, and servants, formed their own unofficial vigilantes' committee and watched Florence's every move, ensuring that she did not personally attend on the patient. He, apart from occasional bouts of delirium, said little except on one occasion to cry out: "There are some strange things knocking about this house!"

May 10 was a day filled with curious incidents. In the morning Michael Maybrick thought he saw Florence pouring medicine from one bottle into another and demanded: "Florrie, how dare you tamper with the medicine!" Later Florence urged James to take some other mixture his nurse had prepared for him and he replied: "You have given me the wrong medicine again." Soothingly, Florence chided him. "What are you talking about?" she said. "You have never had any wrong medicine." That same evening another nurse heard Maybrick's stricken voice complain ambiguously to his wife: "Bunny, how could you do it? I didn't think it of you." Florence answered: "You silly old darling, don't trouble your head about things."

Ebbing away

By the morning of May 11 it was clear that Maybrick's life was ebbing swiftly away. Florence dashed off a despairing letter to Dr. Hopper, James's personal doctor: "My misery is great and my position such a painful one that when I tell you that both my brothers-in-law are here and have taken the nursing of Jim and management of my home completely out of my hands, you will understand how powerless I am to assert myself. I am in great need of a friend. . . . Because I have sinned once must I be misjudged always?"

Soon after completing that letter she fell into a coma, apparently brought on by nervous exhaustion, from which she did not recover for 24 hours. While she lay unconscious a bizarre scenario was

acted out in Battlecrease House: James Maybrick died (at 8.30 on the evening of May 11), his brothers searched their sister-in-law's rooms and found a parcel labelled "Arsenic: Poison for cats", and letters from Brierley. Throughout the house, indeed, they uncovered enough arsenic (on the basis of two grains as a decidedly fatal dose) to have killed 50 people.

Full majesty

For two days Florence Maybrick was kept by her brothers-in-law a virtual prisoner in her own home. No one spoke to her and on Michael Maybrick's orders her children were sent away from the house without being allowed to see her. On the morning of the third day the tramp of feet was heard on the stairs and a posse of policemen, led by Superintendent Isaac Bryning, of the Lancashire County Police, pushed into the bedroom where she lay. Summoning the full majesty of his office, the superintendent gravely intoned:

"Mrs. Maybrick, I am about to say something to you. After I have said what I intend to say, if you reply be careful how you reply because whatever you say may be used in evidence against you. Mrs. Maybrick, you are in custody on suspicion of causing the death of your late husband, James Maybrick, on the 11th instant."

She made no reply and policemen

guarded her bedside until, within a few days, she was moved to the hospital at Liverpool's Walton Jail. A post-mortem disclosed half a grain of arsenic in Maybrick's body—enough to be a fatal dose if taken at one time. Another half grain was found in a bottle of meat juice which a nurse had prepared, but which Florence had taken away from her into another room for a few minutes. None of the juice, however, had been given to James Maybrick.

As soon as the facts emerged after his death there was no doubt about the dominance of arsenic in Maybrick's life. He had been buying an arsenic-based tonic from a Liverpool chemist regularly for at least 18 months, and had increased the dosage until he was taking the equivalent of one-third of a grain of white arsenic every day. He had even admitted to Sir James Poole, a former Lord Mayor of Liverpool, that he habitually took "poisonous medicines". Sir James had warned him: "The more you take of these things the more you require and you will go on until they carry you off."

For all that, Florence Maybrick's trial for murder opened in St. George's Hall, Liverpool, on July 31, 1889, with Sir Charles Russell, Q.C., M.P. (later to be

BLACK-ROBED and looking repentant, Florence Maybrick is pictured standing in the dock in a contemporary print. But her mourning failed to impress the jury.

Radio Times Hulton

TENSE and expectant, a large audience listens to the evidence given at the Coroner's inquest on the death of James Maybrick. It soon became obvious that he had died of arsenic poisoning. But who had administered it? In retrospect it seems almost certain that Florence was responsible, that she not only attempted to kill him but actually succeeded. At the time, however, public opinion, as much as anything, saved her from death. The case evoked enormous interest in the U.S. where there were appeals for mercy, and misgivings about British justice.

Mary Evans

Lord Russell, Lord Chief Justice of England) leading for the defence. The evidence given against her appeared to be damning, and on August 7, after an absence of only 38 minutes, the jury found her guilty and she was sentenced to death.

The verdict, however, caused concern in Britain and the United States. The London *Times* wrote: "It is useless to disguise the fact that the public are not thoroughly convinced of the prisoner's guilt." But even if she had not actually killed her husband she was a "wicked woman" in many eyes, including those of Queen Victoria, who disapproved of any woman who, for whatever reason, was unfaithful to her husband. There was a strong body of opinion which, while it did not wish to see her hanged, thought she should not go free.

Bread and gruel

Petitions against the hanging poured into the Home Office. At 1.30 a.m. on August 23, three days before the execution date, a messenger arrived at Walton Jail bearing an order from Henry Matthews, the Home Secretary, commuting the sentence to life imprisonment. The terms of the order did not relieve the worries in some legal minds. For it said

that although the evidence led "clearly to the conclusion" that Florence *attempted* to murder her husband with arsenic, it left a reasonable doubt as to whether he actually died from arsenical poisoning. In other words, Florence Maybrick was to serve "life" on a charge (of attempted murder) for which she had neither been tried nor convicted.

In the event she served just on 15 years, first at Woking Prison in Surrey, and then at Aylesbury, in Buckinghamshire. She was given the number "L.P. 29" —"L" for life, "P" the code letter for the year of her conviction, and 29 as the 29th prisoner to be sentenced that year.

Such were the conditions of the time that, like all new prisoners, she spent the first nine months in solitary confinement, locked in her cell and required to make at least five men's shirts a week or lose the privileges of letters and visitors. In that time she was forbidden to talk to other prisoners during the one-hour exercise period a day, or to prison guards unless spoken to. Her main diet was bread and gruel and her cell measured seven feet by four feet and contained no bed, chair, or table, but only a hammock and three shelves. Her once-dazzling gowns she exchanged for an anonymous brown dress, marked with broad arrows, and a

red star to show her first-offender classification.

Prominent United States citizens, including President Grover Cleveland and later President William McKinley, appealed to the British authorities for mercy. Even after he became Lord Chief Justice, Lord Russell continued to urge her release, but the pressures were all to no avail. Lord Russell died. Mr. Justice Stephen, who presided at her trial, died. Finally, in 1901, Queen Victoria, who had personally opposed Mrs. Maybrick's release, also died and was succeeded by King Edward VII. Only then would the authorities at last offer the wretched woman a glimmer of hope. She would be released, they said, in three years' time.

Bitter endurance

So, at 6.45 a.m. on January 25, 1904, Florence Maybrick regained her freedom. The once vivacious girl from Alabama was now 41, and bitter endurance clouded the eyes that long ago had set James's pulse racing. With an escort provided by the American ambassador she crossed on the Channel ferry from Southampton to Le Havre in France. From there she went on by train to Rouen, where she was at long last reunited with her aged mother.

Soon afterwards, leaving her mother who was too ill to travel, she sailed from Antwerp to New York in the Red Star liner *Vaderland*—travelling under the assumed name of Rose Ingraham. She had not seen her native country for more than 20 years and the changes, the new buildings in New York, and the bustle of big city life made her feel as though she had stepped into another world. Although she had lost her nationality when she married, the Department of Immigration ruled that she was to be regarded as an American citizen with full citizenship rights.

For a while she was a celebrity, giving newspaper interviews and lectures and writing a book entitled *My Fifteen Lost Years*. The book added little to what was already known about the case. It made no mention of the hotel incident with Brierley, but referred to her husband's infidelities (which, she said, had brought her to the point of seeking advice on a divorce). It also explained her letter's "sick unto death" phrase, of which much use was made at the trial, as a common Southern United States expression for anyone who was seriously ill.

After a while she disappeared from the headlines, and in 1917, aged 55 and reverting to her maiden name of Florence Chandler, settled down in a small house on the outskirts of the village of South Kent, Connecticut. Eventually, some people in the village discovered her true identity but, with a compassion not shown to her by many in her long years of suffering, they kept the information to themselves. They let her dwell as peacefully as she could, surrounded by dozens of cats—her only companions.

She lived on, lonely and forgotten, until she drifted into her final years in a state of personal neglect and squalor. On October 23, 1941, at the age of 76—and 52 years after her husband—Florence Maybrick died and was buried in her adopted village. A wooden cross bearing only her initials, F.E.C.M. (Florence Elizabeth Chandler Maybrick), marks her last resting place.

SENSATION and controversy surrounded the Maybrick case and continued until her death in 1941 at the age of seventy-six. The newspapers were just as interested then as during the trial. The picture (below) shows the young Florence as she appeared to the Victorian public.

Mrs. Maybrick Dies at 76—Her Secret Is Revealed
SAVED FROM GALLOWS: TRIAL STIRRED WORLD

Mrs. Florence Maybrick, whose trial and death sentence for the murder of her husband at Liverpool in 1889 stirred the world, has been found dead in a wooden shack, her home in South Kent, Connecticut. She was 76.

In July, 1889, Florence Maybrick, beautiful 24-year-old American wife of James Maybrick, a Liverpool cotton merchant, was found guilty of murdering her husband with arsenic.

A wife paid for a murder never committed

John Frost/Quartet

Radio Times Hulton/Quartet

WHEN it became known in the spring of 1886 that Adelaide Bartlett was to be tried at London's Old Bailey for poisoning her husband with fatal results—and that her clergyman friend, the Rev. George Dyson, would take his place beside her in the dock as an accessory to the crime—public interest was intense. So many spectators were expected to attend the trial that accommodation had to be specially provided for them in the shape of a stand which was constructed near the dock and blocked up one of the entrances to the court.

In addition to the public gallery, the stand was packed to capacity, mostly by women, who had come to see the pretty French widow on trial for her life, together with the Wesleyan minister whom many people believed to be her lover.

Immense trouble

The trial opened on April 12, 1886, before Mr. Justice Wills, a leading authority on the law of evidence and also a well-known mountaineer, who was later to try Oscar Wilde on homosexual charges and to sentence him to two years' imprisonment with hard labour. It has always been a rule in English poison trials that a Law Officer should appear for the Crown, and in this case the prosecution was led by Attorney-General Sir Charles Russell, a hard-hitting Irishman.

As her leading defence counsel, Mrs. Bartlett had secured the services of Sir Edward Clarke, the most brilliant and sought after lawyer of his day, who was known to take immense trouble with the preparation of his cases. In this instance he had put aside all other work and had spent ten days in the British Museum reading up everything he could discover about the properties and uses of chloroform—the substance which his client was alleged to have administered to the late Mr. Edwin Bartlett.

The Rev. George Dyson was defended by another leading lawyer, Sir Frank Lockwood, who as Solicitor-General was to prosecute in the second Oscar Wilde trial. But Lockwood had little to do for the Rev. Dyson apart from making an application to the court that his client should be tried separately. However, this turned out to be unnecessary, since at the outset the Attorney-General intimated that the prosecution intended to offer no evidence against Dyson and he was formally acquitted by the jury.

In these circumstances it was obvious that the prosecution intended to call him as a witness. While this was expected to strengthen the prosecution's case against Adelaide Bartlett, it was also expected

Murder by Chloroform

Adelaide Bartlett

She was a woman of flashing eyes and passionate temperament. Was she also a skilful poisoner . . . ?

MEN succumbed easily to her beauty. Was the Rev. Dyson also under her powerful spell?

Radio Times Hulton/Mary Evans

to help the defence, since it meant that the minister could be cross-examined on any statements he had made—which would not have been possible had he remained in the dock.

At that time prisoners were not permitted to give evidence in their own defence, and this meant that neither could Mrs. Bartlett testify. Many people thought that this put defendants in criminal trials at a great disadvantage. But when they were eventually able to do so a dozen years later the privilege was to prove a two-edged sword, since if they chose to go into the witness-box they were liable to be cross-examined—sometimes with disastrous results for themselves.

The events leading up to the death of Edwin Bartlett, which Sir Charles Russell outlined in his opening speech to the jury, were full of a dramatic interest which was to be sustained throughout the trial. The prisoner, who was dressed in black as if she was still in mourning for her husband, had been born Adelaide Blanche de la Tremoille in Orleans, and was 30 years old. She was said to be the natural daughter of an Englishman of good social position. Nothing was known of her mother whose name she presumably took, and very little of her early life apart from the fact that she was brought to England as a child.

In 1875 she was living in Kingston-on-Thames, and in the same house there lodged a man named Frederick Bartlett. The latter introduced her to his brother Edwin, who was a grocer. A few weeks later Edwin and Adelaide were married, being encouraged to do so by Adelaide's father, who put up a substantial sum of money in the way of dowry. This enabled Edwin Bartlett to extend his business, so that eventually he owned six shops in the neighbourhood of Brixton and Dulwich in South London.

Domestic unpleasantness

Although Adelaide was 19 at the time of her marriage, her husband—who was some ten years older—considered that her education was incomplete. He therefore sent her to school in Stoke Newington and later to a convent in Belgium, and she would spend the holidays with him in London. In 1887, her schooling being finished, the couple went to live in nearby Herne Hill, where they were joined by the husband's father who had recently become a widower; he was a carpenter and builder also called Edwin.

Shortly afterwards there was some domestic unpleasantness caused by the elder Bartlett accusing Adelaide of having had "intimate relations" with his other son, Fred. The upshot was that he was forced to withdraw his statement and make a written apology. Adelaide never forgot nor forgave the incident.

Her marital relations appear to have been somewhat unusual. According to her, she was induced to enter into a compact with her husband, in consequence of "certain peculiar views" held by him, that their relations "should be of an entirely platonic nature". Apparently the husband held that a man should have two wives—one for intellectual companionship and the other, as he put it, "for service". Adelaide fulfilled the former role, and the arrangement was adhered to, she afterwards told her doctor, except on one occasion which was due to her desire for motherhood.

Handsome pastor

In 1881 she gave birth to a stillborn child, and so severe was her suffering that she resolved to have no more children. Generally, she lived on affectionate terms with her husband, apart from the conditions of the marriage compact which she said distressed her at first. On the other hand, her husband purported to admire her physically and liked to show her off to his male acquaintances, whose attentions to her he apparently enjoyed.

Two years later, they went to live at Merton, near Wimbledon, and it was as the result of attending the local Wesleyan chapel that they met the minister, George Dyson—a handsome and attractive pastor who had recently graduated from Trinity College, Dublin. They became friends and it was not long before the three of them were on Christian name terms.

"Would that I could find words to express my thankfulness to you for the very loving letter you sent Adelaide today," wrote Edwin to George in a letter which was subsequently quoted in court. "It would have done anybody good to see her overflowing with joy as she read it whilst walking along the street, and afterwards as she read it to me. I felt my heart going out to you. I long to tell you how proud I felt at the thought I should soon be able to clasp the hand of the man who from his heart could pen such noble thoughts."

Edwin Bartlett suggested that his wife's education should be continued under the minister's tuition, and this the Rev. Dyson was only too glad to do, spending hours with Adelaide when her husband was at business. When the Bartletts moved to Pimlico, in London, so assured was the reverend visitor's position that an old coat and slippers were kept in the living-

CROWN COUNSEL was Sir Charles Russell, a skilled cross-examiner in court.

Mary Evans

room for him. Indeed the maid became accustomed to seeing them side by side on the sofa, and once she found Adelaide sitting on the floor with her head resting on George's knee.

George visited her when she and her husband spent a long summer holiday in Dover, and since the minister's stipend did not amount to more than £100 a year, Edwin Bartlett sent him a first-class ticket. Eventually, he told the minister that he was making a new will leaving everything unconditionally to his wife, and asked him to be the executor,

to which Dyson agreed with apparent reluctance. He told Bartlett that there was no denying the fact that he was "growing very attached" to Adelaide, and asked him whether it would not be better to discontinue his friendship with them.

Thrown together

"Why should you discontinue it?" asked Edwin, adding that he "hoped they should have some pleasant intercourse", and to facilitate this presented him with a season ticket so that he could come into London regularly. The Rev. Dyson would now kiss Adelaide openly in her husband's presence, walk out with her, and even entertain her in his bachelor quarters.

"My husband threw us together," she said afterwards. "He requested us, in his presence, to kiss, and he seemed to enjoy it. He had given me to Mr. Dyson."

On their return to London in October 1885, the Bartletts went to live in fur-

nished apartments at 38 Clapperton Street, Pimlico, where they occupied a living-room and bedroom, which communicated with folding doors. Edwin Bartlett was a strong healthy man, and three years

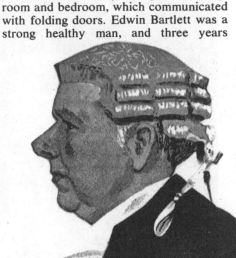

—Mary Evans

DEFENCE TEAM was composed of Frank Lockwood (right) for Dyson and the great Sir Edward George Clarke, whose brilliant performance saved Adelaide from hanging.

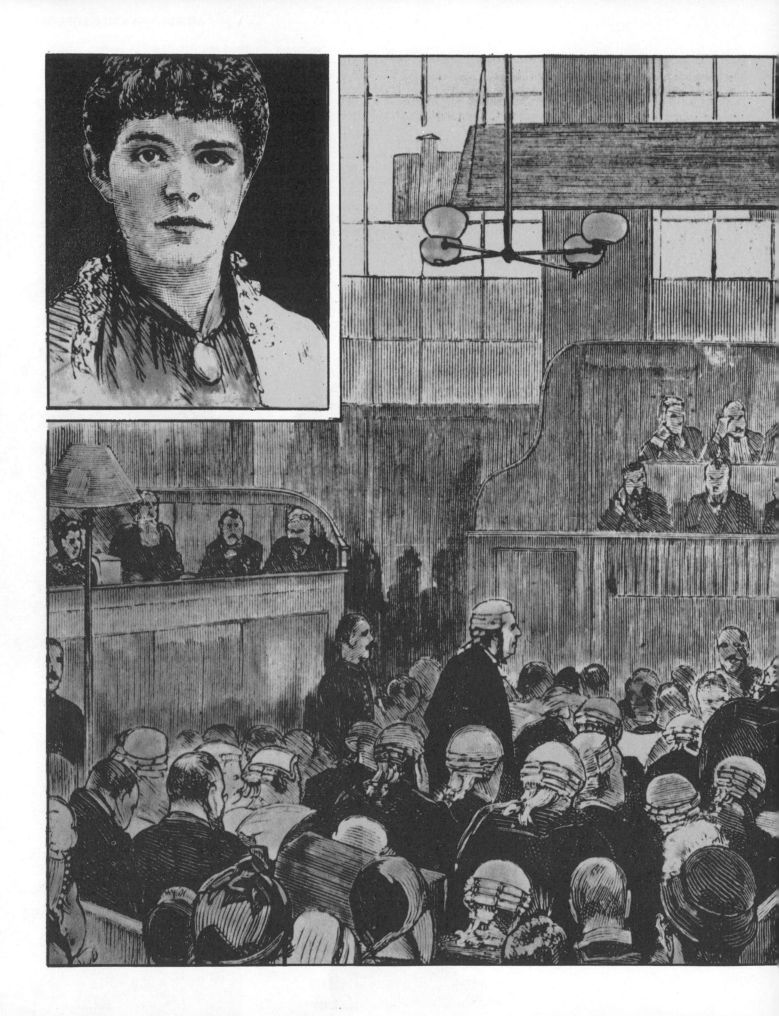

previously he had been accepted by an insurance company as a first-class life — although Adelaide told George Dyson that for some years he had suffered from a painful internal complaint for which she had nursed and doctored him with chloroform to soothe his pain. His teeth also gave him trouble owing to their decayed condition, and he had a number of extractions done at this time.

On December 10, a local doctor, Alfred Leach, who had not previously attended him, was called in and found him suffering from indigestion and also mercury poisoning — which the patient attributed to his having taken a pill of unknown strength and constituents. Dr. Leach also found his teeth in a bad state and diagnosed that he had necrosis of the jaw. Meanwhile, Adelaide continued to nurse her husband with conspicuous devotion, sitting up with him night after night. On being advised by the doctor to get some

Mary Evans

CROWDED COURTROOM . . . The trial was the subject of passionate interest if only for one reason: everyone had heard that the defendant was a great beauty!

rest, she replied, "What is the use? He will not sleep unless I hold his toe."

Adelaide then suggested calling in another opinion, stating that her husband's friends would accuse her of "poisoning" him if he did not get better soon. So a Dr. Dudley was summoned. But apart from the patient's depression, sleeplessness, and the condition of his gums, he did not consider that anything was radically wrong with him. Dr. Dudley consequently told him he should get up and go out every day. Dr. Leach gave him some purgatives, and finding his health better took him out for a drive.

During his illness he was visited by his father and also by George Dyson, who at Mrs. Bartlett's request got her some chloroform. Edwin rapidly improved and on New Year's Eve was well enough to go to the dentist and have another tooth extracted.

Whatever may have been wrong with Edwin Bartlett, he had an excellent appetite. On New Year's Eve he had oysters for lunch, and dined off jugged hare—which he said he enjoyed so much that he could eat three a day. For supper he had more oysters, bread and butter, and cake, and ordered a large haddock for breakfast next morning. After supper the maid made up the fire, and Mrs. Bartlett told her not to go into the room again but to bring some beef tea and leave it outside the door.

Strange chance

At four o'clock in the morning, the landlord, Frederick Doggett, was awakened by Mrs. Bartlett. "Come down," she cried. "I think Mr. Bartlett is dead!" Mr. Doggett, who by a strange chance was Registrar of Deaths for the district, found his lodger lying on his back in bed. He was perfectly cold and must have been dead for two or three hours.

"I had fallen asleep with my hand round his foot," explained Mrs. Bartlett. "I awoke with a pain in my arm, and found him lying on his face. I put him in the position in which you see him, and tried to pour brandy down his throat—nearly half a pint."

When Mr. Doggett entered the room, he detected a strong smell of anaesthetic, and saw on the mantelpiece a wineglass three-quarters full of what smelt like brandy with ether in it. But according to him—and also to Dr. Leach, who arrived shortly afterwards—there was no bottle of chloroform on the mantelpiece. Dr. Leach asked her if her husband could have taken poison. "Oh no," was the reply, "he could have got no poison without my knowledge."

She was told there would have to be a post-mortem on the body and an inquest. She was also told that the rooms must be sealed pending investigation by the authorities, and that she must leave the house. Accordingly, she went to stay with friends in Dulwich, being taken there by George Dyson who had called at the house on the following morning. On the way he asked her whether she had used the chloroform he had procured for her. "I have not used it," she replied. "I have not had occasion to use it. The bottle is there just as you gave it to me."

Fresh bottle

According to her, the bottle remained on the mantelpiece from the time of her husband's death until next morning—when she removed it and put it in a drawer in the bedroom. She added that it was still there when she returned to the house on January 6. She then took it away and threw it out of the window of a train in which she was travelling between London and Peckham Rye.

Meanwhile, the post-mortem examination revealed that Edwin Bartlett's stomach contained over 11 grains of chloroform, "almost as strong as a freshly opened bottle," said the pathologist. At the adjourned inquest which followed, the coroner's jury returned a verdict to the effect that Edwin Bartlett had died from chloroform administered by his wife for the purpose of taking his life, and that the Rev. George Dyson was an accessory before the fact.

There could be no doubt that Bartlett's death was due to the chloroform discovered in his stomach. The question posed by the Attorney-General was, how did it get there? He dismissed any suggestion of suicide or accident. It was clear, Sir Charles told the court, that the deceased was first partially chloroformed and then—when he was semi-conscious—liquid chloroform was poured down his throat.

Peculiar ideas

The first prosecution witness to enter the box was Edwin Bartlett, Senior. He related how he called on his son during his illness, and how he said he was better and hoped soon to be at business again. He also repeated what his daughter-in-law had told him about Edwin's death. "He died with my arm round his foot; he always liked to have my hand on his foot."

Asked by Clarke in cross-examination whether he disapproved of his son's marriage, the witness admitted that he "certainly did not much approve of it". Questioned about the letter of apology he had signed, he stated that he knew it to be false, but he had signed it at his son's request "because it would make peace with him and his wife if I did". Asked in re-examination to elaborate on the charge he had made against Adelaide, the elder Bartlett said that she had run away and been absent for a week or more, during which time he and Edwin were sure that she had gone off with the other son Fred—who had since departed for the United States.

After the landlord and his wife, and several other minor witnesses, had briefly testified, the Rev. George Dyson was called. He was in clerical dress and had closely trimmed whiskers and a heavy black moustache. He described how the prisoner had asked him to get her some chloroform for external use on her husband, which she said she sprinkled on a handkerchief to soothe him. He purchased several small amounts in four separate bottles, telling the chemist in each case that it was required to remove grease stains.

On returning home, he poured the contents of the four bottles into one large bottle to which he transferred the poison label. The next day he gave it to Mrs. Bartlett "whilst out for a stroll on the Embankment". He accompanied her back to her lodgings in Clapperton Street, where she saw her husband who was up and dressed and "seemed brightened" by the fact that he had been for a drive.

Skilful cross-examination

Sir Edward Clarke cross-examined with masterly skill, his questions being purposely friendly and sympathetic. He realized that the more he could associate the minister's actions with those of his client in the dock, the more he would be able to strengthen the instinctive reluctance of the jury to send her—and her alone—to the gallows.

The Rev. Dyson first confirmed that he had met Mrs. Bartlett on January 9 at the house of a Mr. and Mrs. Mathews, the friends with whom she had gone to stay in Dulwich.

"On that day you spoke to her about the chloroform?"

"Yes."

"And she was indignant?"

"Very indignant."

"And she said, why didn't you charge her outright with having given chloroform to her husband?"

The witness agreed that she had used words to that effect, and that it was from her lips that he first heard the suggestion. The minister added that he had not spoken to her since that day.

"Was there any secret between you, or any secret understanding between you, apart from her husband?"

"None," answered the witness emphatically.

"Was there any impropriety between you and Mrs. Bartlett?"

"There was not," said Dyson. However, he added that he had kissed her.

"That would be an impropriety—you do not defend that?"

"No."

"You mean to say," the judge interrupted, "it was only in her husband's presence."

"And out of his presence," the minister admitted after a slightly embarrassed pause.

"You became aware," Clarke continued, "at a very early period in your acquaintance that Mr. Bartlett had peculiar ideas on the subject of marriage?"

Two wives?

Dyson agreed that this was so, and that Mr. Bartlett had suggested there might be one wife for companionship and another wife for service.

"Were both of them to be bedfellows?" the judge again broke in.

"He never mentioned that to me, my lord."

"I want to know," said Mr. Justice Wills, "why you went to three different shops to buy the chloroform?"

"Because I did not get as much as I wanted at one shop."

SEX BOOK . . . The judge made much of the supposed "immorality" of the accused woman and her husband who read books such as the one pictured here. Rather less attention was paid to the chloroform bottle which Adelaide had thrown away!

Quartet

This answer did not satisfy the judge. "Why did you not say to the first man, 'You have given me a little bottle – I want four or five times this quantity'?"

"Because I thought he would want to know what I wanted it for, and I did not wish to enter into a long explanation."

"Why not?" snapped the judge.

"Because I thought he would not understand that Mrs. Bartlett was skilled in the use of medicines."

"Why did you say it was for taking grease spots out of clothes?"

"He asked me what I wanted it for," replied the minister. "I do not defend that, my lord. It was simply that I wanted to avoid an explanation. That was the only idea in my mind."

Mrs. Alice Mathews confirmed what passed at the meeting between Mrs. Bartlett and George Dyson at her house, when Adelaide had been indignant at the clergyman's suggestion that it might be proved that she had given Edwin chloroform. George Mathews, her husband, who followed her, was asked in cross-examination about a certain book which he said Mrs. Bartlett had lent him. It was written by Dr. T. L. Nichols and was entitled *Esoteric Anthropology: The Mysteries of Man.*

It dealt with the physical relations between the sexes and particularly their regulation by birth control. Abstinence was recommended; but various methods of contraception were described. The

ESOTERIC

ANTHROPOLOGY

(THE MYSTERIES OF MAN):

A COMPREHENSIVE AND CONFIDENTIAL TREATISE ON THE STRUCTURE, FUNCTIONS, PASSIONAL ATTRACTIONS, AND PERVERSIONS, TRUE AND FALSE PHYSICAL AND SOCIAL CONDITIONS, AND THE MOST INTIMATE RELATIONS OF MEN AND WOMEN.

ANATOMICAL, PHYSIOLOGICAL, PATHOLOGICAL, THERAPEUTICAL, AND OBSTETRICAL;

HYGIENIC AND HYDROPATHIC.

From the American Stereotype Edition, Revised and Rewritten.

By T. L. NICHOLS, M.D., F.A.S.,

Principal of the American Hydropathic Institute; Author of "Human Physiology the Basis of Sanitary and Social Science."

MALVERN:
PUBLISHED BY T. L. NICHOLS.

witness said that he had not read the book, which had been returned to Mrs. Bartlett by his wife.

However, another witness said she had done so. This was a trained nurse and midwife, Annie Walker, who had attended Mrs. Bartlett during her confinement. She had been recommended to Adelaide by the author's wife Mrs. Nichols, who helped her husband in his work and who had been consulted by Mrs. Bartlett.

"When I visited her after her confinement," said Nurse Walker, "I saw Mr. Bartlett. As far as I could judge, they were living together as man and wife, and they were on affectionate terms together."

Cross-examined by Sir Edward Clarke, Nurse Walker said that she had not used chloroform at the confinement; so far as she knew Mrs. Bartlett had no knowledge of it and its uses.

"You have looked through this book?" Clarke went on, holding up a copy of *Esoteric Anthropology*.

"I have."

"There is nothing immoral or indecent in this book, is there?"

"Not anything." The witness said that the Bartletts had made no attempt to conceal the book, and it lay about their place quite openly.

Dr. Alfred Leach confirmed his professional visits to the late Edwin Bartlett, the treatment he prescribed, and the patient's symptoms after death. He also related the details of his conversation with Mrs. Bartlett, when she had told him of the marriage compact with her husband. The doctor was not a very satisfactory witness, as he was inclined to qualify his answers by self-conscious personal explanations. But if there was one thing that Dr. Leach was clear about—the judge afterwards reminded the jury—it was that when he first saw his patient lying dead there was no bottle of chloroform upon the mantelpiece.

An officer in the Metropolitan Police, who was employed by the coroner, described how he had searched the rooms in Clapperton Street when they had been unsealed. His most interesting discovery turned out to be one of Edwin Bartlett's suits of clothes, in the right-hand trousers pocket of which he found "four or five of what are popularly called French letters".

Medical evidence

The prosecution called two expert medical witnesses, and one of them agreed in cross-examination that there was no recorded case of murder by liquid chloroform. One doctor tried the experiment on six patients and all resisted. The other succeeded only with children, and not with sleeping adults—who all woke up at once. Both agreed that the liquid

would enter the windpipe and cause choking, burning the windpipe and leaving traces. Such traces were not revealed by the post-mortem on Mr. Bartlett.

Finally the prosecution called servants, and others, who testified that the Bartletts habitually occupied the same room. With that the case for the Crown was closed. Sir Edward Clarke rose, and declared that he did not intend to call any evidence for the defence. He then went straight on to address the jury.

His first task was to discredit the prosecution's theory that Mrs. Bartlett had caused her husband's death by forcing chloroform down his throat. If he was conscious, the first attempt must have failed through the patient's resistance. Then, if he became insensible, some of the chloroform must—on the medical evidence—have got into the air passages. But there was no trace of any there. Sir Edward then put forward his theory that Edwin Bartlett had deliberately taken his own life in a fit of depression.

Single act

Later, in his closing speech to the jury, Sir Charles Russell attempted to discount the suicide theory by putting forward an alternative—that the fatal draught might have been handed to the deceased in a glass of brandy and gulped down by him supposing it to be some medicine.

Immediately Clarke was on his feet protesting strongly that this theory had not been advanced before. His protests were supported by the judge, who ruled that it was now too late to bring it up, and directed the jury to pay no attention to Russell's theory.

As soon as Russell sat down, and before the judge began his summing up, Clarke was again on his feet—this time to ask if he could recall Nurse Walker to answer a single question. Apparently the nurse had come to him and volunteered some information. The judge agreed, and Annie Walker again stepped into the witness box.

"At the time you nursed Mrs. Bartlett in her confinement," Clarke asked her, "did you become aware from anything she said to you with regard to its having been the result of a single act?"

"Yes, sir."

The judge leaned forward to ask, "What was it?"

"That it happened only once—on a Sunday afternoon."

"She said so?" the judge persisted.

"Both of them did," replied Nurse Walker. What was more, the witness added, they both said that on other occasions "there was always some preventive used".

"You say you had that from both of them?"

"From both of them," the witness repeated.

Mr. Justice Wills summed up the evidence quite fairly. However, he could not disguise his prejudice against the prisoner, and had some scathing things to say about her and her husband in the context of their sexual relations. First, there were the French letters which were found in the dead man's pocket. "It is an unpleasant subject," said the judge, who plainly disapproved of such articles. "The case is full of unpleasant subjects."

Another such subject was the book *Esoteric Anthropology*, which explained how contraception could be practised, and which the judge stigmatized as "garbage", scattering its poison and doing its mischief under the garb of ostentatious purity.

"And then what becomes of this morbid romance about the non-sexual connection?" asked the judge. "The whole foundation for that baseless illusion is swept away by the one sentence which you heard in the witness-box today," the judge concluded.

Grave suspicion

The jury were out for just over two hours. "Do you find the prisoner, Adelaide Bartlett, guilty or not guilty?" the clerk of the court asked the foreman on his return to the courtroom.

"We have well considered the evidence," the foreman replied, "and although we think grave suspicion is attached to the prisoner, we do not think there is sufficient evidence to show how or by whom the chloroform was administered."

"Then you say that the prisoner is not guilty, gentlemen?"

"Not guilty."

The spectators in court cheered loudly and were soundly rebuked by the judge—who told them their conduct was an outrage, and a court of justice was not to be turned into a theatre by such "indecent exhibitions". Sir Edward Clarke, for the only time in his career, broke down and sobbed in relief. He, too, was cheered when he appeared that night at the Lyceum Theatre to see Sir Henry Irving and Ellen Terry playing in *Faust*.

The future of Adelaide Bartlett and George Dyson is not known for certain. According to one account they eventually married; according to another they never set eyes on each other again. However, one thing is certain, and that is what a distinguished surgeon told the Lord Chief Justice, who passed it on to Clarke with a note of congratulation on his triumph.

"Mrs. Bartlett was no doubt quite properly acquitted," said the surgeon. "But now it is to be hoped that, in the interests of science, she will tell us how she did it!"

The Minister and the Choir Singer

Rev. E. W. Hall and Eleanor Mills

SEX, passion, jealousy and illicit love. These were the ingredients of the horrific murder that rocked highly-moral New Jersey in 1922. The terribly mutilated body of a soprano in the church choir was found beside her preacher lover, under a crab apple tree in a lonely lovers' lane . . .

WHO KILLED the minister and his mistress (left)? The jury cleared his wife (extreme left), her brother William Stevens and cousin Henry Carpender (pictured bottom). Earlier, Charlotte Mills (below) told of letters her mother wrote to the minister . . . letters in which she wrote of "the man who made me smile today" and added: "my heart is his, my life is his . . ."

ONE OF the juiciest scandals in the New York commuter belt reached its climax in a most horrible murder in 1922 for which three persons stood trial four years later in the Court of Oyer and Terminer in Somerville, New Jersey. They were Frances Noel Hall, the widow of one of the two murder victims, and her brothers Henry and William Stevens. The presiding judges at the trial, which opened on November 3, 1926 and lasted a month, were Charles W. Parker, Supreme Court Justice of New Jersey, and Frank L. Cleary, Somerset County Judge. New Jersey State Senator Alexander Simpson acted as special prosecutor, while the chief defence counsel was Robert J. McCarter.

The background to the trial had already received extensive treatment in the press and had aroused enormous public interest, which went far beyond the territorial limits of New Jersey, since it possessed all the features of an exciting movie drama—sex, passion, jealousy, and illicit love between a pastor in a well-to-do rural community and a woman who sang in the choir and was the wife of the church sexton.

Mrs. Frances Hall was a dignified middle-aged woman with greying hair. On the first day of the trial she appeared dressed in a black corded silk coat with a squirrel collar and a black ribbon hat, and she sat with her two brothers, who had been indicted with her, in a row of seats directly in front of the rail in the courtroom. After the all-male jury had been chosen in a remarkably short time, just over an hour, State Senator Simpson opened the case for the prosecution.

Case reopened

Although the murders with which Mrs. Hall and her brothers were charged had taken place four years previously, the case had not come to trial earlier because the grand jury which had initially examined the matter was not satisfied that there was sufficient evidence to indict the defendants. The Governor of New Jersey had ordered the case to be reopened following a newspaper story that a woman named Louise Geist—who had been employed as a parlourmaid in the Hall household, and had subsequently got married—was having trouble with her husband, who was trying to get the marriage annulled.

In his petition for annulment, he stated that she had been bribed by Mrs. Hall and her brother Willie Stevens to give false evidence before the original grand jury; that Louise had accompanied Mrs. Hall and her brother to the scene of the murders on the evening that they were committed; and that she had either participated in the crime or been an accessory to it. The murders had taken place on September 14, 1922, off a quiet road much favoured by courting couples called De Russey's Lane, on the outskirts of New Brunswick, a small New Jersey town about 35 miles from New York.

The prosecutor made it clear from the outset that he blamed the tragedy on Mrs. Hall's desire to catch her husband in a compromising position with Eleanor Mills, the sexton's wife. There were few people in New Brunswick, at least among those who worshipped at the church of St. John the Evangelist, who had not heard gossip linking the names of the handsome Rev. Edward Wheeler Hall and the pretty young choir singer. Indeed there were some grounds for supposing that they were planning to elope together.

Making a date

According to the prosecution, Mrs. Hall overheard her husband making a date to meet Eleanor Mills in De Russey's Lane on the evening of September 14, and she had asked her two brothers to accompany her there. Unfortunately for the defendants, Senator Alexander went on, their crime had been witnessed by a certain Mrs. Jane Gibson, who kept pigs and for that reason was nicknamed the "Pig Woman" by the newspapers.

The bodies of the Rev. Edward Hall and Mrs. Eleanor Mills were discovered by another courting couple, who had gone for a walk on the morning of September 16 and made their gruesome find when the minister and the choir singer had been dead for about 36 hours. The bodies were lying side by side on their backs beneath a crab apple tree, with Eleanor Mills's head resting on the minister's right arm and her left hand on his right knee, as if this shocking tableau had been deliberately arranged.

His head was covered with a Panama hat, while a brown scarf concealed the lower portion of her throat—which had been slit from ear to ear right down to her chin and when the scarf was removed revealed a mass of maggots. She was wearing a cheap, spotted muslin dress, while the minister wore an ordinary double-breasted suit. His pockets were empty and his gold watch was missing. Propped up against the dead man's left foot was one of his visiting cards inscribed in Gothic lettering with his name and that of his church. Also lying on the grass was his pocketbook containing his driving licence and Masonic and Y.M.C.A. cards, some passionate love-letters in Mrs. Mills's handwriting, and two spent cartridge cases. Mrs. Mills had been shot between the eyes as well as having had her throat cut and her tongue and vocal cords removed. The minister had also been fatally shot.

Any notion of a suicide pact was ruled out by the nature of the wounds, by the disappearance of the minister's money and his watch, and by the absence of weapons beside the bodies. There was a rumour which persisted for long afterwards that the minister's penis had been amputated and placed in the choir singer's mouth, but such a mutilation is not borne out by the autopsy report.

The love letters found scattered about the grass were scrawled in pencil on cheap writing paper. They betrayed a most ardent passion on the writer's part. "There isn't a man who could make me smile as you did today," wrote Eleanor Mills in one of them. "I know there are girls with more shapely bodies, but I do not care what they have. I have the greatest of all blessings, the deep, true, and eternal love of a noble man. My heart is his, my life is his, all I have is his, poor as my body is, scrawny as they say my skin may be, but I am his for ever."

The first two witnesses called by the prosecution were John S. Dickson, an accountant with a Wall Street brokerage firm, and his wife; they lived in North Plainfield, a small community about 10 miles north of New Brunswick. Mr. Dickson testified that at 8.30 on the night of the murders a man who he said was Willie Stevens called at his house and asked to be directed to Parker House, an old people's home, where he said he had relatives.

At first the witness thought he was drunk. ("He was agitated. He was anxious to get out of the neighbourhood.") Mr. and Mrs. Dickson accompanied him to the trolley bus stop and on their way their visitor said he was an epileptic. According to Mr. Dickson, he pulled out "an open-faced" gold watch, presumably resembling the Rev. Hall's, to see the time.

A very soft hand

Mr. Dickson also said he had taken his hand. "It was a very soft hand. I would say one that is not in the habit of doing hard work." Mrs. Dickson bore out her husband's testimony in this respect, describing the man's hand as "soft, but very cold and clammy". She caused an outburst of laughter in the courtroom when she went on to state that she had never felt a man's hand before.

Judge Parker banged his gavel on the bench to restore order. "I want to say to this audience that this is a murder trial that is being tried," he warned, "and if there is going to be any hilarity the courtroom will be cleared, and cleared without compunction."

In cross-examination both the Dicksons stated that their visitor was not wearing glasses. Thus, whoever he was, he was certainly not Willie Stevens, who could not move a yard without his special lenses.

QUESTIONS OF DOUBT

Charlotte Mills, the murdered woman's 20-year-old daughter, who was now a newspaper reporter, identified a number of her mother's letters to the Rev. Hall. It had been her habit, said Charlotte, to leave notes for the minister in a large book in his study.

"Where was the large book?" asked Senator Simpson.

"The second shelf from the bottom of the bookcase."

Church divorce rules

After dinner on September 14, according to Charlotte, Mrs. Mills had cut out an article by a well known Episcopal clergyman—who had long advocated liberalization of the church's divorce canons—from that day's New York *World* and taken it to the Rev. Hall's study. She returned home at 7.15 and told her daughter that she had met Miss Opie, a dressmaker who lived next door to Mr. and Mrs. Mills, and Miss Opie had told her that a telephone message had come from Mr. Hall for her. Mrs. Mills then informed her daughter that she was going up the street to phone the minister—apparently there was no phone in the Mills's house—and see if there was anything Mr. Hall wanted. Her mother left the house, said Charlotte, and that was the last she saw of her alive.

The prosecutor then handed Charlotte a second package of letters. She identified these as being in the Rev. Hall's handwriting, and said that her mother kept them in a crocheted bag which used to hang on the back of their living-room door. In addition the bag contained a diary kept by the minister. Charlotte also stated in cross-examination that her father James Mills had been given $500 for the letters and diary by a newspaper company, but she said she did not know whether her father had ever read them.

The four shots

Charlotte Mills was followed on the witness stand by Anna Hoag, who lived close to the scene of the crime: she was a woman of uncertain age with a pale complexion accentuated by brown curls which peeped out from the brim of a modish turban. She said she heard four shots about ten o'clock on the night of the murder. She went on to say that one afternoon in August 1923 a man whom she identified as Henry Stevens had visited her home. He was immaculately dressed in a dark suit and Panama hat, and he called to ask the way to Raritan.

"I asked him to sit down, and he sat on the porch," said Mrs. Hoag. "I thought

THE PIG WOMAN, Jane Gibson, lies on a bed and tells her story (top) to the jury, pictured right going back into the court after a lunch break.

144

But when asked if he had told a detective four years previously that he had quarrelled with his wife because of her affection for the Rev. Hall, the sexton said that he could not remember. The love letters of the unfortunate pair were then read out in court and provided a tasty dish for the spectators and newspaper readers.

After this the prosecution called Louise Geist, the former parlourmaid, whose matrimonial troubles had precipitated the re-opening of the case. It was confidently expected that her evidence would restore the shaken fortunes of the prosecution, but again the Senator was disappointed. She declared that her husband's affidavit was nonsense: he had married her, she said, only in order to learn from her the secret of the murders, and, discovering too late that she did not know it, was revenging himself by bringing these charges against her.

On a stretcher

The Pig Woman was then brought into court on a stretcher and placed in a hospital bed, attended by a nurse and a doctor who kept feeling her pulse. Speaking in a weak voice, she said that a few nights before the murders a thief had robbed her of two rows of Indian corn. Hoping to catch him if he returned for more, she tied her dog to a tree between her shanty and the scene of the crime. Roused by the dog's barking on the night of the murders, she went to the scene but saw nothing.

However, she lost a slipper and returning to recover it she saw two women and two men quarrelling in the lane. One of the couples, a white-haired woman and a bushy-haired man were standing beneath the crab apple tree. "Explain these letters!" the white-haired woman had cried, after which there was a struggle, something gleamed in the moonlight, and the man shouted, "Let's go!" Then the other woman screamed, four shots were fired, and the Pig Woman decided that she had better retire.

"She's a liar!"

Handed photographs of Mrs. Hall and Willie Stevens by the prosecutor, the witness had no hesitation in identifying them as the grey-haired woman and the bushy-haired man whom she saw by the crab apple tree. Meanwhile the Pig Woman's aged mother, who had been tracked down by the defence and provided with a seat near her daughter's bed in court, kept remarking loudly: "She's a liar, a liar, a liar! That's what she is, and what she's always been." There is no doubt the mother was right, and that the Pig Woman had deliberately made up her story for the sake of the accompanying newspaper publicity. Indeed, she claimed she would

the man was sick because he trembled so. And then he got talking that he had been in Florida that winter and he talked on Florida for a while. Then all at once he said, 'Wasn't there a tragedy on this place?' and I said 'I know nothing about any tragedy.' And with that I ran into the house because I was frightened."

After she left the porch, it appeared that Mrs. Hoag's unexpected visitor walked to the pump for a drink of water. "Then I came out to watch him," she went on. "I had my dog with me, and I watched him up the lane and the man nearly collapsed—when he passed the place where the bodies were found, he nearly collapsed." Although, according to her, Henry Stevens told her he was out for a walk, Mrs. Hoag was convinced that there was a car waiting for him in De Russey's Lane. "He must have had a car, because he was so immaculate," she told the packed court.

The prosecution now produced the Rev. Hall's visiting card which had been found beside the bodies, and claimed that it bore an unmistakable thumbprint of Willie Stevens. While fingerprint experts were giving evidence, Senator Simpson

was handed a note informing him that the Pig Woman had been taken ill and would be unable to testify. At the Senator's suggestion the judges left the bench and hurriedly visited the hospital where Mrs. Gibson was a patient.

They returned half an hour later to announce that the state of the Pig Woman's kidneys was indeed serious. The trial continued and the defence was able to show, without much difficulty, that the thumbprint on the visiting card had been fraudulently superimposed. Thus another prop in the prosecution structure was knocked away.

The sexton, James Mills, duly took the stand and stated that Mrs. Hall had called on him before the bodies were found. He suggested to her that her husband and his wife had eloped, whereupon, according to the witness, Mrs. Hall bluntly replied that they were dead. He was severely cross-examined by the defence counsel, who extracted some unexpected admissions, including one to the effect that, despite his original denials, he had read "a good part" of the affectionate letters sent to his wife by her clergyman lover.

Map labels: RARITAN RIVER, BUCCLEUCH, RIVER RD., PARKER HOME, AVE., EASTON, D, MRS. HOAGS HOUSE, MIDDLESEX CO., SOMERSET CO., ING CAR, E, WHERE GORSLINE PARKED CAR, BARN, PHILLIPS FARM, C, WHERE MRS. GIBSON SAW TWO CARS ← PARKED, DE RUSSEYS LANE, B, A, LOVERS LANE, WHERE BODIES WERE FOUND UNDER CRABAPPLE TREE, N, FRAILEY

WHERE IT HAPPENED . . . A detective points to the spot under a crab apple tree where the bodies of the minister and his mistress were found (inset). The plan shows the lovers' lane and other key points mentioned in court as the story unfolded.

be "the Babe Ruth of the trial", referring to a popular baseball player of the day.

It was not difficult for the defence to put up a convincing answer to the prosecution's case. When Mrs. Hall took the stand, she disputed the Pig Woman's account and swore that she herself had played no part in the tragedy. As far as she knew, her husband was devoted to her and his conduct had never given her any cause to suspect his morals. On the other hand, she had known Eleanor Mills as an active church worker and in fact she had helped her with hospital and medical expenses when she was ill. Mrs. Hall went on to say that she knew that her husband had received some letters from Eleanor because he had shown them to her. "They were, as near as I remember," she said, "descriptions of evening services at church."

Mrs. Hall proceeded to describe how her husband left home on the night of the murders, as the result of a telephone call from Mrs. Mills, saying that he must go and see the sexton about his wife's hospital bill. The minister had $50 in his pocket and also his gold watch. Surprised by her husband's long absence, she woke her brother Willie who lived with them

and together they went to the church to see if the Rev. Hall had fallen asleep there. They found the church shut up and in darkness. They then walked on to the sexton's house and finding no light there either they returned home, entering by the back door.

Asked why she had not alerted the police sooner about her husband's disappearance, she replied that she had in fact telephoned them early next morning, without giving her name, and had asked whether there were any accidents in the area which had been reported. She was told that there was none. She then got into touch with several members of her husband's family and instructed her lawyer to carry on with the investigation from there.

Willie Stevens corroborated his sister's account of how she had wakened him in the dead of night and they had gone together to the church and to the Mills's house. He was quite unshaken under cross-examination.

Indeed he scored neatly off the prosecutor who had badgered him with questions as to where he was at a certain time. "If a person sees me go upstairs and doesn't see me come downstairs," he

asked Senator Simpson, "isn't that a conclusion that I was in my room?"

"Certainly," the Senator agreed.

"Well," said Willie Stevens, "that's all there was to it."

In the middle of the fifth week, Senator Simpson appealed to the judges to order a new trial on the ground that the jury-men were not paying proper attention to his arguments. His motion was refused. Counsel's final speeches on both sides matched each other in extravagance. The defence went so far as to suggest that the Pig Woman might have shot the Rev. Hall and Mrs. Mills and cut the latter's throat under the erroneous impression that they were the thieves who had stolen her corn. Not to be outdone, Senator Simpson declared that Mrs. Hall's lack of emotion at the death of her husband showed that she was a Messalina, a Lucretia Borgia and a Queen ("Bloody")

THE WITNESSES . . . Pig Woman Jane Gibson (right) and Emil Nelson (below) both claimed they saw the killing, but they were not believed. A detective examines Mrs. Mill's blood-stained clothes.

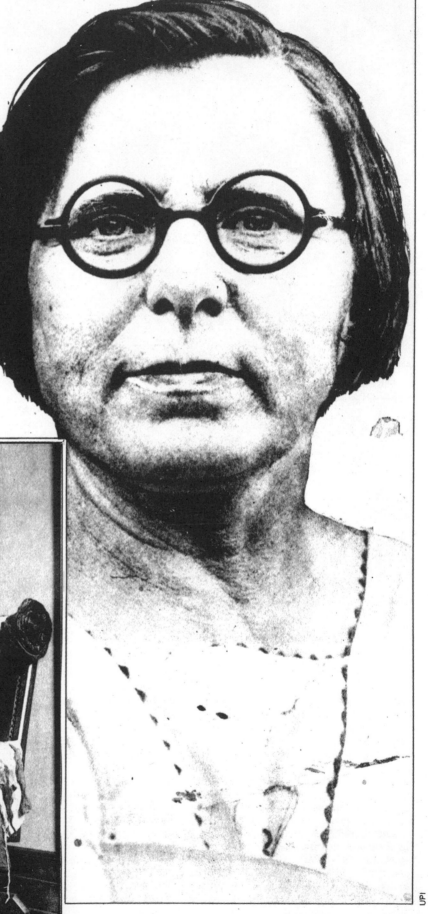

Sunday Times

Mary. "Has she ever batted an eyelid?" he asked the jury with some heat.

On December 3, 1926, the jury returned a verdict of not guilty, after deliberating for five hours. Mrs. Hall, her two brothers, and her cousin, Henry Carpender, who had taken care of the Rev. Hall's funeral arrangements and was being held on a charge of complicity in the murders pending separate trial, were all immediately released. James Mills, the sexton, remarked that he was not surprised by the result—money, he said, could buy anything. This was a dig at the defendants who had spent many thousands of dollars in clearing themselves of the baseless charges brought against them. The expenses of the prosecution were still greater, as the taxpayers

WERE THEY GUILTY? One theory is that the moralistic Ku Klux Klan assassinated the couple for breaking the order's strict rules on sex.

of New Jersey were soon to discover.

The killer or killers of the Rev. Hall and Mrs. Mills were never brought to justice, and to this day the case remains one of the unsolved crime mysteries of the United States. The most plausible solution has been put forward by William Kunstler, a New York lawyer, who has made a profound study of the crime. It is that it was the work of the Ku Klux Klan, which organized the slaying of the clergyman and his mistress for their flagrant violation of the order's rigid standards of sexual morality.

There were many New Jersey branches of the Klan at the time and Klansmen were particularly active in the state. The killing bore all the signs of a ritual Klan murder, the deliberate juxtaposition of the bodies to emphasize their adulterous relationship, and the severing of the soprano's singer's vocal chords to make the same point as forcefully as the emasculation of a southern Negro for raping a white woman.

There was also the persistent rumour of the treatment of the minister's genitalia. At all events, if the Kunstler theory is true—and no one has come up with a better one—the admitted circumstances of the murders indeed formed a most terrible warning to other would-be violators of the Seventh Commandment: Thou shalt not commit adultery.

The Lonely
Body on the Beach

Starr Faithfull

Even in death she was beautiful. But what lay behind her mysterious death? As police and press investigated, a bizarre story emerged of rape, drugs and tragic sexual inadequacy. Did this lovely, but unloved, girl commit suicide, as some claimed, or was she brutally murdered . . . ?

IN THE already warm dawn sunshine of June 8, 1931 Daniel Moriarty, a beach-comber, went strolling on the golden sands of Long Beach, about twenty miles out of New York, and found a body. Even in death the corpse was impressive. It was that of a young girl, with long brown hair framing a beautiful face, and the expensive silk dress which was its only garment clung damply to the curves of a magnificent figure. But however attractive she may have been, the girl was dead, and Moriarty paused only long enough to drag the corpse clear of the waterline before stumbling off across the dry sand to phone the police.

Finger marks

The time between Moriarty's call and the positive identification of the dead girl was short; checking quickly through the files of the New York Missing Persons Bureau, the police found only one description which tallied. Three days before, on the morning of June 5, a Mr. Stanley E. Faithfull had reported that his 25-year-old step-daughter—romantically named Starr Faithfull—had not returned home the night before.

He had checked out her usual friends and acquaintances unavailingly, and had been calling the Bureau for news at regular intervals ever since. By mid-day of June 8, Mr. Faithfull had identified

the Long Beach corpse as that of his missing daughter, and an autopsy—the first of three which were to be performed on the girl—got under way.

Like the identification, the autopsy took very little time to perform, and by that evening the assistant medical examiner for Long Beach was able to make his report. Starr Faithfull had died by drowning. Her body had been in the water about forty-eight hours. There were no traces of alcohol, but she had taken between one and two grains of veronal—possibly enough to cause unconsciousness but not enough to kill her. She had eaten a large meal shortly before dying, and there was sand in her lungs, indicating that she had been breathing as she lay with her head in the shallow water at the edge of the beach. Her upper arms were badly bruised, the bruises being in the shape of finger marks, and—last but by no means least in the opinion of the medical examiner—she had been raped.

Like other aspects of the extraordinary Faithfull case, the sexual angle was to cause a great deal of argument, for two days later, at a further autopsy, doctors insisted that they could find no evidence at all of "criminal assault"—but it was enough for the District Attorney of Nassau County, under whose jurisdiction Long Beach came. Elvin N. Edwards, the D.A., had just enjoyed considerable

WASHED UP . . . Starr Faithfull had, according to her last letters, ruined her life, and she no longer wanted to live. But was this the end she desired?

publicity for his part in the trial and execution of a top gangster named "Two Gun" Crowley, and he relished the idea of being in the limelight again: he called a press conference and announced that he was treating the case as murder.

The first newspaper reports dwelt on the point that the dead girl was an "heiress, the brown-haired, brown-eyed product of a Boston finishing school who preferred to be alone, reading volumes on philosophy and kindred subjects". But the following morning, when the press had had more time to investigate, this rather prim picture was discovered to be far from complete. She was, in fact, the daughter of a Boston woman of good family who had divorced Starr's father, Frank W. Wyman, in the early 1920's to marry Stanley E. Faithfull, a retired manufacturing chemist and would-be inventor.

On her re-marriage, the former Mrs. Wyman had changed not only her own name but those of her two daughters, Starr and Tucker—three years younger than her sister—to Faithfull, and had gone to live with her new husband in his small town-house at 12 St. Luke's Place, Greenwich Village. There the family

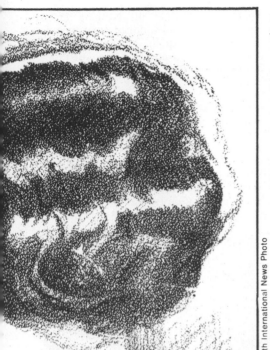

Both International News Photo

still resided, rather cramped by Mr. Faithfull's valuable collection of Chippendale, Sheraton, and Empire furniture, and his large library of well-bound books.

That the entire family was eccentric to some degree became apparent as the investigation progressed. But in the first few days police and press alike were primarily interested in the peculiarities of Starr Faithfull herself. They discovered that she had been an odd mixture of romantic and "good time girl", not so much a tramp —as some newspapers suggested—as a high-spirited manic-depressive type who, during her "high" periods, sought out the company of glittering people to dance and drink the evenings away.

She had been twice to London, once with her mother and Tucker and once on her own, and while there had cut a dash among the semi-aristocratic, "gay young things" set of Mayfair and Chelsea. Unfortunately since her last voyage the family fortunes—also the subject of press speculation—had dwindled, and in 1931 Starr could not afford a European trip.

Instead she had begun to take a vicarious delight in haunting the New York docks as the great luxury liners were leaving, joining in last night parties aboard, and often coming ashore only as the ships prepared to sail. Although not a regular drinker, Starr did, on occasion, become drunk. Those were the days of Prohibition, and her ex-chemist stepfather, realizing the dangers of "bootleg" liquor, often made her a flask of Martinis to take with her on these jaunts.

Hapless doctor

Pursuing Starr's fascination with the docks as a line of inquiry, the investigators quickly discovered that she had made a stir there just ten days before her body was found. It appeared that she had formed an attachment, some months previously, to Dr. George Jameson-Carr, ship's surgeon aboard the Cunard liner *Franconia*. It was a completely one-sided affair, but every time the *Franconia* docked Starr went to press her affections on the somewhat hapless doctor.

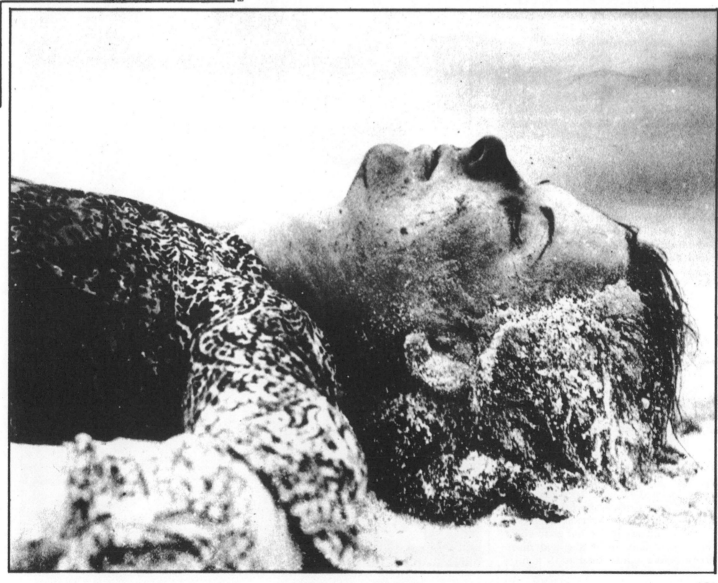

AT HOME with the Faithfulls (right). Apparently it was a highly eccentric family, although sufficiently wealthy to possess a stately New York house (above).

On May 29, a few hours before the liner was due to sail, Starr had staggered drunkenly up the gang-plank and sought out Dr. Jameson-Carr in his quarters. After trying to reason with her, he had asked Starr to leave; in fact she had hidden among the passengers, and it was not until the *Franconia* was some distance down the bay that she was discovered—much to the surgeon's embarrassment. The captain had signalled a tug-boat to come alongside, and Starr, still reeling drunk, had been shipped back to the dock. Dr. Jameson-Carr had sailed on with his ship, and thus ceased to be of immediate interest to the detectives.

Juicy scandal

But the incident took on new relevance when Starr's movements on June 4, the day of her disappearance, were traced. She had left home with only three dollars in her purse at about midday, in reasonably good spirits. No one in her family had asked where she was going, and she had not volunteered the information. During the afternoon she had been seen on the docks, where the two Atlantic liners *Mauretania* and *Ile de France* were preparing to sail.

A little later she had gone aboard the *Mauretania* and had left it shortly before departure time; a number of other witnesses claimed to have seen her boarding the *Ile de France* shortly afterwards, though their claims were never proved. No one could say if she *had* gone aboard the French ship, or if she had disembarked before sailing time at 10 p.m.

Supposing, reasoned the reporters on the case, Starr Faithfull had again stowed away aboard one or other of the ships, and had remained hidden until it was passing Long Island, the narrow 118-mile strip of land which runs due east and west off the coast of New York and Connecticut, part of whose shores was Long Beach? Supposing that when passing Long Beach she had jumped or fallen overboard?

Both District Attorney Edwards and Stanley Faithfull protested at this explanation; the lawman was convinced that she had been murdered, while her father was equally convinced that she would not kill herself. Nothing loath, the newspapers abandoned their suicide theory in favour of the more sensational one of murder. But they still clung to one angle; if it was murder, then surely Starr Faithfull must have been thrown from a passing ship; after all, there was no record of her having visited Long Beach or known anyone in the area before.

Investigations continued. The next item to emerge was a juicy piece of scandal. During the previous summer, almost exactly a year from the date of her death, Starr Faithfull had been found in a New York hotel. Guests had heard screams and called the police; when a patrolman

SOMEBODY paid a great deal of money to silence inquiries about Starr's past sexual life. The family lawyer (right), Charles Rowley, would reveal nothing. Above: Starr's dog waits for her in vain.

burst into her room, he found Starr naked, drunken, and bleeding, upon the bed, while a young man dressed only in an undershirt stood glaring at her, his fists clenched. On the bedside table stood a half-empty bottle of gin. The young man had given his name as Joseph Collins, proving his identity by showing his army discharge papers. Amazingly, in view of the fairly serious bruisings and lacerations to Starr's face, the patrolman had told him to clear off, and Collins had disappeared for good.

At Bellvue Hospital, where she had spent the rest of the night, Starr had screamed and shouted until her parents arrived to take her home. She had been vague about the circumstances of her beating: "I was drinking gin as far as I know . . . I don't remember . . . I suppose somebody knocked me around a bit."

Almost simultaneously with the "hotel beating" story came the revelation that, when Starr Faithfull was nineteen, she had spent nine days under observation in a Boston mental hospital and, although discharged and reported to be "much improved", she had, at the time of her death, still been under regular psychoanalysis. Rumour had it that her mental troubles were bound up with sexual inadequacy of some kind. One or two papers hinted that the Collins affair had been the result of Starr employing Collins to have sexual intercourse with her, and then being overcome by fear at the last moment, causing him to attack her through frustration.

The sexual line of inquiry bore fruit when police came across a diary or journal which she called her "Mem Book". Written partly in shorthand, and with only initials mentioned, the book was a record of her sexual activities in real life and fantasy—some of which were so erotic that even the New York tabloids refused to print them.

But the Collins incident, Starr's mental history, and the diaries clearly indicated one thing—that sex had played a prominent and possibly tragic part in the girl's life. Ever since the start of the case the press, the police, and District Attorney Edwards had been trying to discover the source of the Faithfull family income, and had each put forward various theories. The more conservative pointed out that both Mr. and Mrs. Faithfull had had capital at some time, she through inheritance, he through his chemical business. While more sensational speculators suggested that the family were either blackmailers or lived from the proceeds of running an international drug ring. The blackmail theory gained currency in a curious way, although the truth of the Faithfulls' money matters was never properly disclosed.

Probable link

In her diaries, Starr had constantly alluded to "A.J.P.", presumably one of her lovers. Her feelings towards him appear to have been mixed; sometimes she hated A.J.P., sometimes she wrote of him affectionately, but for the most part, even when writing of their sporadic sexual life, she seemed to fear him. A typical entry ran: "Spent night A.J.P. Providence. Oh Horror, Horror, Horror!!!"

It was only when Mr. Faithfull, while declining to take any fee, agreed to give his own recollections of Starr to a news agency that a probable link between the family income and the "sex diaries" became established. According to Stanley Faithfull, his step-daughter had been seduced at the age of eleven by a middle-aged Boston businessman, whom Mr. Faithfull referred to only as "X". This "X" had been the father of some girls who were Starr's schoolfriends, and one day had stunned her with ether and had intercourse with her.

Congressman

Apparently the relationship had persisted over the years, although Mr. and Mrs. Faithfull had known nothing about it until Starr had confessed to them when she was in her late teens. They had noticed that she was nervous, often refused to leave her room for days on end, occasionally insisted that she could not go swimming because she would "have to expose herself in a bathing suit".

Finally, after spending two days with "X" in a New York hotel room, she had told her mother about the seduction and what had followed; one of the odd omissions in the Faithfull case was that no one seems to have asked why, if Mr. Faithfull was so quick to report his daughter's disappearance at the age of twenty-five, he had apparently done nothing about her absence for two days when she was barely out of childhood.

Barely was the newspaper report cool from the wires when assiduous reporters had linked "X" with "A.J.P." and had found a likely culprit: he was Andrew J. Peters, former Congressman, former Mayor of Boston, and a distant relative of Mrs. Faithfull. Furthermore, his family and the Faithfulls had at one time been close, Starr had played with his children, and he had certainly spent time alone with

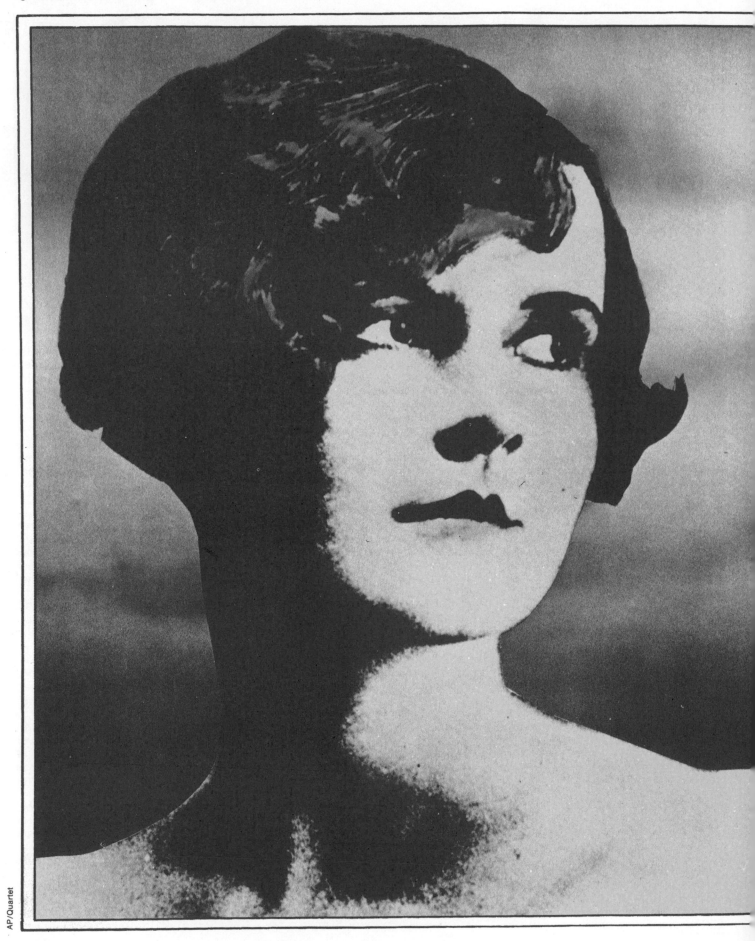

Starr. Further digging revealed that a "considerable sum of money" had been paid to Starr's parents for signing a formal release to an unnamed individual, "quitting him in lengthy terms of all liabilities for damage done to Starr".

When approached, Mr. Faithfull agreed that he had been paid $20,000 for signing such a document, and that all of it had been spent on medical and psychiatric care for the girl. Subsequent reports said that the sum had been $80,000, and that this was the mysterious source of the Faithfull family income. The firm of Boston lawyers which negotiated the agreement only remarked laconically: "If Faithfull wants to say that it was only $20,000, then we are satisfied to let it rest at that."

Mr. Peters' only comment was a formal denial issued to the press that he had ever had improper relations with Starr Faithfull. He refused to comment on the matter of the document Mr. Faithfull had signed, and—presumably because of a strong alibi—was allowed to drift out of the case.

About a week went by while these facts were laboriously gathered. During that time Frank Wyman, Starr's real father, arrived in New York and, with his ex-wife and her husband, sought and received permission from the authorities to cremate the body. As the family group were kneeling around the coffin in a Long Island mortuary, a police car screamed to a stop outside, and an excited representative of District Attorney Edwards leapt out. On the D.A.'s authority the funeral was cancelled; yet another post-mortem had been ordered, on the grounds of new evidence. While reporters waited outside the autopsy room, the third examination of Starr's remains was made. Finally Edwards came out to read a statement.

Three letters

"Gentlemen," he said to a hushed audience, "I know the identities of the two men who killed Starr Faithfull. They took her to Long Beach, drugged her, and held her head under the water until she was drowned. I will arrest both of them within 36 hours."

Unfortunately for the thousands of avid followers of the case, the statement faded into anticlimax; when reporters chased up the matter two days later Edwards mumbled something to the effect that the lead was false. But on June 23, a fortnight after the body's discovery, the most startling development of all occurred: Dr. George Jameson-Carr arrived back from England to reveal that Starr Faithfull had written him three letters between May 30—the day after she was shipped so unceremoniously ashore from the *Franconia*—and June 4, when she disappeared from home. One

LEAVING for the crematory. The cremation was stopped at the last minute to allow a further examination of Starr's remains. Left: the beauty in life.

was a formal note, apologizing stiffly for her disorderly conduct and exonerating him from all blame. It was dated June 2. The other two, rambling and pathetic, were clearly suicidal.

The first, dated May 30, began abruptly: "I am going now (I have been thinking of it for a long time) to end my worthless, disorderly bore of an existence—before I ruin anyone else's life as well. I certainly have made a sordid, futureless mess of it all . . . I take dope to forget and drink to try and like people, but it is of no use." She went on to say that she was "mad and insane" over Dr. Jameson-Carr, and took allonal to try and alleviate her feelings. She was looking forward to dying, now that her decision was made: "The half hour before I die will, I imagine, be quite blissful."

The third and final letter, written on June 4 and posted at 4.30 p.m., began almost cheerfully. She had made up her mind to "put this thing through" but was worried about being prevented at the last moment. "If one wants to get away with murder one has to jolly well keep one's wits about one. It's the same with suicide. If I don't watch out I shall wake up in a psychopathic ward, but I intend to watch out and accomplish my end this time. No ether, allonal, or window jumping. I don't want to be maimed, I want oblivion."

However, the most important part of the letter came a few sentences further down, when Starr described what she imagined would be the pleasures of dying. She loved to eat, she said, and promised herself one "delicious meal with no worry over gaining . . . I am going to drink slowly, keeping aware every second. Also I am going to enjoy my last cigar-

ettes. I won't worry because men flirt with me in the streets—I shall encourage them—I don't care who they are. I'm afraid I've always been a rotten 'sleeper'; it's the preliminaries that count with me. It doesn't matter though."

Again she underlined her passion for Dr. Jameson-Carr: "There are no words in which to describe this feeling I have for you. The words love, adore, worship have become meaningless . . ." The letter was signed simply: "Starr." Dr. Jameson-Carr had been in Belgium when news of Starr Faithfull's death reached him. Finding the letters when he returned to England, he had made his way as soon as possible to New York, without pay from Cunard, who were annoyed with him for getting his name in the papers. A kindly man, he was upset by the whole affair, but he felt the letters should clear the matter up.

Which is what they did. Despite Mr. Faithfull's claim that the letters were forgeries, half-a-dozen handwriting experts testified that they were written by the same hand that wrote the diaries. Starr's sister Tucker admitted that while in London, Starr had tried to commit suicide, using twenty-four grains of allonal, but had been found and revived. There was, of course, no question that the ship's surgeon who appeared to have driven her to death could have had anything to do with the events of her death itself. The matter was put down to suicide, and the case was closed.

Some reporters remained dissatisfied

with the coroner's verdict. One of the most prominent of these was Morris Markey, who founded the "Reporter at Large" column for the *New Yorker*, and was a highly respected investigative journalist. At the height of the Faithfull case, Mr. Markey had interviewed the Faithfull family and established an easy relationship with them; he also kept copious notes of the case on file. In 1948 he finally published a pet theory of his, one that had been growing for seventeen years, in which he sought to show that by the most extraordinary of coincidences, Starr had been murdered on her "suicide night".

First, he took the last letter, the suicide note written on June 4. In it, Starr had set out with macabre relish the things she planned to do before killing herself. She was going to enjoy a "delicious meal" and indeed a "big meal" was found undigested in her stomach. There were no traces of alcohol in her system—despite her assertion that she would drink slowly and pleasurably—but there were small traces of veronal—a barbiturate very similar to allonal—in her body, although she had said that she would not use allonal to kill herself.

"More provocative," pointed out Mr. Markey, were "several other things which she dropped into her last letter". She had said that she would not worry about "flirts" and would, indeed, encourage them; she had mentioned the pleasure of being rude to people, telling them exactly what she thought of them; and finally she had confessed that she was, in her own words, "a rotten sleeper".

Bearing these points in mind, Mr. Markey recalled the Collins episode. On that occasion, he asked, would it be too far-fetched to suggest that Collins found himself in a bedroom with a beautiful, naked girl who was, for psychological reasons, unable to let him make love to her, and that Collins, frustrated at having found a "teaser", beat her up in rage?

DID the good time girl (above) commit suicide? What was the mystery behind the money paid to her parents (left)?

What if a similar but more tragic incident had happened on the night of June 4? Perhaps, in her carefree, "ante-mortem" mood, she picked up a "flirt", a stranger, and suggested that they go to Long Beach. The great transatlantic liners could be seen from there, five miles out, glittering palaces in the blue dusk, full of laughing, happy people such as she herself had once been. She allowed her pick-up to buy her a good meal, but decided not to blur her last enjoyment with drink after all. Maybe she had decided to allow herself the ultimate in pleasure—teasing a sexually aroused male—"a male", as Mr. Markey put it, "who lay eternally in her mind as the male who had hurt and frightened her and savagely disillusioned her, so long ago in Boston".

It seems probable, in view of her past history, that she usually carried some form of barbiturate with her; perhaps on this evening she decided to give herself a final "lift" with a couple of grains of veronal; perhaps instead of taking the man to a room she had led him out onto the sands, to watch the Europe-bound ships go by for the last time.

"And then," said Mr. Markey, "I think she teased this unknown man beyond endurance . . . he mauled her . . . then he was frightened . . . and decided that she would never tell of it. So he took her down to the water's edge and held her head under for a while." In the end, as Mr. Markey put it: ". . . Starr Faithfull was foiled of her final purpose as she had been foiled of everything else in life. She was not even able to accomplish her own end."

International News Photos

Index A

Acknowledgments

Front of jacket: A.P.
Back of jacket: L.E.A.
Pages 2–3: Radio Times Hulton Picture Library/Popperfoto
Page 4: Syndication International, Radio Times Hulton/Quartet